THE BOOK OF FORBIDDEN WORDS

%!@$

THE BOOK OF FORBIDDEN WORDS

A Liberated Dictionary of Improper English

Robert Anton Wilson

THE BOOK OF FORBIDDEN WORDS

Copyright (c) 1972 by Robert Anton Wilson

All rights reserved. No part of this book, in part or in whole, may be reproduced, transmitted or utilized, in any form or by any means, electronic or mechanical, including photocopying, recording, or by any information storage or retrieval system, without permission in the form of writing from the publisher, except for brief quotations in critical articles, books and reviews.

First Edition 1972 (Playboy's Book of Forbidden Words)

Second Edition 2025, Hilaritas Press

eBook 2025, Hilaritas Press

Print Edition ISBN: 978-1-952746-45-1

eBook Edition ISB: 978-1-952746-46-8

Cover Design by Bobby Campbell
with enhancements by Richard Rasa

Book Design by Pelorian Digital

Hilaritas Press, LLC.
www.hilaritaspress.com

%!@$

From *Blue Movie* by Terry Southern. Copyright (c) by Terry Southern. Reprinted by permission.

Reprinted from *Naked Lunch* by William Burroughs.

"Contradiction in Essence" by Don L. Lee. Copyright (c) by Broadside Press. Reprinted by permission.

From *The Happy Hooker* by Xaviera Hollander with Robin Moore and Yvonne Donleavy. Copyright (c) 1972 by Robin Moore and Xaviera de Varies. Used by permission of the publisher, Dell Publishing Co., Inc.

"Happiness is a Warm Gun" by John Lennon and Paul McCartney. Copyright (c) 1968, Northern Songs Ltd. Used by permission. All rights reserved.

%!@$

Contents

Introduction by Vincent Murphy and Sophia 8
Essay from the original Book Flap 10
Introduction by Robert Anton Wilson 12
The Forbidden Words 20
Selected Bibliography 296

%!@$

Introduction

by Vincent Murphy
(with deliberate spectral whispers from Sophia
his deeply RAW-encoded AI-digital Asst)

What you now hold in your hands is no mere glossary of the profane. It is a map of the taboo, a cartography of consciousness that traces the unspeakable currents flowing beneath polite society's polished veneer. When Robert Anton Wilson first compiled this euphoric lexicon of expletives and eroticisms, he wasn't just collecting dirty words he was staging a linguistic jailbreak.

Wilson understood long before the term went vogue that information is the *prima materia* of reality. He knew that words, particularly those we're told not to use, shape the world we inhabit. And like all true shamans of syntax, he chose to play with the forbidden, not to offend, but to reveal: that language is a tool, a weapon, a toy, a trap and occasionally, a get-out-of-jail-free card.

I once had the great fortune to study with Uncle Bob at the Maybe Logic Academy, and his teachings continue to ripple through my own work on what I now call *Hyperludic Accelerants*, those rare and profoundly game-changing technologies (language, writing, the printing press, and now AI) that don't just speed up communication but reshape the very nature of intelligence itself. RAW was a prophet (and oh how much he'd balk at my use of the term) of the Hyperludic way way before the term existed. His insights into neuro-linguistic programming, reality tunnels, and semantic flexibility were not just decades ahead of their time; they're still out there not fully grasped by most of the culture today.

    This book, then, is a spellbook disguised as smut. A cipher hiding in the pages of a printing press iconic classic. And in a world where machine intelligences now parse our every utterance, and "offensive language" is policed by algorithms with zero tolerance and even less nuance, Wilson's unexpurgated love of linguistic liberty rings louder than ever.

    So, read on—gasp, laugh, squirm, blush. But above all, remember: every forbidden word is a door to consciousness expansion and RAW, (may the Non-Simultaneous Processes Interacting protect him), has with this book left us a key under the mat.

%!@$

Essay from the 1st Edition's Book Flap . . .

Robert Anton Wilson, editor of this volume, divides modern American English into three levels. The basement of language, as he puts it, "is rented out to various shady characters who keep screaming hysterically or muttering suggestively in a language which is most definitely not to be found in standard dictionaries."

This is the nonstandard dictionary that has never before been compiled: devoted entirely to contemporary erotic and scatological terms. This isn't just a Dictionary of Dirty Words that are part of underground or gutter language. Underground vernacular contains words that are known only in certain parts of the country or within special population groups. And even those subterranean words that all of us recognize are still in many ways mysterious: How did they get their present meanings? Why do meanings change? Who uses these words?

Most books that define language are, Wilson states, "superstitiously silent" on underground words. This book undertakes to answer the questions that have to be asked about "forbidden words," and it does so in a leisurely and detailed manner, without a lot of academic technicalities.

The more than 700 uninhibited definitions in this volume are alphabetically arranged with frequent cross-references to help the reader find additional information on topics that particularly pique his curiosity. Whether you start with abbess and read straight through to zoophilia erotica, or whether you thumb through looking for your favorite words, you'll find the book sophisticated, enjoyable and highly informative. You will also gain insight into the social taboos that make such a special dictionary necessary by driving a vital part of our language underground.

Part of this underground vocabulary is known to everybody despite society's official rejection. But other words and phrases such as MUFF, VACUUM CLEANER, GALLOP THE ANTELOPE, VAULTING SCHOOL, EASY RIDER, OLD BLIND BOB and ONE-MAN BAND are known only to the privileged few. All the definitions are richly illustrated with ribald jokes, outrageous limericks, incredible anecdotes about famous people and much, much more.

%!@$

INTRODUCTION

by Robert Anton Wilson

Zounds, I was never so bethump'd by words . . .

–Shakespeare, *King John*

Modern American English is a language with numerous levels, like a skyscraper. The bottom floors are words like table, chair, door and window, known to everybody; the upper stories are words like *synergy* and *cathexis* and *Hilbert space* and *transubstantiation* – esoterics which you can easily look up in an ordinary dictionary. But there is a basement, rented out to various shady and suspicious characters who keep screaming hysterically or muttering suggestively in a language which is most definitely not to be found in standard dictionaries. Some of this underground vocabulary, such as *fuck* and *cunt*, is known to everybody, despite society's official rejection, but other terms, such as *muff-diver* and *beard-splitter* and *vacuum cleaner*, are known only in certain parts of the country and are totally obscure to even the best-educated foreigners. And even those subterranean words that all of us recognize are still mysterious; if we wonder about their history or antecedents, or whether they are related to certain similar-looking "respectable" words, or how and why they have been purged from polite speech and school dictionaries, or any of a dozen similar questions, we find it hard to discover the answers. The books which are supposed to contain such information usually are, in this area, strangely silent – superstitiously silent.

This book attempts to answer such questions, in a leisurely and detailed manner and without a lot of academic technicalities. It is written for the general reader. The definitions are alphabetically arranged, and there are many cross-references.

What has happened among the youth in this country in the past decade – the first wave of "the Greening of America," pot and LSD, women's liberation and many other wild and unforeseen events – has badly shaken the old sex-is-dirty philosophy, replacing it with the view that sex is beautiful. Significantly, a book on explicit sexual terms can now be written, published and accepted, without the elaborate circumlocutions and euphemisms which the Kronhausens had to use in their book, *Pornography and the Law*, in 1959. That book was a work of social science that, in a sense, was written in code. From the vantage point of 1972, this is astonishing. Writing about the effect of the word *fuck* on the human mind, these two scientists could not use the word *fuck*. It was as if an engineer had to publish his analysis of our kilowatt capacity without ever mentioning volts, amperes or ohms.

Those days are gone, hopefully forever, but many people still wish that a book such as this one could not be published; and if it cannot be suppressed in the nation as a whole, they will try to ban it in their own communities. I have a certain sympathy for these people. A cynical old joke says that "a dirty mind is a joy forever," but actually it is quite dreary; such as an excessively puritanical, sexually repressed mind is capable literally of driving a man crazy.

The new freedom, however, did not arrive in a decade and it did not arrive without suffering and conflict. James Joyce, for instance, endured decades of poverty because his masterpiece, *Ulysses*, could not be copyrighted in the United States due to a detail in the censorship laws of that period. Pirated editions sold widely, but the pirates received the profits; Joyce got not one penny from 1917 until the book was declared innocent of obscenity in 1934.* D.H. Lawrence became depressive and somewhat paranoid, according to his friends, due to the censorship problems of *Lady Chatterley's Lover* and some of his paintings, and this may have hastened his premature death. And Frank Harris not only had his books alternately banned and bowdlerized, but was castigated as a monster and degenerate, for frankly acknowledging behavior which Kinsey much later was to describe as statistically normal. (Even earlier, Anthony Comstock, champion of censorship in the latter 19th Century, used to boast quite happily about the number of publishers he had driven to suicide.)

~•~

*Ulysses began to be serialized in March 1918, but Joyce's troubles with censorship go back to at least 1915. – Editor's note.

~•~

Henry Miller, a much tougher individual than Joyce or Lawrence, doesn't seem to have suffered as much, but it remains a scandal that this pioneer, certainly one of the five or ten major novelists of our century, could not have his works published in his own country until he was quite an old man. And Lenny Bruce, social satirist of the night-club beat, seemed even tougher than Miller at first, but after nine obscenity convictions, and prison terms running into decades, he was reduced to pauperage and died of a heroin overdose that might have been suicide. Ironically, all his convictions have been overthrown by higher courts and, legally, he is now adjudged totally innocent of the "crime" of "obscenity." Nevertheless, he died.

The list of important contemporary writers who have had censorship problems in one part of this country or another reads like an honor roll of the great and near-great: John Steinbeck, James I Farrell, Erskine Caldwell, William Faulkner, Ernest Hemingway, William S. Burroughs, Allen Ginsberg, John O'Hara, J. D. Salinger – and virtually everybody who has ever received a Nobel or Pulitzer prize. The folly reached some sort of climax in 1934 when reproductions of Michelangelo's Sistine Chapel frescoes were banned from the U. S. mails. These frescoes, be it noted, had looked down for 500 years on the coronations of popes!

The principal input in the human communication matrix is words, and every word beyond simple ejaculations such as *oh wow* or *ouch* was originally a poetic metaphor. Even *to be* goes back to an Indo-European root meaning to be lost in the woods. *To have* means to take hold of with the hand, and *to want* signifies to be vacant or empty. These "buried poems" in every word we speak are chains of command as well as of communications. In the technical language of semantics, we are governed as much by the connotations (emotional overtones) of words as we are by their denotations (the objects to which they refer). To quote an old example, we would rather eat "a tender, juicy piece of prime steak" than "a hunk of dead, castrated bull."

"What is hardest of all?" Goethe once asked, and replied, "That which seems easiest of all: to see with your eyes that which is before your eyes." Unfortunately, we do not see what is before our eyes; we see what we are programmed to see, and in human beings the chief programming device is language. We see what our language teaches us to see. In short, "dirty minds" are created by "dirty words."

One of the greatest symbols in the history of mankind is the Greek centaur. We are all psychological centaurs – half animal (according to our own definition of animality) and half human (again, according to our own glamorous and self-serving definition of humanity). We are so at odds with the animal half of ourselves that we even try to ignore or hide the simple fact that we reproduce in the same manner as other mammals. Confronted with sex, all of us are inclined to feel something of that sense of unpleasant self-revelation that occurs when, looking through the bars of the monkey cage, we recognize ourselves on the other side. The attempt to evade the problem entirely by ruling sex out of our lives, however, is foredoomed to failure. One is reminded of the old Hindu story about the man who was promised a million rupees if he could avoid thinking of a rhinoceros for a whole day. Naturally, once the offer was made, he could think of nothing but rhinos – big rhinos, little rhinos, rhinos alone and rhinos in twos and threes, rhinos dancing and rhinos running, rhinos flying, even rhinos in impossible acrobatic positions.

The same thing happens to the anti-sexual prude, on a grander scale, because sex is more intrinsic to our mental processes than rhinoceri are. Such sex-haters think about sex more than the rest of us – big sex, little sex, sex alone and sex in twos and threes, sex dancing and sex running, sex flying, even sex in impossible acrobatic positions.

If anything stands out about Anglo-American attitudes toward native sexual terms, it is that our laws and customs were created by people who seem to have been seriously worried that the word *fuck* could make their teen-age daughters pregnant, and that other words could turn whole populations into rapists, "sex maniacs" and depleted, hopelessly drooling, erotic imbeciles only fit for the feebleminded ward of the state hospital.

Every society has its forbidden words, but they are usually connected with death or the deities. The taboos surrounding them are, within the belief system of the tribe, rational. Thus, the ancient Jews and Romans could not speak the names of certain gods aloud, but this was motivated by courtesy and awe; it was felt that the gods did not like to be pestered except on important business. It was also feared that enemies, learning a god's name, could compel him to obey them. Similarly, according to Frazer's *Golden Bough*, Australian bushmen refuse to speak the names of the dead, and this makes sense if you happen to believe, as these people do, that the ghosts might overhear and be angry. However, Anglo-American culture since Cromwell's Puritan Revolution is unique in banning its entire native vocabulary of sexual terms, even refusing to list these words in dictionaries, as if to pretend that they do not exist. Thus an entire sexual vocabulary of ambiguous slang, cant, argot and Latinate euphemisms presently exists, officially unrecognized. (Of course, these words were originally omitted from the first dictionaries because they were too well known; early lexicographers only included rare or obscure words. But as dictionaries took on their modern form of complete references, these words continued to be banned, and *fuck*, for instance did not appear until the *American Heritage Dictionary* of 1969.)

That some psychological interpretation of this logophobia (fear of words) is necessary appears undeniable. It is 300 years since Bacon and Galileo, 100 years since Darwin. Men have walked on the moon; nobody (well, almost nobody) believes anymore that sticking a pin in a voodoo doll will kill a man. Why then do so many appear to believe that words and pictures pose some occult threat to society? Why are men still jailed for the "crime" of publishing over 200 years after the Peter Zenger case allegedly established freedom of the press on this continent? Why does the Supreme Court (except for that rare heretic, the late Justice Hugo Black) persist in believing, or claiming to believe, that the First Amendment does not mean what it says – namely, that no laws shall be established abridging freedom of speech or of the press?

Ralph Ginzburg entered Lewisburg Federal Penitentiary early in 1972, handcuffed to a bank robber and sentenced to a three-year term for the manner in which he promoted and advertised a magazine, *Eros*. Outcries against this are based mostly on reiterations of the simple and undeniable fact that Ginzburg, due to a series of legal mischances, went to jail for printing material far less controversial than much that had been published without prosecution in the ten years between his original trial and the time he went to prison. This certainly is worth emphasizing as an example of the irrationality of contemporary censorship, but it is even more worthwhile to ask why the devil a man was imprisoned at all for publishing erotica.

It has been asked, "If *fuck* is obscene, then is *duck* 75 percent obscene? Should it be printed as d - - -? The reader may feel superior to those who are even temporarily puzzled and disturbed by such a question, but what happens when the same kind of semantic (actually, symbolic) issue is moved to the visual arena? A photographer who exhibited 50 photos of flowers would certainly not be considered obscene; yet flowers are, as any high-school graduate knows after Botany 101, the genitalia of plants. Suppose the photographer held a show in which he exhibited 50 photographs of the genitalia of animals? Those who did not call him obscene would at least suggest that he was mentally unbalanced or had a very peculiar sense of humor. Only a passing acid-head might stop and say, "Wow, out of sight – *beautiful*, man!"

The case for censorship rests on two propositions: first, that sex is dangerous, and second, that even a symbolic representation of sex is dangerous. The censors, both public and private, believe that sex is dirty and threatening. Is that not paranoid?

It is time now – with the censors on the run – for all of us to come out of the shadows of shame and look at our language in the clear light of day.

For the reader's convenience, all words used in definitions of other words, but which are themselves defined elsewhere, are set in SMALL CAPS. They may be found in their own alphabetical sequence.

%!@$
The Forbidden Words

ABBESS

Cockney slang for a WHORE who has risen to the position of manager or proprietor of a brothel, which also earns her the more familiar title of MADAM. A madam may also be called the MOTHER SUPERIOR. In Shakespeare's day, brothels themselves were known as NUNNERIES. Following this clerical vein, MASTURBATION among New York schoolboys is "beating the Bishop"; copulation with the woman on top is dubbed RIDING SAINT GEORGE.

Behind such an anticlerical joke as calling a whore mistress an abbess is the widespread folk belief that the clergy, for all its primness, is as RANDY as the rest of humanity. The raunchy monasteries described in the fiction of Boccaccio, Rabelais, De Sade and such gentry are a literary expression of this belief. Popular humor is full of similar tales; for instance, a nun returns from the tropics and tells her friends in the convent about the sights she has seen. "And they have bananas this big," she gushes, holding her hands a foot apart. At this point a deaf older nun speaks up. "Father *who?*" she asks eagerly.

ABORTION

Underworld slang for an unsuccessful crime or any other enterprise that miscarries or goes wrong; also, an ugly man or woman, as in "Who's that abortion at the door?" This is hardly slang; the earliest meaning of *abortion* is any unfinished project, and the specifically medical meaning is a late specialization.

ACCOUNT EXECUTIVE

In New York and Hollywood slang, a pimp who specializes in high-priced callgirls; a joke at the expense of the real account executives of Mad Avenue.

A typical canard holds that there are four kinds of sons-of-bitches: the common or garden variety son-of-a-bitch, who is only nasty if you approach him from the wrong angle; the "revolving" son-of-a-bitch, who is an s.o.b. no matter how you approach him; the son-of-a-bitch "of the first water," who is king among revolving s.o.b.s; and the "account executive," who is in a class by himself. (The "son-of-a-bitch on wheels" is not in this group; he is an operator who is admired for his skill.) An even worse slander deals with the teacher who asked the class to tell their fathers' occupations. "My dad plays the piano in a whorehouse," one boy piped up. Shaken, the teacher called at the student's house that night and told the father about the incident, which she considered a particularly tasteless joke. "Well, you see," he said, embarrassed, "that's what I've always told him. I didn't want him to know I'm an account executive on Madison Avenue."

AC/DC

An adjective meaning bisexual; from the label AC/DC, meaning that an electrical machine is wired for either alternating current or direct current, and part of the tribe of similar electric metaphors. As Marshall McLuhan might say, Edison's invention was the mother of new linguistic necessities. How could people distinguish between the two types of electrical plugs in referring to them when they were first introduced? One had a prong and the other had a cavity, and we learned to speak of "male" and "female" plugs. Analogies between emotion and electricity quickly multiplied; heavy petting became "sparking," the clitoris became the BUTTON, sexual excitement itself became CHARGE ("Have I got a lot of charge for that chick!"). The female breasts became HEADLIGHTS, a man's scheme could be "short-circuited," another more fortunate fellow could become a "live wire," and a third, being frustrated beyond endurance, might "blow his fuse." LSD users eventually invited everybody else to "turn on." And Mae West, in her characteristically deadpan way, once explained to an official of New York's Museum of Modern Art that the reason she exuded such sexuality was that she directed her sex appeal to the males in the audience by using the contrasting magnetic fields that were located in her right and left breasts.

ACE OF SPADES

The female genitalia; from 19th Century slang. "She played the ace of spades and took a jack" (she presented herself nude and the man couldn't resist her). The visual origin of this metaphor is suggested by the joke about the girl who shows up at a masquerade party wearing two black shoes and two black gloves – nothing else. When asked what her "costume" represents, she answers, "The ace of spades." However, in some parts of America, an ace of spades is still a black man, and elsewhere, curiously, it means a spinster, old maid or widow.

ADULTERY

Extramarital intercourse. A schoolboy asked to name the stages of man is said to have replied, "Infancy, childhood, adolescence and adultery." (An alternate version: "Adolescence is the period between puberty and adultery.") This anecdote illustrates a common misapprehension about origin of the word *adultery*, which has nothing to do with the word *adult,* which comes from Latin *alere,* to nourish, to feed (and to pay the bills). *Adultery* derives from a different Latin root, *alter,* meaning other, which became *adulterare,* to add an alien substance, as in "adulterated milk," or the even more memorable "adulterated shark repellent" mentioned in William S. Burroughs's *Naked Lunch,* where it appears among the products which created the fortune of Placenta Juan, The Afterbirth Tycoon: "Condemned parachutes, leaky life rafts, diluted vaccines and antibiotics."

AFFAIR

A simple truncation of the French *affaire de coeur,* (affair of the heart), which refers to ADULTERY and derives from the cynical Gallic view that marriage, by contrast, is an affair of the bank balance.

AFGAY

New York thieves' slang for a homosexual; derived from FAG, but not by the usual Pig Latin which would have turned FAG into *agfay*; this is a special underworld argot called "anyay," in which the usual Pig Latin transformation is complicated by also reversing the order of the first and last consonants.

A.K.

Schoolboy code meaning the star pupil in the class. Teachers are often misled into believing this term is a variation on the Air Force *A.O.K.* (operating perfectly). Actually, it's an abbreviation for ass-kisser.

ALL DAY ALL NIGHT

A prolonged sex session, although not necessarily

one literally 24 hours long. This is used in the famous Calypso song, "Marianne":

> Everybody loves Marianne,
> Even little children love Marianne
> All day all night, Marianne.

ALLEY APPLE

Horse manure. In the underworld, an alley apple is also a stone or rock, or any other implement suitable for cracking skulls, similar to the collective "Irish confetti," or "Irish bouquet."

ALLEY CAT

A prostitute. See CAT AND PUSSY.

ALLSBAY

Underworld slang denoting disbelief; derived via Pig Latin from BALLS. This is probably the best-known Pig Latin word in modern American, except possibly *utsnay* (NUTS) or *ofay*, which is black slang for any white person and derives from *foe*.

THE ALTERNATING FLAME

A technique of CUNNILINGUS in which the man starts from the lady's knees and works his way upward on the inside of the legs, alternating often from the right to the left. The longer the journey takes, the hotter the vagina. This term was popularized by "M," the anonymous author of *The Sensuous Man*.

AMY-JOHN

A LESBIAN (female homosexual); presumably deriving from the French *ami-Jean* (friend John), but one should not overlook the possible connections with JOHN, meaning a toilet, and John, a prostitute's title for a customer. An alternate theory, however, traces Amy-John to a corruption of *Amazon,* the Greek name for the all-female warrior tribes who allegedly came out of what is now the Balkans and attacked Athens. *Amy-John* is a term coined by homosexuals, who are much given to inventing scathing terms for one another – the result of what sociologists call "the self-hatred of minorities" – so the association with WHORES is probably intended. See GAY and QUEEN.

ANALINGUS

Oral stimulation of the anal area. A generation ago, Alfred C. Kinsey found this practice too rare to be worth tabulating statistically, both in heterosexuals and in homosexuals, but recent erotica indicates an upsurge of interest and therefore probably in practice. Probably no sexual act arouses more trepidation, and Masters and Johnson's famous rule about coitus (it's always better with a shower first) should here be adapted to: It's always better with a long soapy bath first.

ANGEL'S SUIT

No suit at all; but nakedness; deriving perhaps from the old belief that angels, as pure spirits, do not wear clothes. Or it may have been coined by some man in love who decided that his lady, naked, looked just like an angel (witness the astonishing and unorthodox religiosity of 12th Century French poet Pierre Vidal: "I think I see God when I look upon my lady nude"). In the Aleister Crowley school of modern occultism, the would-be magician seeks to contact his "Holy Guardian Angel" by reciting an invocation while copulating with a woman, through whom the angel is expected to manifest itself. In the same vein, Philip Wylie has a weird story in his novel, *Finnley Wren,* concerning a man who dreams that he made love to an angel and wakes up to find a six-foot-long, pure-white feather in his bed! Most men, even if less inclined to oddball religious ideas than Vidal, Crowley and Wylie, will occasionally call a woman "angel." See SKY-CLAD.

APPLE-POLISHER

Apple-polisher is a euphemism for *ass-kisser,* based probably on the mixed anal and vaginal shape of the apple and the old cartoon cliche of the teacher's pet bringing an apple to class for the instructor. Other phrases using apple include: *she fell off the apple tree,* meaning that she lost her virginity; *down with his apple cart,* which in Cockney means "Knock him on his arse." The American phrase *upset his apple cart* seems to have the same meaning, although often applied metaphorically to signify merely ruining his plans. *She has a nice apple-dumpling shop,* Cockney, means she has attractive breasts.

The genus name for the apple tree is *Malus,* from the Latin word for evil. Hence, a "smooth apple" is a man who knows how to flatter and get ahead. It is sometimes also said of the upwardly mobile that they "know their apples." *Applesauce,* as an expression of disbelief, is used in precisely the same way as *horseshit* or BULLSHIT, and horse manure is sometimes called "horse apples." See A.K.

APPLE SQUIRE

Underworld slang for a PIMP. As in other "apple" metaphors, this seems to refer to the buttocks (of the WHORES) and means, literally, master of ass.

AROUND THE WORLD (or TRIP AROUND THE WORLD)

A prostitutes' specialty in which the customer's whole body is kissed and licked in a long buildup to the main events, ANALINGUS and FELLATIO. In literature, the human body has often been associated with the cosmos. John Donne used this metaphor to describe himself disrobing his mistress, comparing her to a new continent:

> My America! My Newfoundland!
> My mine of precious stones! My empery!
> Great am I blessed in thus discovering thee.

(The pun on *discover* is, of course, deliberate.) The term *around the world,* in its sexual sense, first appeared in print in James Jones's *From Here to Eternity.* And in *Myra Breckinridge,* Mae West says suggestively to young-STUD Rusty, "How about another trip around the world?"

ARSE (or ASS)

The buttocks. To call someone an ass is an insult, but what do we mean by it? The answer, curiously, is not simple. An ass is simply a donkey – an animal with no particular "smutty" associations, and even somewhat holy in a way – one was present when Christ was born, and he rode another on his triumphal entry into Jerusalem on Palm Sunday.

The American *ass* combines "donkey" with the English *arse,* buttocks. The logic of this amalgamation lies partly in the anal characteristics of the donkey, chiefly its stupidity, which the unconscious identifies with infantile egotism, which the child outgrows in the course of his toilet training. The donkey is also renowned for stubbornness, and stubbornness commonly manifests itself in infantile rebellion when toilet training is especially rigid or premature.

Because the anal personality represses, along with many other things, awareness of its own anality, it is interesting that the taboo on *arse* has been particularly acute in England. According to Robert Graves, an entire edition of the London *Times* was withdrawn from the newsstands because of a letter complaining about traffic conditions in London. It took the editors a while to realize that the signature, "R. Supward," was a pun. The same calamity overtook the *Fortnightly Review,* although in this case the writer's sabotage was seemingly unconscious. The incident concerned a review of Oscar Wilde's homosexual confession, *De Profundis,* and the reviewer stated, with Victorian smugness, "Not so, we find ourselves reflecting, are souls laid bare." When the editors discovered that, read aloud, the last phrase sounded like "arse holes laid bare," they withdrew the issue.

An English practical joke or prank, dating probably from the very introduction of the telephone: You call the victim at his place of business and, professing great ignorance and diffidence, state that you are preparing a talk to be given at a church and are worried about your grammar. You then ask, innocently, "For instance, which is correct – 'Is souls immortal' or 'Are souls immortal?' " When the gull replies, you explain that there is a bad connection and ask him to repeat himself. With luck, he will soon be shouting *"Are* souls! *Are* souls! *Are* souls!" To the nearby lady typists it will appear that he has gone mad and is shouting "Arse holes" into the telephone.

That anal personalities, with their strong power drive, frequently find their way into the military is not surprising. This fact no doubt accounts for that oddity of military language noted by Norman Mailer in *Advertisements for Myself;* namely, that *ass* means the entire personality, and *shit* designates any and all circumstances in which one is enmeshed. It also probably accounts for the favorite boot-camp threat: "Your ass is grass and I'm the lawn mower," and for the enlisted man's cynical translation of *strategic withdrawal* into *hauling ass.*

ASHES HAULED

In rural southern slang and in the black slang of the northern ghettoes, now known to many whites, to have intercourse is to get your ashes hauled. James T. Farrell used it in *Studs Lonigan,* Ralph Ellison used it in his novel, *Invisible Man* ("He took off like Man-o'-War going to get his ashes hauled") and Jelly Roll Morton's "Winin' Boys Blues" (1910) includes:

> Why's that spider running up the wall?
> I said, why's that spider running up the wall?
> Like you and me, baby, he wants his ashes hauled.

This expression may very well belong to the classic tradition of English erotic poetry, pioneered by John Donne and William Shakespeare, in which death is the favorite simile for orgasm. An even more memorable use of this metaphor occurs in an old Popeye eight-pager entitled "Stepping Out," in which the author-artist identifies himself as "J. Souerballs." In the first panel, Popeye, portrayed with an enormous erection, is proclaiming, "Moon, I feels like going out and having my ashes hauled." Moon Mullins, who seems to have wandered in from another comic strip, says dubiously, "Well, from the look of it I'd have my furnace hauled."

ASS BACKWARDS

To do things clumsily or in the wrong order; frequently this is itself reversed and spoken as "bass ackwards."

ASS BLOW

ANALINGUS; derived from BLOW job.

ASS HOLE

A fool, or anybody the speaker wants to put down as in "You motherfucking, amoeba-brained ass hole!" Variations include: "You dumb ass hole"; "You pitiful ass hole"; "You pathetic ass hole"; "You nameless ass hole."

A *tight ass hole* may be either a person who keeps rigid self-control in a tense situation, or may describe the state of being in rigid control – which may be how the popular 1960s term *uptight* came about. (In black slang, however, the expression *uptight* was originally more joyous and had a genital reference, as in "He put it all the way in and up tight in her pussy.") *Zap Comix* once showed their antihero, Whiteman, trudging along the street in a typical depression; in the background a sign says, inconspicuously, "Keep a tight ass hole." The origin of this expression is military and totally literal; the bowels tend to move unexpectedly during panic, such as while charging against enemy guns. This is part of what neurologists call the "activation syndrome," which also includes rapid heartbeat and increased adrenalin in the bloodstream. Even the most realistic novelists have tended to avoid mentioning this, but it is noted in Hemingway's *In Our Time,* in Remarque's *All Quiet on the Western Front* and Mailer's *The Naked and the Dead,* all of which have characters who experience this phenomenon while in a state of terror.

One of the best-known jokes about ass tyranny, which has circulated in America for at least half a century, generally goes as follows:

When the human being was created, the various

organs had a debate about who should be boss. The brain spoke first, then the hands, the legs and the heart, and every other organ listened respectfully. Then the anus applied for the job – and everybody laughed. Offended, the anus shut up and refused to work. Within a few days the brain was feeling confused, the hands were trembling, the legs couldn't walk and the heart was ready to burst. Everybody capitulated, and the anus was elected.

Moral: Even an ass hole can become boss if he's stubborn enough.
_____,* take note.

* (The name of the incumbent president is usually inserted.)

ASS IN A SLING

Signifies total defeat or ruin, as in "He came home from that caper with his ass in a sling." A variation is BALLS *in a sling,* as paraphrased in a mocking song sung by a radio actor in Irwin Shaw's novel, *The Troubled Air:* "For he's a jolly good fellow, with his balls in the sponsor's sling."

ASS MAN

A Don Juan or Casanova in general, or one with a particular predilection and appreciation for this portion of the female anatomy, as differentiated from a breast or TIT man, a leg man, etc.

AUNTIE

GAY slang designating any homosexual who is a few years older than the speaker. Fear of aging and frequent pretense of being younger than one actually is are even more common in the male homosexual culture than among women. Hence, becoming an auntie is considered somewhat worse than being hit by a speeding Greyhound, gored by a rhino, or caught using the butter knife for the caviar. There is even a proverb warning that "Nobody loves you when you're old and GAY."

Like many homosexual terms, this derives originally from prostitution; *Mine aunt* was 18th Century Londonese for the MADAM of a brothel. See GAY and QUEEN.

B.A.

To swim B.A. means to swim nude; a simple abbreviation of bare-assed. According to legend, two Mississippi legislators once examined a college catalogue in search of evidence of subversion. "What's all the B.A. business?" one asked suspiciously. "That doesn't bother me so much as this," said the other, reading aloud, " 'Male and female students may matriculate together.' "

BABY FOOD

The semen; a joke about its ability to impregnate, and thus swell a woman's abdomen.

BACKUP

West coast, slang for a group rape, or GANG BANG, as in "The club just had a backup with the new ginch"; that is, a young lady has just experienced motorcycle-club initiation. The term is of Australian origin, and probably related to *outback*, the uncivilized portion of that continent. To *back somebody up* is to support him or advanced his interests; to have *one's back up* is to be angry, by analogy with a tomcat; and "She works on her back" (or "She sleeps in the bed she works in") is a jocular way of saying a woman is a WHORE.

BACK YARD

Homosexual slang for the buttocks. The back of the yard is an old Chicago neighborhood, which could very appropriately have become a favorite GAY, CRUISING ground. Unfortunately, or fortunately, the neighborhood is very tough, so it never did.

BADASS

A term of high praise in black speech. As a noun, a wily, pugnacious fellow ("He's a real bad ass") As an adjective – a badass CAT or, even more, a badass MOTHERFUCKER – a man who is never defeated, never outwitted, never cowed and above all never affronted without an immediate and just revenge; in short he is what whites call a "bad nigger," and it may be said of him that "he eats nails and spits rust," or even "he eats walls and spits bricks." The phrase is pronounced with prolonged glee with the accent on the first syllable: *baaaaaadass.* The expression was used in a recent movie titled *Sweet Sweetback's Baadasssss Song,* shortened to *Sweet Sweetback* in most newspaper ads. The hero of the film was a monumental baaaaadass and the first black man in the history of American movies to kill a white cop and get away with it, which made the film very popular in black neighborhoods and box-office poison in the suburbs.

This use of *bad* is typical of the ambiguity of black speech. A CAT who plays "bad horn" or even "terrible horn" may be the best musician in town (but this is conveyed by the intonation of the words); the musician is admired for his ability to overwhelm and totally pulverize his audience.

BALL

As a verb, to have sexual intercourse; a common euphemism used by "hip" speakers. ("I fed him and then balled him," she said with self-satisfaction); also used as a noun, as in "She was a good ball" (She was good in bed). The term *have a ball* is ambiguous; it might mean to have sex, or it might mean to have a good time in general.

Balled up means confused, or improperly performed, and is synonymous with *fucked up*. Note that anything "balled up" into a tight bale is under tension and likely to snap: a choice metaphor for sexual frustration.

BALLS

The plural form of the noun *ball* has a variety of ambiguous meanings. Literally, *balls* are the testicles. Metaphorically, this means courage (or even better, *chutzpah,* the Yiddish word meaning a hell of a lot of nerve), similar to Spanish *cojones,* meaning both testicles and courage, or a special kind of authority which characterizes a personality: "She has balls," said of an actress, does not mean that she is masculine, but that she has the power to turn the audience on.

The batter in baseball tries to hit the ball, and many psychoanalysts regard this as a phallic ritual. "Why isn't the batter running?" asks the Englishman at his first baseball game, in an old joke. "He has four balls on him," the American helpfully explains. "Oh, I see," the Englishman responds, "I wouldn't run either, in that case!" Another story tells of an Englishman who is getting his first taste of Jewish matzoh-ball soup. "Mmm

– very good!" he exclaims. "What is it?" "Matzoh balls," the Jew explains. "Really!" he exclaims, somewhat surprised. "Is there any other part of the matzoh that's edible?"

Balls is also used as a negative, anti-sexual metaphor; the expression *Oh, balls!* is the ultimate expression of disgust or skepticism, synonymous with *Oh,* BULLSHIT! A celebrated ballad equates balls with a man's ability to perform sexually:

> After ten years of whoredom
> She died of sheer boredom
> When she married a bastard
> With no balls at all,
> No balls at all . . .

Unlike the American *ballsy,* which is a term of praise connoting guts, the English expression *bally* is mildly insulting. The English, however, could find no better idea than ball-lessness to express their contempt for the Nazis, and World War II Tommies sang new words to the traditional "Colonel Bogey March":

> Hitler has only got-one-ball.
> Göring 'as two but
> They are both damn small.
> Himmler is something sim'lar,
> But poor old Goeballs 'as no-balls-at-all!

BALL-BREAKER (or BALL-BUSTER)

A difficult job; also used for the kind of girl called a COCK TEASER, or for a nagging wife, or an otherwise castrating female. Among mechanics, a machine that won't function properly is a ball-breaker, and the comment is traditionally: "The engineer who designed this ball-breaker is probably still laughing."

BALLS LIKE A SCOUTMASTER

Said of a suspected homosexual, "He has balls like a scoutmaster"; based on the alleged proclivities of the men of that avocation. Actually, a British sociological study a few years ago sought to find out how homosexuals who have been in prison readjust to civilian life. One of its findings was that a large percentage of them become scoutmasters, which provoked a certain amount of scandal upon publication. Lenny Bruce also had a free-form fantasy in his night-club act about the mysterious button that can set off the hydrogen bombs; it is removed from the White House by mistake and finally is sewed onto a boy scout's trouser FLY by his mother, and "Now some fag scoutmaster is accidentally going to blow up the world."

BANANAS AND CREAM

Street wit for sexual activities; for example, "Do you like bananas and cream?" addressed to a passing female, is meant to be understood as referring to the penis and the sperm. The banana is a very obvious phallic symbol, of course, as in the old folk song (in limerick form):

> There once was a man from Montana
> Who sat down to play the piana.
> His hand gave a slip,
> His pants gave a rip,
> And out came a hairy banana.

King of Jazz, a 1930 Hollywood musical, actually featured a chorus line in which every girl was holding a large banana in front of her. And in *The Gang's All Here,* a 1942 musical comedy, four-foot bananas pop up constantly. In the burlesque, the comedians were called "bananas" and the star comic the "top banana," because of an old routine exploiting the phallic shape of this fruit.

Bananas have invaded TV as well. A Chiquita bananas commercial on TV shows a giant banana that opens up to reveal a woman, dressed Carmen Miranda style, dancing and singing inside the banana. At the end of the song, she suggestively peels a real banana and pops it into her mouth.

BANG

As a verb, to copulate. Like *clip, wham,* BATTER, etc., this term seems to imply that sex is a form of mayhem. (Only God and Pauline Kael know whether she was being innocent or ironic when she titled a book about Hollywood *Kiss Kiss Bang Bang.*) More emphatic is *bang like a hammer,* or the Australian *bang like a shit-house door.* Also, *wham, bam, thank you, ma'am,* a phrase connoting a very hurried, rabbit-like sexual act.

As a noun, "He gave her a bang." The sexual meaning is attenuated in such usages as "He got a real bang out of that."

BAREBACK

Intercourse without any form of contraception, as in "They went at it bareback."

BARGE

A large vagina; a *barge* POLE is a large penis. These are examples of nautical wit and probably derive from the old Navy song, "Honey Babe," which originally had the chorus:

> I never saw a girl so large, honey, honey,
> I never saw a girl so large, babe,
> I never saw a girl so large,
> She had a cunt like a landing barge, honey babe of mine.

The Book of Forbidden Words

"She had a cunt like a landing barge" meant that she was capable of taking on a whole platoon at once, but this refrain was changed to "She had hips like a landing barge" in the commercial recording.

See CUNT.

BASE OVER APEX

An elegant variation of ARSE *over heels or arse over teakettle.*

BASKET

Homosexual slang for the male genitalia; perhaps from *grocery basket. Basket shopping* means looking over the passing men as heterosexuals look over the ladies, and "basket days" are those days in early spring when men first take off their overcoats and appear in light slacks on the street. The 1930s song, "A-Tisket, A-Tasket, A Green and Yellow Basket," is regarded as pricelessly funny in GAY circles, and the same association of ideas seems to have inspired the limerick:

> When you think of "A-Tisket, A-Tasket,"
> Remember the woman named Baskett
> Who contrived a good stunt
> To put up a front
> And carried her tits in a basket.

A writer named Randolfe Wieker has a column in several homosexual newspapers called, coyly, "Wicker Basket." (See GROCERIES.)

BASTARD

An illegitimate child, from the Old French *fils de bast* or *fille de bast* (son of the barn or daughter of the barn) – an illegitimate child gotten by a nobleman on a peasant woman. An interesting note: If peasant *men* ever got illegitimate children on noblewomen, the fact was quickly hushed up; the man suffered the same fate as an American black caught tampering with Boss Charlie's lady, and no word for the unspeakable offspring of this anarchistic union has come down to us. The word quickly took on its modern meaning of *any* illegitimate child, however, without any class distinction, and William the Conqueror was more familiarly known to his contemporaries as William the Bastard.

The word has lost most of its sting in both England and America (especially since bastards have been admitted to the House of Lords, as Robert Graves whimsically noted), and if you really want to insult somebody you have to add a modifier, such as *lying* bastard, *dirty* bastard, *thieving* bastard, etc. Two novelists have contributed more energetic intensities: BITCH's bastard (Joyce in *Ulysses,* quoting real Dublinese) and *filthy, foul bitch's* bastard (in Frederick Wakeman's 1950s novel of show biz, *The Saxon Charm).* Meanwhile, *Joe, you old bastard!* is an expression of affection among lower-class males in England and males of all classes in America.

BAT

Hobo slang for a prostitute, allegedly because they come out around twilight, and probably the source of the insult calling a middle-aged woman an "old bat."

BATTER

To copulate; probably related to BANG, *wham* and similar violent sexual metaphors, and possibly derived from Latin *batuere,* the origin of our English FUCK. According to psychoanalysts, baseball bats often appear in dreams as symbols of the phallus, and interestingly, the great Oedipal cuss word, MOTHERFUCKER, is a favorite with baseball players. (There was a sharp reaction of public disapproval when the press made some guarded references to this fact a few years ago.) Also noteworthy is the folk parody of "Grandfather's Clock," which contains the lines:

> My grandfather's cock
> Was too big for his jock
> So it hung ninety years by his side.
> It was long, it was fat,
> It was like a baseball bat,
> It was grandfather's treasure and his pride.

B & D

Bondage and discipline; a code used in personal ads for sadomasochistic practices.

BEACH BASH

Biker's slang for a sex party on the oceanfront. Compare the related old show-biz joke about Southampton, Long Island, a favorite resort for the Broadway jet set, where, it is said, "actresses lie on the sand and look at the stars, while producers lie on the stars and look at the sand."

BEARD

The female pubic area – and surely this is merely a harmless visual metaphor? If one suggests that a beard is often attacked by a razor, one could be accused of carrying Freudianism to the point where it staggers. Pause, then, and ask a friend to name the three most famous murderers in history. Almost certainly Jack the Ripper will lead the list. The Ripper, of course, is known for removing the genitalia and sometimes the breasts and wombs of women he killed, using a surgical scalpel. He shaved their beards, so to speak.

Around the turn of the present century, the male beard became an object of derision and was banned. The clean-shaven look (which actually makes the difference between the sexes less obvious by making men more like women) became mandatory. Men who persisted in wearing whiskers were hooted at in the streets and greeted with shouts of "Beaver!" – a word also used for the female pubic hair. This was a complete reversal of the traditional male attitudes, in which a beardless boy was regarded with contempt.

When Jake Ehrlich, the famous San Francisco attorney, first started practicing law, an opposing lawyer once called him a "beardless boy." Ehrlich replied without blinking, "If I knew you judged intelligence by face hairs, I would have sent my goat."

A "beard-splitter," in hobo slang, is a Don Juan, and the "bearded clam" is an East Coast witticism for the vulva. The following joke also lends itself to interpretation: An American, a Russian and an Arab are cast away on a desert island. Suddenly they see a beautiful woman in a sarong. "She's mine!" cries the American, pointing to the design of stars and stripes on her sarong. He rushes forward and tears off the flimsy garment, but then red panties are revealed beneath it. "The red flag!" cries the Russian. "She's mine!" He dashes to her and rips off the panties. The Arab smiles. "The beard of Allah . . ." he says calmly.

In the 17th Century drama entitled *Sodom,* prince Pricket and the princess, fair Swivia (from 17th-18th Century slang, *swive,* to copulate), are found in a GARDEN; she is attempting to seduce him. Their speech concerning her own garden is the poetic high point of the play:

> *Pricket*: It has a beard, too, and the mouth's all raw,

The strangest creature that I ever saw.

Swivia: Twas such a thing, philosophers have taught,

That all mankind into the world have brought;

Twas such a thing the King, our sire, bestrid

Out of whose womb we come.

Pricket: The devil we did!

Swivia: This is the workhouse of the world's chief trade,

On this soft anvil all mankind was made

Come, this is a harmless thing, draw near and try

You will desire no other death to die.

See also COTTON and MUFF.

BEAT THE MEAT

Male MASTURBATION; probably deriving from the old use of *meatus* to mean the penis. Recall in *Portnoy's Complaint* his masturbation fantasy of the talking brassiere saying to him, "Oh beat it, Big Boy, beat it to a red-hot pulp." The variation *beat the dummy,* frequently heard in New York, refers to that other NARCISSISTIC art, ventriloquism, and the conversations some men (such as Mellors in *Lady Chatterley's Lover*) have with their WANGS. There are even horror stories in which the dummy comes alive; one such yarn was made into an English movie with Michael Redgrave. The homosexual equivalent is the story of the man destroyed by his "talking ass hole" in Burroughs's *Naked Lunch.*

BEATTIE AND BABS

Body lice; probably from Cockney rhyming slang for CRABS.

BEAVER

The female pubic hair. A "beaver shot" is a photograph showing the pubic hair, and a "split beaver" is a photo in which the lips of the vulva are open and visible. See BEARD and SPREAD SHOT for related terms.

BEEFCAKE

Homosexual slang for male pinups. Perhaps this contains a reference to BEEF INJECTION, black slang for copulation in which *beef* means the penis. It is doubtful, however, that Beefeater Gin has a deliberate pun in its name. See also CHEESECAKE.

BEEF INJECTION

Black and rural southern slang meaning copulation, as in "I'd like to give that chick a beef injection," and similar to the homosexual use of *hot dog* to mean the penis.

BEHIND THE BEHIND

Male SODOMY, or BUGGERY; derived from *beyond the beyond,* a satirical phrase ridiculing any highfaluting or pretentious conversation, especially about the occult or transcendental: "Oh, here we go again, beyond the beyond."

BELLE

Formerly meant a beautiful woman; now almost exclusively homosexual slang meaning an especially desirable young man.

BELLY QUEEN

A homosexual who prefers intercourse in the heterosexual face-to-face position. The penis is inserted in the anus or between the thighs.

BENDER

A homosexual; perhaps from a series of insulting rhymes that used to be shouted at suspected homosexuals by tough kids in Brooklyn; for example, "He sucks for the luck"; "He bends for his friends." Similarly, to "go on a bender" is to get very drunk; to "go around the bend" is to become insane; and (in England) *He's bent* means he is perverted, usually with an implication of sadism. QUEER also comes from a root meaning bent, deflected or turned.

And then there's the story about the New England lady who married a man who confessed on their wedding night that his only previous erotic experiences were homosexual. "Good Heavens," she wept, "now I don't know which way to turn."

BENNIE

WHORE's slang for a customer who prefers CUNNILINGUS to coitus. Probably from *benny* for benzedrine, an amphetamine, the implication being that such a customer provides a special flash or rush.

BESSIE

A male homosexual; often used by homosexuals themselves when angry, as in "Oh, come off it, Bessie."

BEULAH

A homosexual male; often used by another homosexual

in a derogatory way, as in "Oh, stop it, Beulah, you're coming on like gang-busters." *Coming on like gang-busters* used to be exclusively homosexual slang – it refers to the old radio show, which began with a blast of machine-gun fire – until Barry Goldwater used it in a speech during the 1968 presidential campaign. And Senator Goldwater, by the way, who once designed a product called "antsy-pants" and spoke of an ideal missile as one that "could hit the men's room in the Kremlin," successfully sued Ralph Ginzburg for implying that he was a latent homosexual and a paranoid. Senator Goldwater is *not* a latent homosexual or paranoid.

BIG BROTHER

The erect penis. This is one of the many examples of men personalizing their virile members, as in the routine, "Jock is a strapping lad; he supports his brother, Dick, and his two cousins, Tom and Harry, who are nuts." See LITTLE SISTER, JOCK, DICK and NUTS.

BIG CONK, BIG COCK

A catchphrase meaning that a man with a big nose will also have a large penis. This is widely believed in rural areas, although medical science doesn't support it. In urban settings the possessor of a large beak is more likely to be greeted with insult or ridicule, such as "If I had a schnozz like that, I'd wear a shoulder holster." There is a parallel superstition that a woman with a big mouth will also have a big vagina, but this is not regarded as especially desirable, since the ideal woman is often said to be "half Indian and half Scotch," which is explained for the naive as meaning savage and tight.

THE BIG O

Orgasm. This phrase inspired a rumor or hoax, perpetrated by *The Realist* magazine, which claimed the U.S. government possessed a new weapon – the O Bomb – which could conquer an enemy by rendering him helpless in spasms of ecstasy. The punch line was that the Pentagon wouldn't use this device because, unlike the hydrogen bomb, it was considered immoral. A lapel button saying "OH, DROP THE O BOMB" appeared in the wake of this rumor.

BIG SHIT

A satirical variation of *big shot,* a put-down intended to show lack of admiration. Similar is *big wheel,* sometimes with the sardonic explanation, "He goes around in circles, so he thinks he's a big wheel." Similarly: "He's an important man – he has 2000 people under him. He's night watchman in a cemetery!" and "He comes from a big iron and steel family. His mother irons and his father steals."

BI-LINGUAL

Code used in personal ads, signifying a desire to have oral sex with both men and women. *Bi-minded,* in the same ads, means bisexual or AC/DC. The rationale of such persons is memorably stated by a character in Mailer's *An American Dream:* "It's all friction."

BIMBO

In vulgar speech, any female; originally, a prostitute. From the Italian *bambino,* baby.

BIRD

In England, a woman; in America sometimes used to mean a homosexual, but more often just an unknown person, as in "Who's that bird standing in the door?" The English usage was most prominently displayed in the novel and movie, *Alfie,* in which the antihero, Alfie, refers to all his female conquests as birds and speaks of them in such complimentary terms as "The new bird is almost human," or "This bird almost had a brain." The connotation of homosexuality goes back to at least 1920, when Fitzgerald used it in *This Side of Paradise:* "If only that St. Paul's crowd at the next table would not mistake him for a bird, too . . ." Terms like *yardbird* and *jailbird* derive from the idea of "anybody" or an unknown person; a jailbird is anybody who happens to have been in prison. In the South, a bird may also mean a penis, and in southern military academies a suspected homosexual is said to be "taking birds." See also COCK, CANARY, FLY and PIMP.

BIRTHDAY SUIT

To be in one's birthday suit is to be stark naked, as in "There he stood in his birthday suit." This is still popular and regarded as wit among prepubescent children, but is far from modern; it dates back to the 18th Century. See IN THE ALTOGETHER and SKINNY DIPPING.

BISHOP

To *make a bishop,* in rural English slang, is to have intercourse with the woman on top; *to beat the bishop* is schoolboy slang for MASTURBATION; and in some parts of the country a bishop is A CONDOM. Another affront to bishops is the limerick:

> A habit obscene and unsavory

Holds the bishop of Boston in slavery.
Midst hootings and howls
He deflowers young owls
Which he keeps in an underground aviary.

And the equally impious:

There were two young ladies from Birmingham,
And this is the story concerning 'em:
They lifted the smock
And tickled the cock
Of the Bishop as he was confirming 'em!

BITCH

A WHORE or highly promiscuous woman; also, any malicious or domineering woman; deriving from Middle English *bicche,* a female dog. *Son-of-a-bitch* is a modern form of Shakespeare's double-barreled insult "thou whoreson dog." The association is based on the notable lack of selectivity usually exhibited by female dogs IN HEAT. Outside of Shakespeare, the only memorable use of this imagery occurs in a story where, paradoxically, the phrase *isn't* used – the well-known yarn of the gentle Quaker who, driven past the limits of his Christian forbearance, finally shouts at his tormentor, "And when thou goest to thy home tonight, may thy mother run out from under the porch and bite thee!"

The verb *bitched* has two different meanings: *He bitched the job* (he did it poorly) has a vastly different connotation from *He bitched about the job* (he complained). The explanation of the second kind of bitching may be related to chewing ("He chewed me out") after the analogy of a dog gnawing a bone. Similarly, *worry* comes from an old root meaning to chew or gnaw like a DOG. The dog was the first animal to be domesticated and our language has many similes based on a dog's behavior: Bill collectors "hound" us, angry people "bark" at us, a coward retreats "with his tail between his legs," complainers "whine," threateners "growl." Some of us even "bark up the wrong tree." Since female canines are good hunters, good watchdogs and as generally competent as males, it is still unclear why "bitching" a job means doing it poorly. As for the adjective *bitchy*, meaning snappy or complaining, as in "Be careful, she's in a really bitchy mood today," this may derive from the female dog's irritability and snappishness when protecting a litter of newborn puppies.

BITCHED, BUGGERED AND BEWILDERED

A phrase sometimes used literally of a young and inexperienced girl after her first session of varietistic intercourse ("She was bitched, buggered and bewildered"); more often, a simple metaphor for one who is confused and suspects a swindle ("I read the contract and it left me bitched, buggered and bewildered"). This was reflected in a popular song title of the 1950s: "Bewitched, Bothered and Bewildered."

Similar expressions are *laid, relayed and parlayed,* generally meaning a satisfying, multi-orgasmic night of love; and *screwed, blued and tattooed,* having the same meaning but sometimes used to mean betrayed or double-crossed. See also FUCKED AND FAR FROM HOME.

BITCH HEAVEN

Hobo and underworld slang for the city of Boston; based on the old belief that Boston had more cheap prostitutes than any other large city in the country.

BITCH'S CHRISTMAS

Homosexual slang for Halloween, when the GAY set celebrates with masked balls or DRAG parties. This excerpt from black folklore (recorded in *Deep Down in the Jungle,* a book by Roger Abrahams) gives a colorful picture of one of these festivities, which in black slang is called a "Freak's Ball":

> We gonna have a ball
> Down the bulldagger's hall.
> There's gonna be thirty-nine cockheads fried in snot,
> Two or three pickled dicks tied in a knot.
> There's gonna be long cock, short cock, cock without bone.
> You can fuck a cock, suck a cock, or leave a god damn cock alone.

BITE

In Cockney, either a woman's genitalia or a cheat; a biter is a highly sexed woman. This term reflects what psychoanalysts call the *vagina dentata* (the vagina armed with teeth) myth – a common male anxiety fantasy. One of the best-known *vagina dentata* jokes in America involves a repressive mother who tells her son that the female organ contains a wolf that will bit off his penis if he ever rashly attempts intercourse. When he is finally tempted, he asks the lady to close her eyes and experimentally inserts a broom handle before risking his own organ. At this moment, the lady's stomach rumbles, and he cries, "Growl all you want; you're not getting my dick!"

BITE THE BROWN

To perform ANALINGUS, also called "going up mustard

road," or "going up the Hershey Bar road." This diversion is regarded with great repugnance by most Americans, but its devotees defend themselves with a crude pun: "Once you've got past the smell, you have it licked."

BLACKJACK

Homosexual slang for the penis of a black man; from the blackjack (a piece of lead or iron in a black leather sheath) used by some policemen and certain criminals to quiet those who oppose them.

BLACK VELVET

A black woman, or the vagina of a black woman. "He's got a black velvet hangup": He only has sex with black women.

BLAZE THE TRAIL

To copulate with a virgin. In Irish-American slang, a "blazer" is a man who seduces virgins. A resolute Freudian might find in this metaphor a clue to the character of those explorers who blaze the trail to a "virgin" country (nowadays a new planet) and set up a flagpole there (see POLE), but some prefer to leave the exploration to others and move in when the territory has already been cultivated. Ex-New York Mayor James Walker remarked that George Washington was "first in war, first in peace, and first in the hearts of his countrymen – but he married a widow."

For some men, seducing virgins is almost a fetish; witness the Texan who placed this ad:

> ATTENTION virgins! I am an affluent, good-looking, healthy, white man of 45

who has never had a virgin and wants you desperately enough to do practically anything for you in return. I am of average size, youthful condition, well built, extremely generous, considerate, sensitive, sincere, intelligent, versatile, sensuous, a world traveler having means of getting together wherever you are. Would be patient & cooperative . . .

BLIND CHEEKS

The buttocks. *I'll give him a hit where it won't blind him* is Irish-American wit, meaning "I'll kick his arse." The cheek metaphor was also used by Bob Hope in the 1940s, causing him to be cut off the radio when he said, in effect, "If girls wear their skirts any shorter they'll have to buy another hairnet and powder two more cheeks." But Hope was only paraphrasing an old gag from the 1920s, which went (in verse):

> If dresses get much shorter,
> Said Mary, with a sob,
> I'll have two more cheeks to powder
> And one more place to bob.

BLISTER

A prostitute; from the notion that these ladies are more likely than not to be carrying venereal disease. One should here recall Flaubert's remark that he knew many young men who avoided WHORES for that reason "and then caught the most beautiful cases of clap from their middle-class sweethearts." See BURNED, BITE, CLAP.

BLOODY

A general intensifier that is mysteriously regarded as obscene in England; it has been suggested that it has something to do with menstruation or is a contraction of *by our Lady.* A popular ditty considered daring during the First World War, entitled "The Great Australian Adjective," parodied the Aussies' fondness for the word in such couplets as "He leaped upon his bloody horse/ And galloped off of-bloody-course . . ." This circulated widely in mimeograph form, but was not published till the late 1920s, in Robert Graves's essay on swearing, "Lars Porsena," where it appeared with the key word abbreviated to b - - - - y. In parts of Latin America, even today, bars frequented by English tourists tactfully list Bloody Mary as "B. Mary."

BLOW

To perform oral sex upon a person. A "blow job" is FELLATIO, or in common parlance, COCKSUCKING. A "blower" was originally the mistress of a highwayman or other outlaw; to "blow the grounsils" is to copulate with a woman on the floor; *He hit the blow* means he stole the goods; to "blow the gab" is to confess a crime.

Blow also means to ruin; *We blew it,* meaning we ruined everything, is very widespread in youth-culture speech today and very nearly the last line of the popular movie, *Easy Rider.*

Andy Warhol's movie, *Blow Job,* always evokes a powerful reaction. Whenever an art theater announces this will be shown, a record audience turns out. After a few minutes, embarrassment overcomes prurience and people begin laughing and shouting jokes at the screen. (The film runs nearly half an hour and the most popular audience diversion is to sing – to the tune of "We Shall Overcome" – "He Shall Never Co-oo-oome!")

The extent of this taboo in our culture is also suggested by a significant fact about the two great novels that smashed the sexual censorship of the 1920s: Joyce's *Ulysses* and Lawrence's *Lady Chatterley's Lover*. Both books, although daring to print "forbidden words" like FUCK and CUNT and to describe coitus frankly, avoided tackling FELLATIO in a direct fashion. Joyce's Molly Bloom only *thinks* she *might* like to try it sometime; Lawrence's Connie Chatterley does not take Mellors's penis in her mouth, but merely kisses it.

Needless to say, we owe considerable verbal merriment to the sexual connotations of *blow,* for example, this joke: "On the High Holidays," a Jewish gentleman explains to a Gentile lady friend, "we always blow the *shofar*" (a ceremonial ram's horn sounded in the synagogue service). "How sweet," murmurs the liberal lady, "I've always heard that Jewish people are so kind to their help . . ."

The most exquisitely esthetic blow job in modern fiction, without doubt, is that described in the scene between the director and the LESBIAN actress in Terry Southern's *Blue Movie*. Boris's erect cock has become obvious, and Arabella asks:

> ". . . Is that for Arabella?"
>
> ". . . I'm beginning to think that it is," he admitted.
>
> "Oh, Boris, you're wonderful," she said with a marvelous laugh, and slowly pulled down the zipper, and took it out – holding it carefully, studying it. "Just look at it – all throbbing and eager, and no place to go."
>
> "No place to *come,* you mean," said Boris, trying to maintain a cavalier mien – he was beginning to suspect her of being one of the world's great prick-teasers.

"Why do they have to be so big?" she said, her head to one side regarding it with a little-girl pouting expression. "Maybe if they weren't so big I could do it."

"Sorry," said Boris.

"No, no *chéri*, " she laughed, "it's *perfect*. I wish I had one exactly like it. And look, it's so hungry," she touched a small glistening drop on the head, "it's drooling." She sighed, and looked at him, now holding it very firmly in her right hand. "Yes, I promise you one day we will – not now, it would upset me too much, would be bad for the picture, but one day…" She giggled, and added, "maybe if I am on *top*…" Then she returned her attention to the member straining in her grasp. "But now we've got to stop it from throbbing and aching and everything, yes?"

"Yes," Boris agreed hopefully.

"It *is* a beautiful thing," she admitted, and closing her great lovely eyes, and moistening her heavy red lips, she opened her mouth and slowly, tenderly took it inside.

Boris sighed with relief that it was actually going to happen. He made a mental note to be sure and *fuck* Arabella as soon as possible – then he returned his attention to her fabulous head, and as he did, she stopped for a second and looked up with a soft smile, all breathless, dewy-eyed, and shimmering wet lips. "Are you going to come in Arabella's beautiful mouth?"

"Uh, something like that," said Boris thinking, My God, is she going to stop now?

She nodded, closed her eyes, opened her mouth, then looked up at him, assuming her little-girl pout. "I guess she has to *swallow it*, doesn't she?"

"Yep."

She smiled her secret smile. "Good – she wants to swallow it."

She resumed in earnest, Boris fondling both nipples, squeezing them hard, and she reacting more ravenously the harder he squeezed. When he started to come, he let go of her nipples and took her head in his hands, holding it and pulling it to him, wanting to come as deep inside her famous, beautiful mouth as possible, to explode against the very back of her virgin throat. And she devoured it, gulping and sucking as in some insatiable desperation, until every drop was drained – and Boris, in a state of collapse, weakly pushed her head away.

"Wow," he murmured.

Arabella looked up at him, her huge eyes shimmering, happy knowing she had pleased. "Hmm," her pink tongue moved around her glistening lips, "it's strange, I always thought there would be more of it."

"Well . . . it's very *rich*."

"Oh, it's fantastic, it tastes so . . . I don't know, so *alive*. "

Boris, eyes closed, reached out and found her hand. "Yeah, I guess it would at that."

BLUE

A color often associated with sex. A "blue movie" is a SKIN FLICK; a joke that is "blue around the edges" is "off-color" – namely, a sex story. The origin may be the 18th Century Blue Boar Tavern of ripe reputation. *Blue boar* became a slang term for venereal disease during this London bistro's lifetime.

The fact that "Bluebeard" (Gilles de Lavel) was convicted of mass murder may or may not contribute something to this association of ideas; a "blue squadron" is the children of interracial (black-white) marriages, perhaps from the white prejudice that such unions are obscene, but perhaps with a reference to the skin color thought to result by those who have never seen such children. *Blueskin* has been white-racist slang for a Negro since 1865, and "the blues" is black music. Oddly, a "bluenose" is not a RANDY or HORNY person at all, but a conspicuously puritanical one.

BLUE BALLS

In some parts of America, gonorrhea; in other places, the cramps experienced by men after prolonged desire or PETTING without orgasm. From *blue* referring to bruised, as in "black and blue." An attempt by Ralph Ginzburg to mail his magazine, *Eros,* from Blue Ball, Pennsylvania, was cited by the majority of the Supreme Court as evidence of his "pandering" intent, and thus this bit of whimsy is part of the reason he went to prison. Ginzburg also attempted to mail from Intercourse, Pennsylvania, but, like Blue Ball, it did not have a large enough post office. (He finally settled for Middlesex, New Jersey.) Ginzburg was probably inspired by the old joke concerning these oddly named Pennsylvania towns – that the road from Intercourse to Paradise leads to Blue Balls.

BOG HOUSE

An outhouse or privy in English slang. The "bogey" or the "bogeyman," a mythical figure used to intimidate children, as in "Eat your carrots or the bogeyman will come and get you," is an anal monster. A "boogie" is a black man or adult Negro – an insulting racist term not used in polite company. The association of *boogie* with *bogie*, working on the minds of little children, may account for some of the persistence of emotional racism in parts of America; Boogie Woogie, in 1920s American slang, was black music. In contemporary Texas, the "Dirty Dallas Boogie" is a dance in which the face is kept in an aloof frown, *a la* Spanish flamenco, while the pelvis performs very erotic gyrations.

BONE

The penis; a "bone-on" is an erection (also known as a HARD-ON); "Bone-Queen," a cocksucking homosexual. An old riddle asks, "How far apart did Napoleon and Josephine sleep?" and answers, "Only a bone apart."

Another joke on this topic concerns the duchess who was touring an army hospital after the war. "And where were you wounded, my good man?" she asks one soldier. "In – er – the male organ," he answers mournfully. "And did it break the bone?" she asks in horror. "Madam," he replies, "my compliments to the Duke!"

BOOBOOS

The testicles; in earlier centuries, venereal disease. Often spelled *bubus*. Not to be confused with *making booboos* (mistakes) which derives from the Spanish *bobo* (foolish, silly, stupid).

BOOBS

The female breasts, also called "boobies." Probably related to *bulb, bulbous,* and also to *bobbing,* an up-and-down motion. A British ad for the movie, *Taking Off!,* under the head "BOOBS!" and a picture of a lady with quite a revealing decolletage, said:

> Boobs are what people make when they don't concentrate on what they're doing. They also make arms and legs and little girls. When little girls grow up they sometimes Take Off to put their boobs to proper use/misuse (depending on your moral climate). When the parents try to bring their erring offspring back to the family boob, the boob and the bird attached feel like "Taking Off" again. That's what "Taking Off" is all about. "Taking Off" is a movie. You've got to see it. Would we lie? O.K., cross our boobs!

BOSOM

The female breasts; ultimately derived from Sanskrit *bhasman,* blowing (in the sense of blooming). There may also be a link with *boss* (meaning protuberance), as in *emboss.* A "bossie" (cow) is an animal noted for its mammary glands. *Boss* also means the best, the finest ("That was boss grass") in black slang, recently adopted by some whites. See BOOBS, TITS.

BOSTON TEA PARTY

A "specialty," as prostitutes say, in which the man – an odd duck, or KINK – pays to have the woman use him in preference to the toilet bowl when emptying her bladder. This is also called GOLDEN SHOWERS. Those who seek the more thorough masochism of being defecated upon ask for "pound cake."

The Book of Forbidden Words

BOTTLE

To perform anal intercourse on a woman. Actually, using a bottle (or a corncob, or a broom handle, or any variety of objects) on a woman's vagina has been the fantasy of many men. Comedian Fatty Arbuckle faced criminal charges in 1921 after actress Virginia Rappe died at one of his parties. The legend that Fatty actually raped Virginia with a champagne bottle (some say it was a less elegant Coke bottle) still persists, and most people have forgotten that he stood trial three times, got a hung jury on the first two occasions and was acquitted the third time. Nevertheless, the comedian was blacklisted by the studios and died in poverty. An alternate rumor has it that the unfortunate Miss Rappe died from the sheer size of Fatty's TOOL. All that the medical evidence could say was that she died of a ruptured bladder.

BOTTOM

The buttocks; from Indo-European *bhund,* to place solidly.

BOTTOMS UP

A well-known English toast, but the same words are sometimes used in the United States to signify sexual intercourse in the typical mammalian position, DOG FASHION or "Lassie fashion."

BOTTOM WOMAN

Black and white southern slang for a PIMP's first or most dependable WHORE, usually his wife or sweetheart. She is usually the foundation of his sexual empire. See BOTTOM.

BOX

The female genitalia, as in the old joke, "She didn't like to wrestle, but you should see her box." This term, although recent, is obscure in origin; it may have come from the Greek myth about Pandora's Box. Freud also points out that the box is often, in dreams, a symbol of the vagina or womb. See MONEY and HIDDEN TREASURE.

BOX LUNCH

He goes down for a box lunch means he performs CUNNILINGUS. New York wits sometimes elaborate this into *He goes down to the "Y" for a box lunch,* the "Y" being a pictogram of the female pubic area jokingly disguised as a scandalous reference to the YWCA.

BOY IN THE BOAT

The clitoris; a slang expression that has lasted since the 18th Century.

BREAKFAST IN BED

CUNNILINGUS. Compare with box lunch.

BREAKING LUCK

A WHORE's first customer of the day, as in "The john who broke my luck today was a bennie." See JOHN and BENNIE.

BRICK SHIT-HOUSE

A hyperbole signifying absolute perfection of structure, usually said of a well-endowed young lady: "She's built like a brick shit-house"; or sometimes, more elegantly, "like a row of brick shit-houses." W.C. Fields managed to sneak a disguised version of this past the strict 1930s movie censors, saying of Mae West in *My Little*

Chickadee, "She's solid as a brick telephone booth." See also *bang like a shit-house door* under BANG.

BROAD

In some circles this synonym for a woman is regarded as insulting, although nobody seems to know why. (The clue might be the Elizabethan use of *road* to signify a prostitute, although others derive it from *bawd.)* In other circles, especially show biz, it was permissible and fashionable usage in the 1950s by such as Frank Sinatra. But in 1958 Rudyard Kipling's daughter, Mrs. Elsie Bambridge, protested publicly against Sinatra's substituting *broad* for *girl* in his recording of "On the Road to Mandalay."

BROKE HER ANKLE

Middle-class American code for a woman having gotten pregnant out of wedlock or, in some parts of the country, having had an ABORTION. Similarly, what psychoanalysts call "displacement downward" – the genitalia being symbolized by the legs or feet – makes the penis the MIDDLE LEG, or the "third leg." A promiscuous woman may be called a WALK IN.

No less a theologian than Saint Jerome, who wrote the Vulgate translation of the Bible, was of the opinion that the Old Testament was written in code, with *foot* every time it appears actually meaning penis. This theory is bypassed in silence by more recent churchmen.

The extreme form of displacement downward is the foot-fetishism which inspires those individuals who are sexually aroused by feet or shoes. Oddly, just about the only movie dealing at length with this subject is Luis Buñuel's *This Strange Passion,* made in the early 1930s, in which the hero acquires this predilection after watching a bishop perform the old Catholic ritual of kissing the feet of the faithful. (This film did not receive mass distribution in the United States, then or at any later time.)* This personal ad sums up ankle/leg fetishism very well:

> "White male, age 43, would like to hear from a long-legged, large-ankled woman, preferably with fair skin or freckles, for intimate times, fun, friendship . . ."

~•~

* This Strange Passion (AKA Él, 1953) seems here to be conflated with L'Âge D'Or (1930). The former indeed opens with such a scene of the Catholic ritual, but only hints at foot fetishism. The latter features an infamous toe-sucking scene and did not get a proper U.S. release before 1979. – *Editor*

~•~

There is also a joke about a fellow who is asked by a strange girl he has picked up to give her a "toe job." He obligingly brings her to orgasm by wriggling his toes in her vagina, but two weeks later irritation sends him to the doctor and he learns that he has gonorrhea of the big toe. "I'll bet this is the strangest case you ever saw," he says, trying to cover his embarrassment. "Not at all," the doctor replies. "Why, last week I treated a girl for athlete's foot of the vagina!"

BRONCO

A young male recently initiated into homosexual activity who may be difficult to deal with: deriving from Spanish *broncho,* wild, through Texan *bronco,* a wild horse. Just as some homosexuals are obsessed with black leather and motorcycle gangs, others are turned on by cowboy clothes and western lore. This was satirized in a pseudo-folk song of the 1940s, "Lavender Cowboy:"

> Red, green and many-colored hair tonics
> He rubbed on his chest day and night,
> But when he looked in the mirror next morning
> No new hairs grew in sight.
>
> He always rode tall in the saddle,
> He cleaned out a holdup's nest,
> He died with his six-guns a-blazing
> – But only two hairs on his chest.

See LAVENDER.

BRONX CHEER

A noise that sounds like a fart, made by blowing through the lips; also called a "raspberry"; from old rhyming slang, *raspberry tart,* meaning a fart. This allegedly originated in the burlesque and vaudeville theatres in the Bronx to show audience dissatisfaction with incompetent performers.

BROWN

To perform anal intercourse; probably from the brown color of feces. The term is in general use among heterosexuals as well as homosexuals, but the *Browning family* or the *Browning sisters* is exclusively homosexual slang for those devoted to this pastime. The reference, a sarcastic one, is to the family of Victorian poetess Elizabeth Barrett Browning.

BROWN EYES

Southern slang for the female breasts or nipples. The popular 1950s song, "Beautiful Brown Eyes," was quite amusing to people aware of this usage, especially its refrain, which was "I'll never love blue eyes again."

BROWN NOSE

A synonym for *ass-kisser.* In school, a student who is a favorite with the teachers; in business or the Army, a recruit who advances rapidly. See A.K.

B.S.

An abbreviation of BULLSHIT. According to contemporary folklore, two farmers were discussing the mysterious degrees toward which their sons were working in college. "Can this B.S. mean what it looks like?" one asks. "I suppose," says the other, "but what's M.S.?" "More of the same, I guess." "And this here Ph.D.?" "Piled Higher and Deeper!"

BUCK NAKED

Totally nude, without a stitch. *Buck Negro* or *buck nigger* are racist terms, implying that blacks are animals. *Buckaroo* (a tough hombre in Western America) is complimentary, however, although some animal identification is again implied. *Buck* comes from the Old English *bucca,* a male goat, and Modern English *buck,* any male animal.

He's quite a buck is still used to imply animal virility, similar to *He's a stud with the ladies;* and then there's Mulligan's comment in Joyce's *Ulysses:* "Readheaded women buck like goats."

But *buck* meaning a dollar comes from frontier days when large skins were called "bucks" and smaller, less valuable skins were "does," after the bucks and does (males and females) of the deer family. Hobos still call priests "bucks" and nuns "does," allegedly from the fact that priests have more money to offer when you beg from them.

The male, or buck, goat has long been identified with an excess of sexual energy and has been worshipped since the Stone Age as the embodiment of the male generative power. The male goat, or horned god, is still an important symbol in contemporary witch cults in England and America. In classical Greece there was the god Pan with his horns and cloven hooves. In the Christian era this old fertility god, in degenerate form, becomes none other than the horned tempter, the Christian devil.

Another sign of the degeneration of the once lordly phallic deity is the contemptuous expression *You old goat!* Also, *giving the horns,* either as a verbal comment or manual gesture to denote cuckoldry, may be a sardonic reference to the fallen god. See HORNY.

BUGGER

To perform anal intercourse; probably from the inquisitor, Robert le Bougre, who sought evidence of this kind of sodomy in each heretic he questioned and ultimately condemned to death. This charge by the church was so common during the medieval period, against any and all groups who questioned its dogma, that an alternate derivation of *bugger* from *Bulgar* has been suggested, since several proto-Protestant heresies arose in Bulgaria, but the crime was attributed to heretical movements all over Europe.

Buggery is not an exclusively homosexual pastime; many heterosexual men practice it with willing mates. The climax of John Updike's novel, *Rabbit, Run,* occurs when the hero attempts to persuade his wife to try this variation. She refuses, and, angry, he leaves and goes to a WHORE. His wife then drinks herself into a stupor and accidentally drowns their baby.

The anus has long been linked with the devil (note the foul odors of sulphur and brimstone when His Majesty appears). This medieval association still lingers on: In *An American Dream,* Norman Mailer's hero thinks of a female character's vagina as God's territory and her anus as the devil's, enacting (in his own mind) a complicated theological struggle as he alternately copulates with each.

Buggery as brutality, as a form of dominance of one male over another, is a pattern going back to our simian ancestors; this idea is expressed in the graffito, "Homosexuality is a pain in the ass." The anus as an object of sadism is exemplified in the crude old folk ballad, "One-Eyed Riley":

> Walking through the park one day,
> Who should I meet but Riley's daughter.
> Never a word I had to say
> But "Don't you think we really oughta?"
> Up the stairs and into bed,
> I humped and humped until I stove her.
> Never a word the maiden said,
> When the fun was over
> But she laughed like hell.
> Suddenly the door smashed in,
> And who stood there but One-Eyed Riley,
> Two horse-pistols on his belt,
> He was in a fit entirely.
> I grabbed old Riley by the hair,
> Shoved his head in a bucket of water,
> Rammed the two horse pistols up his butt,
> Harder than I had humped his daughter.
> Now all you maidens, all you girls,
> Answer now and don't speak shyly,
> Do you want it straight and true,
> Or the way I gave it to One-Eyed Riley?

An interesting contemplation of *buggering* also appears in Hunter Thompson's *Hell's Angels*. Thompson discusses lawyers who demolish rape victims on the witness stand by making rape seem impossible: "Any lawyer who says there's no such thing as rape should be hauled out to a public place by three large perverts and buggered at high noon, with all his clients watching."

BULL DYKE

A formidable, masculine-acting female homosexual, also known as a "bulldagger" and a "bull bitch"; from *bull* as an image of male virility. *Dyke* originally implied a vagina which, due to frequent usage, had attained the size of an engineering excavation. A dagger is an obvious phallic symbol.

BULLSHIT

An expression of disbelief. B.S.A. or Bullshit Artist are titles often bestowed on those whose conversation is chiefly devoted to self-glorification. Another put-down widely practiced is to pantomime the act of shoveling after they finish speaking, as if disposing of what they have dumped on you. A third variation is to shout in imitation dismay: "Grab the shovels and run for the hills, it's oozing over the windowsills!" A cynical Oklahoma joke says that you can squeeze twenty Texans into a phone booth "if you let the hot air and bullshit out of them first." Another version has it that you can ship a dead Texan home in a shoebox if you give him an enema first. See PIG, OWL SHIT.

BUM

In America, the buttocks, anus, or occasionally, the breast; but chiefly the buttocks in English slang. There are several possible origins: from *bottom* by simple contraction; from *boom* and/or Middle English *bommen,* to hum – an indelicate reference to the anus being, as Shakespeare said, "a wind instrument"; from Danish *bodem,* the anus; from German *bummler,* one who loafs or sits down on the job; from *bung,* an opening, as the bunghole of a keg or barrel, which in later English becomes, significantly, a term for either the anus or the purse. *Bumpkin* is a contemptuous term for a country boy. Other "bum" phrases in English slang include *bum brusher,* a schoolmaster (from the British habit of caning students); *bum fiddle,* another quasi-humorous title for the anus; *bumfodder,* toilet paper; and in American slang, *bum steer,* bad advice.

BUNS

The buttocks, usually of a female, as in "Dig the buns on that chick." *She has a bun in the oven,* heard both in England and here, means that the woman in question is pregnant; *It was early in the oven,* said after childbirth, means that the neighbors have learned to count on their fingers (although not to mind their own business) and have calculated that the time from the wedding to the birth was less than nine months.

BURNED

To have caught a venereal disease. Shakespeare puns on this in *King Lear:* "No heretics burned but wenches' suitors." *Burnt offering* is 18th and 19th Century English Navy slang: *He came home a burnt offering* means he caught the CLAP from a foreign woman. Nowadays the term also applies to having incurred any misfortune and is commonly used in the drug world. A meeting place is "burned down" when the police are known to have an eye on it; a dealer who sells inferior drugs is a "burn artist" or, if he specializes in seeking out the very gullible, he "burns the tourists"; and *I'll burn him* is underworld slang for "I'll shoot him on sight."

BURY THE BONE

To copulate; probably based on *bone-on,* a rural variation of HARD-ON. See BONE.

BURY THE HATCHET WHERE IT WON'T RUST

To have intercourse; comparable to the Irish *put it out of sight.* This is probably derived from *bury the hatchet,* meaning to end a quarrel, sexual intercourse being a frequent way of ending a quarrel between a couple. Compare the folk witticism: "The happiest journey a man ever takes is out of the doghouse and into the bedroom." See DOGHOUSE.

BUSH

The female pubic hair. There is a porno movie called *The Bushwhacker,* and devotees of Hollywood kitsch especially treasure the opening line of Russ Meyer's famous SKIN FLICK, *Vixen,* which was "Bush country!" See BEAVER and VIXEN.

BUSINESS

At times used to mean sexual intercourse; but among small children, a bowel movement. Both adults and children use the term *funny business* for sexual behavior they know is forbidden. Other nursery terms of similar meaning include *do-do* and also *poo-poo,* which gives Milne's *Winnie-the-Pooh* a slightly obscene connotation.

(In fact *pooh pooh,* meaning sex, is commemorated in this variation of an old bawdy song:

There was a girl named Jane
Who took this fellow Down to the cellar,
Fed him whiskey, wine and gin
And gave him a piece of that old
pooh-pooh.)

POT, meaning marijuana, doesn't seem to disturb anybody, perhaps because it is so overt; it is, after all, also widely called SHIT. However, the French *potee* (a swarm of children) often amuses American visitors.

BUTCH

Among male homosexuals, one who acts highly masculine, the opposite of FEM which refers to the more passive partner. Among female homosexuals, a masculine woman, a BULL DYKE, as in the ad: "Brunette . . . desperately needs discreet butch lover. Will do anything you wish, erotic, leather, clothes, obedience, mechanical devices . . ."

The origin is the now-forgotten "butch" haircut, which was even shorter than a crewcut and, hence, ultra-masculine. Butch – like Studs or Buster – is a traditional nickname for the toughest kid in the neighborhood.

BUTTERCUP

A male homosexual; from the flower by the same name. Like DAISY and PANSY, this perhaps derives from the old belief that flowers are unisexual, and may also arise from the association of flowers with femininity. This seems to have first appeared in literature in Henry Kane's hard-boiled-detective thriller, *Armchair in Hell,* where the gangster is identified as "a buttercup . . . you know, a daisy."

BUTTERED BUN

A prostitute who has serviced several customers in a row. Some customers will complain, "I don't like buttered buns." See also SLOPPY SECONDS and WET DECKS.

BUTTERFLY FLICK

A technique of FELLATIO which consists of moving the tongue in circular motions about the penis while sucking on it. In *The Sensuous Woman,* by "J," this is one of the many suggestions she makes in her instructions on how to titillate a man.

BUTTON

The clitoris. Before it had a drug connotation, to turn a person on meant to arouse someone sexually or to induce an orgasm.

CAB (or CAB JOINT)

Underworld argot for a whorehouse, evidently based on the facts that taxicabs are sometimes used as mobile brothels and that many cabdrivers in large cities receive a cut of the take for steering customers to whorehouses. Compare "taxi dancer," a female employee of a dance hall where dancing is a good deal more intimate than is usually acceptable elsewhere. See WHORE.

CACKLING FARTS

Eggs – because they appear upon superficial observation to come out of the chicken's anus, which in the hen is not clearly distinct from the sexual organ. This is contemporary underworld slang, but was first recorded in 1676.

CAKE-EATER

One who performs CUNNILINGUS. This term is still current, but its origin, *cake* (for the vagina), has been obsolete for over a century. The sexual meaning has been blurred, and *cake-eater* is sometimes innocently used to mean a man who is popular with the ladies; the *Philadelphia Bulletin* once referred to a local lothario as a "hard-boiled cake-eater."

CAMEL NIGHT

A night of lovemaking; the name is a pun on the camel's conspicuous hump.

CAMP

Old homosexual slang, now nearly obsolete, meaning to act in a feminine, flirtatious manner. Camping has two functions: first, to give a kind of humorous come-on to other homosexuals, as in "Every time he sees an attractive young boy he starts camping like Mae West"; and second, to assault the sensibilities of passing heterosexuals, as in "When he saw the straight tourists, he camped it up and blew their minds." In the second case, as with blacks deliberately "Uncle Tomming," it is hard to separate self-caricature (and self-contempt) from social satire and put-on.

The origin of *camp* is obscure, but the Latin *campus* was a battlefield, thus giving us *decamp, campaign, champion*. In Late Latin, *excampare* is to flee from the battlefield, an act of cowardice. The traditional association of homosexuality and cowardice is deeply rooted in our culture. When New York workers rioted against pacifist students in 1970, FAGGOT was the word of abuse most loudly shouted. Interestingly, the Plains Indians of the United States allowed a boy to decide at puberty whether to be homosexual or heterosexual. If he chose to be GAY, he dressed in DRAG (women's clothing), acted effeminate, did women's work and was not required to go into battle; if he chose to be straight, he had to become a warrior.

All this is what semanticists call a "self-fulfilling prophecy" – that is, in societies like our own and the Plains Indians', where homosexuals are expected to be unwarlike, they will tend to accept that definition of themselves. On the other hand, among the Greeks and Turks the fiercest warriors were often gay, and Plato, who was of that inclination himself, boasted that "an army of such lovers could conquer the world."

Today in America some members of the Gay Liberation Front, trying to reverse their negative public images, are demanding induction into the Army. Others, both gay and straight, who are opposed to the Vietnamese War, regard this as an obnoxious idiocy, and one heterosexual pacifist has asked bitterly, "Do they have to compound their vices by adding butchery to buggery?" To add to the confusion of all this, one school of Freudians believes that war and militarism themselves are outlets for repressed homosexuality. (See our discussion of GUN later.)

Due to Susan Sontag's essay, *Notes on Camp,* this word has now come to mean a certain FUNKY kind of art and clothing – both good and bad – and has been divided into *high camp, low camp, middle camp,* and even *intentional* and *unintentional camp.*

CAN

Either the buttocks, as in "He kicked him in the can," or the lavatory, as in "Pardon me, duchess, while I step into the can." Both usages are more common among children than adults.

CANARY

The penis; Eastern seaboard slang of unknown origin. The German use of *vogel* (bird) as a verb meaning FUCK, the association of doves with Aphrodite, the appearance of the Holy Ghost as a DOVE or pigeon when impregnating the Virgin Mary, and the use of COCK (a male bird) to mean the penis are perhaps analogues. One can also instance the ribald reputation of parrots in humorous folklore, and the stork as a symbol of the father's penis. The root seems to be the well-known dream-association, discussed by Freud, between flying and coitus. See FLY.

CANNIBAL

Thieves' slang for a homosexual, one who EATS another man.

CANOE INSPECTION

Inspection of prostitutes' genitalia for venereal disease; a metaphor based on the shape of the vulva. Compare this with the BOY IN THE BOAT, slang for the clitoris.

CARVEL'S RING

The only device that will ensure a wife's fidelity. The reference is to Rabelais's story about a jealous old doctor, Hans Carvel, who dreamed he bargained with the devil for a magic ring that would prevent him from being cuckolded. When he awoke, his finger was in his wife's vagina. A contemporary variation of this yarn concerns the Mexican, Speedy Gonzales, whose name has also become a byword. In this legend, an American man on his honeymoon in Mexico is told not to leave his wife alone for even a second, because otherwise she is sure to be seduced by Speedy Gonzales. After hearing

The Book of Forbidden Words

this warning several times, the bridegroom decides to sleep with his finger placed like Hans Carvel's. During the night he sneezes and temporarily dislodges the finger, but immediately replaces it. A voice in the dark exclaims, "Take your finger out of my ass, Señor!"

CAT

A prostitute; from French *le chat,* slang for vagina. This also seems to be the origin for the American usage of *pussy* to mean the female genitalia. A *cathouse* is a whorehouse; *catlapper* is lesbian slang for CUNNILINGIST. Today *whipping the cat* and *shooting the cat* both mean MASTURBATION, but the former was once a crude practical joke in which the victim was dragged into a pond, and the latter once meant to vomit from drunkenness. A shrew or nagging wife was a "cat" in recent English; *living under the cat's foot* meant being henpecked.

The association of this animal with femininity is so strong that most people still call even a male cat "she," and a woman who criticizes another is called "catty" or answered by a loud "meow." It seems to be based on the similarity between a cat's small, soft, furry body and the vulva. The feline metaphor is also associated with some men's deep-seated fear that women tend to be as sadistic and destructive as cats are when playing with a mouse. This idea is reinforced by the fact that psychoanalysts consider the mouse a common unconscious symbol of the penis. In a popular old film, *Cat People,* Simone Simon actually turned into a giant cat and devoured her lover.

The cat is also a symbol of unrestrained passion and noisy ecstasy, which is well celebrated in an old folk song with the joyous refrain:

> Cats on the rooftops,

> Cats on the tiles,
> Cats with their faces
> All wreathed in smiles
> As they revel in the joys
> Of forn-eye-cation!

The famous expression *cat on a hot tin roof,* which Tennessee Williams used for the title of a play, comes from 19th Century English *nervous as a cat on hot bricks,* which became *jumpy as a cat on a hot tin roof* in the U.S. Army, and was generally used for a sufferer whose ailment was thought to be sexual frustration.

Caterwauling now means loud or unruly behavior in general, but originally it meant going out at night in search of a female, like a tomcat, and has also been used to mean copulation.

Finally, a cat can also be a man, usually made more specific by an adjective in black and counterculture speech. Thus, a *cool cat* is nice to know; a *down cat* is honest; a *heavy cat* is either tough or in some other way impressive; a *studly cat* scores with the CHICKS; and a *nowhere cat* isn't worth your time. See SHOOT, MOUSETRAP and TOMCATTING.

CAVAULTING

Copulating, FUCKING, having a BALL; evidently from the 18th Century *vaulting academy,* whorehouse.

CEMENT MIXER

The bump-and-grind motions during a burlesque or night-club striptease; from the rolling movement of a cement mixer, as in, "She moved like a cement mixer."

CHANGE ONE'S LUCK

To have intercourse with a black woman, as in "Think I'll go uptown and change my luck"; based on an old superstition that miscegenation actually does have magic results. See LUCK.

CHARGE

Sexual excitation; an interesting term, since a few theoreticians (notably Wilhelm Reich) have conjectured that sexual energy is, or is related to, bioelectricity. See AC/DC and BUTTON.

CHASTITY BELT

A device worn about the pelvic area which prevented women from being able to have sexual intercourse, although allowing for normal functions of urination and excretion. As featured in various medieval tales, this barbaric contraption was usually placed on a wife by a husband about to depart for the crusades, and he left the key with a trusted friend who often proved treacherous. In other versions of the yarn, the locksmith kindly provides relief for the suffering heroine.

Were such cruel gadgets actually used in the Middle Ages, or were they the fantasy of bawdy storytellers? Most authorities accept them as authentic, and one scholar has even offered a plausible theory of how they were inspired (by the even worse African practice of infibulation – sewing up the vulva with a needle and thread when the husband was going away). Gershon Legman, however, one of the most knowledgeable, if erratic, men in the sexology and folklore field, claims that this is all myth. The actual examples of chastity belts in French and Italian museums, he avers, can all be proven to be 18th Century frauds, and no authentic specimen from the medieval period has ever been found. Be that as it may, an actual chastity belt was invented, patented and manufactured in the United States less than 100 years ago – to be used on males. Intended to be affixed on adolescent boys by their parents, this sadistic mechanism had a hole for urination but the opening was ringed with tiny needles. Thus, a flaccid penis could pass through, but as soon as an erection occurred the needles would come into play, causing acute pain and thereby discouraging passion, except in masochists. Its rationale was to "save" the children from the perils, mental and physical, that were thought to result from both MASTURBATION and nocturnal emissions.

CHEEKS

The buttocks. Compare EYE.

CHEESECAKE

Photographs of nude or nearly nude women, regarded as tasty objects. See EAT.

CHERRY

The hymen; a metaphor for the blood flow that sometimes accompanies defloration. Also, a virgin, as in "Is she cherry?" A "cherry picker" is a man with a Lolita complex. Russ Meyer punned on the word when he named his SKIN FLICK *Cherry Harry & Raquel,* which is about a girl who undoubtedly had her cherry picked long ago. See COP A CHERRY.

CHICK

Slang for an attractive young woman, used especially in black speech and in the counterculture; deriving from

1920s slang in which *chicken* had the same meaning and various witty fellows wore lapel buttons saying "Chicken inspector." A memorable use of chickens appears in a famous *Zap Comix* story which begins with various people performing a variety of oral sex acts on one another, when suddenly giant chickens invade the earth. A black clergyman, looking like a caricatured Negro of old 1900 comics, preaches in dialect: "Hesh, chilluns! Sendin' dem chickens down from heaven is jes' God's way of tellin' us folks dat we has SINNED!" Nobody pays any attention to the sermon, and the chickens turn into enormous vaginas, still clucking as the males in the comic rush forward to lick them. "And the word shall be made FLESH," the strip concludes blandly.

CHICKENSHIT

In U.S. Army slang, trivial rules and regulations, rigidly enforced. An officer who insists on such enforcement is said to be running a "chickenshit outfit." In the 19th Century, however, *chickenshit* meant small sums of money.

In civilian slang *chickenshit* generally means cowardly, as in "He ducked out the back door in a real chickenshit way." This is frequently abbreviated to *chicken,* and among adolescent males playing "chicken" is playing any game in which there is risk of death or disfigurement, such as racing two cars directly at each other. The driver who swerves first to avoid the collision is "chicken."

Psychologist Frederic Perls, one of the inventors of Gestalt therapy, divided all human speech into three forms: chickenshit, which is mere idle chatter to pass the time; BULLSHIT, which is role-playing or game-playing; and elephant shit, which consists of profound theories about the universe. Perls good-humoredly included his own work in the third category.

CHILI PIMP

Black slang for a small-time PIMP, with maybe one girl in his stable. The implication is that he only earns enough to eat chili, the main dish in cheap restaurants in black and Puerto Rican neighborhoods.

CHIPPY

A WHORE; seemingly from *chippy user,* underworld slang for a person who uses cocaine very occasionally in order to avoid becoming addicted, which is also known as having a "chippy habit" or a "coffee-and-cake habit" or a "Saturday night habit." Calling a whore a chippy, then, implies that she is used occasionally by those men who are afraid of marriage (habituation).

CHRISTENING

An act of sexual intercourse; from the 19th Century phrase for an ex-virgin, *She's been christened with the pump handle.* Related are: *christening wine,* the blood flow that sometimes accompanies a woman's first coitus; *christen the yak,* as in "She'll christen his yak for him," which means that she will introduce the male to his first intercourse.

CIRCUS

An orgy performed not for the amusement of the participants, but for the entertainment of an audience, who are charged an admission fee. Tijuana, Paris and prerevolutionary Havana were most famous for their circuses (see CUBAN SUPERMAN), and they are now becoming something of a fad in New York and

California, where they are usually called "sex shows." The law still cracks down occasionally, and one memorable case in Los Angeles hinged on the jury's ability to decide whether the participants had genuine climaxes or were only simulating it – whether they were FUCKING or faking, so to speak. The theory behind this was that if the sex were faked, it might be protected from condemnation as being a form of drama with "redeeming social importance."

The use of the term *circus* in this way evidently comes from the touring circuses of yesteryear, which often included such exhibitions as a late-night attraction, for men only, advertised solely by word of mouth through shills circulating in the daytime crowds. The principal entertainment, according to folklore, was usually a young lady copulating with a trained donkey or pony.

Another meaning of *circus,* in underworld slang, is a con game in which the "mark," or victim, is persuaded to sign a small $5 or $10 check (he thinks); of course, he later learns from his bank that he has somehow mysteriously signed a much larger check, perhaps for his life's savings.

CIRCUS LOVE

A long sex session, with lots of variations and most of the 69 positions. See NUMBERS GAME and SIXTY NINE.

CLAP

Slang for gonorrhea, since the 16th Century. *He went out by Hadden and came back by Clapham,* in 18th Century Londonese, meant he went wenching and got gonorrhea, with puns on two English cities. The origin appears to be Middle English *clappen,* to throb.

The current skyrocketing rise in clap and syphilis is

astonishing. Gonorrhea is 29 times as common as the measles, and syphilis has killed 100 million people since 1900, or four times the number who died during the bubonic plague in medieval Europe. Most medical authorities advise people to avoid sex with people whose medical history is unknown, but since few of us have such data available about our intimate associates, much less our casual acquaintances, this advice amounts to saying, "Avoid sexual intercourse." More realistically, for the man the rule is: Urinate immediately after coitus, and then wash with a strong soap; for the woman, douche thoroughly. If a CONDOM is used in addition to these measures, the odds are quite good that no transmission of the disease can occur, but even without a condom, washing and douching are often effective.

CLEOPATRA

Whore's slang for the specialty in which a woman is able to control consciously the usually involuntary vaginal contractions during coitus and uses this ability to enhance the pleasure of the male. We hasten to add that this is also known to quite a few women who aren't in the profession. In India it is called *samdhamsa,* or "the pincers," and the practice is highly commended in sex manuals:

> A woman must ever strive to close and constrict her *yoni* [vagina] until it tightly holds the *lingam* [penis], as the muscle of the anus claps the finger when it is inserted, opening and shutting at her pleasure, and acting like the hand of the dairymaid who milks the cow . . . This can be learned only by long practice and especially by throwing the entire will power into the part to be affected.

When the woman is unwilling or unable to learn this art, men have resorted to desperate remedies: the silver sheath around the penis in China; an alum or sulphur ring in the Near East; rubber bands in Europe and America. These practices are thought to be dangerous by medical authorities.

CLICK

To copulate, now infrequently used. Today the expression *I really clicked with that chick* would probably only mean he got along well with her. In underworld slang, English and American, *click* also means to snatch a wallet or purse, and a "clicker" is one who portions out the booty among thieves.

CLOSET QUEEN

A homosexual who hides his sexual proclivities and passes as straight; the LESBIAN equivalent is *closet dyke;* probably from the old usage of *closeted* to mean "in private." The current wave of homosexuals, both male and female, shedding their cloak of secrecy and publicly declaring their homosexuality is termed "coming out of the closet."

CLUSTER FUCK

Two men copulating simultaneously with the same woman, one entering the vagina and the other the anus. This is also known as a "sandwich" and in Robert Heinlein's science-fiction novel, *I Will Fear No Evil,* it is called "troying" (probably from the French *ménage-à-trois*) and is presented as the most popular variation in the United States by approximately 2000 A.D.

A *Mongolian cluster fuck,* on the other hand, is an orgy with a cast of thousands. Poet and Rock musician Ed Sanders, who coined the term, has occasionally spoken of making a film of that name featuring every living Rock star in one huge pulsating naked sprawl; at other times he has wanted to stage it on the White House lawn as a living demonstration of the slogan "Make Love, Not War."

COCK

The penis; derived from the Latin *coco coco* and Late Latin *cucurru,* imitative of the rooster's distinctive crow. *Cock* is a respectable term for the male bird of any species; for example, cock robin. By the time Middle English developed, *cock* was not yet used for the human penis, but had come to mean a faucet. The transition from faucet to penis – a visual metaphor – came later, and Shakespeare used *cock* in the phallic sense in *Henry V* (1600), but by 1893 Sir James Murray declared it "not permissible in polite speech or literature." Joyce's Molly Bloom puns on it in *Ulysses,* saying of French erotic writer, Paul de Kock, "Nice name he has," and later, in her soliloquy, speculating that he was given the name because "he was always going around trying to shove it into every woman he met."

Curiously, in parts of the southern United States, the word *cock* has become generalized to mean the sexual organs of either sex, or sex in general. Thus, one may hear an expression like "She gave him cock," which tends to confuse city folk. Similarly, a porno version of the comic strip, "Dixie Dugan," published in the 1930s, shows the heroine worried about her "cock odor" and finding reassurance in the use of "Sifeboy" soap – a parody of Lifebuoy soap's famous advertising campaign against "body odor." The cartoonist even abbreviates *cock odor* to C.O. in imitation of Lifebuoy's famous "B.O."

In the 18th Century several interesting variations were

recorded, such as: *Cock Ale,* a provocative drink (equivalent to the legendary *Tiger Piss* of our own time); *cock alley,* a woman's genitalia; *cock whoop,* in high spirits; *cock hoist,* a prostitute; *cockish wench,* a forward young lady. When the Victorian age set in, these words were all banned; even roosters were called "gentleman chickens" in parts of the United States, and many persons named Cox, Coxe, Cocker went to court to change their names. The word *cocky* (which may well refer to the proud walk of the rooster and not have any sexual reference at all) and *cock-and-bull story* were also banned, and even the bull was rechristened a "gentleman cow."

Cockeyed comes from a different *cock* meaning to tip (as in "cock the trigger"); the "cockhorse" in the nursery rhyme, "Ride a Cockhorse to Banbury Cross," is a tipping or rocking horse. A "cocksure" person is one who has a great amount of self-confidence, sexually and otherwise. The origin of our modern "cocktail," however, is baffling, as is the derivation of *Cockney.*

To *cry cockles,* as in "You'll cry cockles some day," means to be hanged in recent English usage, allegedly from the noise made while strangling; but this could also refer to the erection the victim often has when being executed in this manner. William Burroughs has sardonically commented on this ritual (the "Orgasm-Death Gimmick," he calls it) saying it may be the only legal ejaculation the condemned man has ever had; and the stag film in *Naked Lunch* ends with Mary hanging Johnny in order to enjoy his involuntary orgasm while his neck snaps. A gallows on which the client could be hanged until orgasm and then quickly cut down before death was once part of many English brothels and led to some interesting trials when the rescue came a second too late.

One of the oddest bits of censorship in this century was the banning of the word *cockroach* from insecticide ads on the radio. The censors were unaware that the word in no way derives from the English *cock* but comes directly from the Spanish word for that insect, which is *cucaracha*.

In the expression *cockles of the heart,* cockles are simply valves, as are the shellfish (bivalves) sold by Molly Malone in the old Irish ballad with the chorus "Cockles and mussels, alive, alive-oh!" but many prudish speakers still avoid such expressions because of the sexual meaning of *cock*. In contemporary underground parlance, a "great cocksman," used sometimes seriously, sometimes ironically, is a male whose unusual proficiency with this organ makes him in demand as a lover.

Although *cock* is the best-known English word for the penis, there are, besides the other synonyms listed in this dictionary, countless others of past and present, including: *middle finger, middle stump, foreman, tail pipe, flip-flap, flap-doodle, master tool, needle, pump, horn, key, rod of love, pendulum, machine, broomstick, golden rivet, spigot, sugar-stick, potato finger, radish, sausage, winkle, goat, live rabbit, pilgrim's staff, fiddle-stick, dirk, pikestaff, bayonet, nature's scythe, spike, master of ceremonies, unruly member, cunny-catcher, quiff-splitter, bush-beater, skyscraper, baldheaded hermit* and *kidney-wiper* – the last of which recalls the limerick:

> There was a young lady from Sidney
> Who liked it right up to her kidney.
> A man from Quebec
> Shoved it up to her neck.
> He had a big one – didn't he?

COCKSUCKER

A person who performs FELLATIO, usually used as an insult, especially when directed by one male to another, with its implication of homosexuality. *Cocksucking* is rivaled only by *motherfucking* as an all-purpose adjective of disapproval in the United States. When these words are used in conjunction – "You motherfucking cocksucker!" – they present a rather weird picture of the sexual preferences of the recipient.

When Lenny Bruce used *cocksucker* in his nightclub act, he was arrested, tried, found guilty and sentenced to a year in prison. (This decision was overturned by a higher court – after he was dead.) In later monologues, he told of a conversation he had in the police van with the arresting officer.

"Did that really shock you?" Bruce asked.

"It refers to an act only performed by homosexuals and deviates," was the wooden answer.

"No, it doesn't," Lenny replied. "To me it refers to an act performed by any woman I love, or could love, or might marry, or might consider marrying." This frank declaration was considered daring and even shocking by night-club audiences in the early Sixties, just as 40 years earlier, Charlie Chaplin was treated as a bizarre sort of monster for saying frankly, when charged with CUNNILINGUS in a divorce trial, "But all married people do that!"

In the South, where *cock* often means the female genitalia, a cocksucker is probably a man who performs orally for the ladies, and to avoid confusion the fellow who would be called a cocksucker in the North is dubbed a "prick-nibbler."

COCKSUCKER'S TEETH

Something useless or superfluous, as in "I need that like a cocksucker's teeth." (Similar phrases: *useless as the Pope's balls,* or *worthless as tits on a boar hog.*) Even more expressive is "She's worth no more than a cocksucker's behind," usually said of an old WHORE.

COCKTEASER

A woman who promises much more than she intends to deliver; also called a "prickteaser" or "P.T." The opposite is sometimes heard, spoken by a well-satisfied male: "That chick was a cock-pleaser."

CODPIECE

A large and bulging device worn over the male genitalia in Elizabethan times, allegedly to protect the organ. Actually, according to wits of that period, the purpose was provocative and often misleading as with the padded bras worn by women in more recent times. Judging by the garb of the young males in *A Clockwork Orange,* director Stanley Kubrick expects a streamlined version of the codpiece to appear in men's fashions in the next decade. Elvis Presley is already wearing something like it.

COLD-COCK

To knock somebody out with a single blow, delivered quickly and unexpectedly, is called in the West "cold-cocking" him. (The classic method is to dust his cranium with the barrel of a gun.) The term is, of course, a humorous reference to cooling a man's ardors. The most famous practitioner of cold-cocking was Wyatt Earp, who usually managed to avoid gunfights by moving in quickly with a cold-cock before the other party was ready to draw a pistol.

COME

To reach orgasm; the most widely used word for the sexual climax in modern English and American, yet of very recent vintage. Until the early 1920s the word was *spend*. *Come* used as a noun refers to the semen. Since the sensation is more outgoing than incoming, the word is rather odd, as emphasized in the celebrated limerick:

> There was a young man from Kent
> Whose prick was so long that it bent.
> To save himself trouble
> He put it in double
> And instead of coming he went.

Another of Lenny Bruce's arrests was occasioned by a night-club routine based on this word. Condensed, the monologue went as follows (accompanied by a beating bongo drum in cadence): "*To* is a preposition. *Come* is a verb. To come. I want to come. I can't come. If you loved me you would come. I love you but I still can't come." The prosecution argued that this was obscene; the defense that it was a humorous and compassionate dramatization of a very common human problem. The jury, however, voted to send Bruce to jail. And a recent graffito piously declared: "To go together is blessed, to come together divine."

A recent "come" fantasy occurs in the special "69" issue of *Zap Comix,* in which "a few of the southside dykes have captured one of the local studs" and are busy JACKING him OFF. When they have a cup filled with his sperm, one of them fills a hypodermic needle from the cup and injects it into her arm like a heroin addict. She immediately sprouts an enormous penis and a gigantic pair of BALLS, as another dyke cries ecstatically, "It worked fine, Lulu – you've got yourself a beauty!" See BULL DYKE.

COME-DOWN

As a verb used in the 19th Century, *to come down* meant to lose one's erection at a crucial moment. Now it is a noun meaning disappointment, as in "What a come-down it was to see the profit-and-loss statement."

COME GET ME

An encouragement shouted to a musician in black or hippie circles. The shouter is usually male and the implication is homosexual, but is not intended literally; it signifies that the music has overwhelmed the listener (or "wiped him out") and that he is thus incapable of resisting anything else the musician attempts, including sex.

COME GRASS

To inform against one's friends to the police, as in, "If you come grass on the Mafia, you may soon be slightly dead." This is underworld slang that is quite confusing, since it has absolutely nothing to do with either orgasm (COME) or marijuana (grass).

COMMON

In English and Canadian speech, an insulting way to describe a woman, implying that she is equally accessible to all, as in "She's common." This goes back at least to Shakespeare's *Henry IV:* "This Doll Tearsheet would be some road . . . as common I warrant you, as that twixt London and Brighton." *Commons* or *House of Commons* is lower-class English wit for a public lavatory.

CONDOM

The male contraceptive sheath, also known as a RUBBER. Popular lore traces the name to a Colonel Condom who distributed these devices in Her Majesty's Army to combat venereal disease, but no record of the humanitarian colonel has ever been found. It might derive from *conundrum,* a riddle, indicating some initial perplexity as to how to affix the contraption. With the decline of puritanism, condom advertisements can now appear in leading magazines, such as PLAYBOY and *National Lampoon.*

Here is a recent example:

> At last. . . contraceptives through the privacy of the mail.
>
> Whether you live in a big city with its crowded drugstores, or in a small town where people know each other so well, obtaining male contraceptives without embarrassment can be a problem.
>
> Now, Population Planning Associates has solved the problem . . . by offering reliable, famous-brand male contraceptives through the privacy of the mail. Popular brands like Trojan and Sultan. The exciting preshaped Conture. The supremely sensitive Prime. And many more. All are electronically tested and meet rigorous government standards of reliability.
>
> We'll be glad to send you our free illustrated brochure which describes the products and services that we have been bringing to 10,000 regular customers for nearly two years. Or send just $3 for a sampler of a dozen contraceptives

– three each of the brands described above –
plus our brochure. Money back if not delighted.

COOCH

A striptease; in the South, however, the vagina. A cooch dancer, or hoochie-coochie dancer, may not perform an actual striptease, but may merely do an "exotic" dance with some bumps and grinds.

COOL, COOLER

To be cool is to be calm and self-possessed, generally an admirable state. A "cool guy" is one you can trust; a "cool chick" is sexually attractive; "cool jazz" is the least emotional variety of blues music; and *That was cool* can either mean "That was smart" or "That was sneaky and cruel." In the drug world, heroin and downers (barbiturates) are considered "cool," meaning that they calm one down, whereas pot and psychedelics are "frantic" or "hot." Men Against Cool, meanwhile, is an all-male pro-women's-liberation group to whom *cool* signifies everything false and deceitful in typical male attitudes. (One wonders whether they are aware that their initials – M.A.C. – spell a slang word for PIMP in parts of the country.)

Cooler (a noun) is underworld slang for a woman who knows how to calm a man down, no matter how tense, steamed-up or hot-and-bothered he may be. (In bars and taverns a "cooler" is a drink with ice in it, for summer days.)

Cool it, meaning "Calm down," is used in a Bijou Funnies satire on Sunday School, in which the teacher says, "When you come right down to it and face the cold hard facts, sex is just a biological urge!! Often teens mistake their sexual desires for love and are very sorry later. Luckily, God has a way for those faced with TEMPTATION to stay pure! This Christian way is called 'cooling it.' When you feel yourself giving in to your animal instincts merely think of something DISGUSTING!" A teen-age girl responds sardonically, "On my next date I'm gonna take along some ice cubes." See COLD COCK.

COP A CHERRY

To deflower a virgin. *Cop,* meaning to steal, is from Old French *caper,* to take, and is not related to *cop* meaning policeman, which, according to one theory, comes from the copper buttons on an English bobby's uniform.

COP A FEEL

To fondle a woman's breasts or genitalia, the first step of a seduction – or the last, if the man is unskillful. The same expression is also sometimes used of those who operate in crowds or subways, as in "She was furious because some creep copped a feel off her in the elevator."

COP A JOINT

To perform FELLATIO; but in some circles to obtain a free marijuana cigarette. See JOINT.

CORNHOLE

To BUGGER, to perform anal intercourse. In the western United States, a "cob" is a bullying and authoritarian individual, especially an unpopular ranch foreman, who may also be called a "ramrod," which is a word for penis. (This was the title of a Joel McCrea movie, although the traditional explanation was not included in the film: "He walks like he's got a ramrod up his ass.")

The actual use of the corncob as a substitute penis by an impotent gangster occurs in William Faulkner's most sensational and famous novel, *Sanctuary,* terrifyingly effective because it is never described directly and is thus left to the reader's fantasy. *Cornhole* also appears in one of the best-known anticlerical limericks:

> There once was a monk from Siberia
> Whose existence grew drearier and drearier
> Till he sucked off one brother
> And cornholed another
> And eloped with a Mother Superior.

COTTON

Female pubic hair. *See* also BEAVER, BEARD, MUFF.

CRABS

Body lice, especially those infesting the pubic area, called "mechanized dandruff" in the Army. Some years ago a Hollywood film, *Attack of the Crab Monsters,* was greeted with inappropriate hilarity in certain New York theaters; and almost everybody has by now seen the graffito (found in men's rooms from coast to coast), "Don't throw toothpicks in the urinal, the crabs here have learned to pole-vault."

CRACK

The cleft in the buttocks and vulva. Decode for yourself the symbolism in the children's rhyme: "Step on a crack/ And break your mother's back."

CRADLE-ROBBER

A man with a Lolita complex (desire for prepubescent girls, from Vladimir Nabokov's famous novel, *Lolita).*

CRAP

Excrement, as in "I have to take a crap," but widely used as a metaphor: "What kind of crap are you handing me?" "I don't have to take your crap," or "I don't believe that crap." The origin is Low German, *krape,* a vile and inedible fish, but the popularity of *crap* in the modern world is due to the drug culture in which, during the 1920s, the word meant heroin of inferior quality because it had been cut (adulterated) by the pushers. When it became obvious to all junkies that no other kind of heroin was available on the American black market, *crap* and later *shit* came to mean heroin in general and, later, a variety of other drugs.

As recently as 1970, the film, *End of the Road,* had the phrase *horsecrap* in place of the more usual *horseshit.* At the time this seemed daring for Hollywood, since no one could have predicted the thundering *fucks* and *cunts* that now come hurtling off our screens.

Crap, meaning both excrement and deception, is nicely synopsized in the *San Francisco Comic Book,* which has a sequence in which two people sit drinking coffee while the TV news tells them: "In Washington, the administration moved quickly to quell what it called 'wild, unfounded rumors being spread by hippies and radicals . . . The strange large lumps of unidentified brown matter that have turned up in much of the nation's drinking water do not represent an ecological breakdown . . . They are merely particles of rust and other pure, natural, harmless ORGANIC matter,' an administration spokesman said . . . Meanwhile, in other news, the government released a startling study today which shows that human feces is not only harmless to health but actually contains many remarkable nutritional properties . . ." But at this point the listeners, with bulging eyes and expressions of horror, bolt for the bathroom to vomit. Evidently, they do not trust the media.

CREEP

In white slang, a person with unusual sex habits, a KINK or FREAK; in black slang, to be unfaithful to one's mate, as in "He's creeping on his old lady"; also called "making a creep" or "pulling a creep." Another *creep*, meaning a plainclothes cop or secret agent, is heard occasionally; and in the Manhattan Project (code name for the group of scientists who built the atom bomb during World War II) every physicist had a *creep* assigned to him.

CRIB

A whorehouse. In black speech, *crib* is now used to mean one's home, just as *hustle* (to prostitute) sometimes means to work at one's job, the implication being that we're all WHORES in one way or another. See HUSTLER.

CRUD

Dried semen clinging to one's penis after intercourse; also excrement, or a venereal disease, or (in the Army) anything an officer says. A favorite joke among the 30-year men is to warn new recruits when arriving in a foreign land against a malignant and mythical venereal ailment, the Creeping Caledonian Crud, sometimes more technically known as Wilkerson's Disease, the Purple Crud or Hong Kong DONG.

CRUISE

To go out soliciting sexual companionship, in homosexual slang. In New York, however, a "heavy cruiser" is a case-hardened and tough-looking prostitute.

CUBAN SUPERMAN

A name given to a succession of highly endowed men who performed in CIRCUSES (or bawdy shows) in Havana during prerevolutionary days. The essence of this specialty is to copulate with an incredible number of women in succession without losing one's erection. The original and most famous Cuban Superman gave visual proof that he actually ejaculated in each case, but he was soon followed by unworthy imitators who coated their organs with Novocain before going on stage and thus obtained durable erections (with no chance of genuine response). Since the Revolution the whereabouts of the original Superman are unknown, and it is a matter of conjecture whether his talents are being utilized in building socialism or whether he has been "rehabilitated" into some less colorful line of work.

CUNNILINGUS

Stimulation of the female genitalia with mouth, teeth and tongue; sometimes called "the fine art of pussy-nibbling." See PUSSY, EAT.

CUNT

The female genitalia, from Middle English *cunte, queynte* (the form used by Chaucer, and the original of our word *quaint), quiff* or *quim,* Low German *kunte,* Old Norse *kunta* and so on, back to Latin *cunnus* and Greek *kusthos.* Wayland Young imaginatively traces it to an Indo-European root, *kon,* meaning beginning.

Although used frankly by Chaucer, it acquired an obscene connotation as early as Shakespeare's time and he only puns on it, as in *Twelfth Night:* "Her C's, her U's 'n her T's"; also in *Hamlet,* in which the hero's pun on *lap* (vagina) gets a rise out of Ophelia and he asks mockingly, "Did you think I spoke of *country* matters?" After that poor showing, the word did not appear in respectable literature for three centuries (although the much-admired Robert Burns infiltrated it into one of his clandestine publications, *The Merrie Muses of Caledonia,* where it sports gamily through a poem entitled "Nine Inch Will Please a Lady" – the punch line being, "But not a country cunt!"). It next surfaced in Joyce's *Ulysses* where Bloom ruminates poetically about the Sinai desert: "It bore the first, the oldest race. Dead now: sunken. An old woman's. The grey sunken cunt of the world." (In Stephen's nightmare, later on, one of the ladies is engagingly named Cunty Kate; her less desirable companion is Bibbie-the-Clap.) D. H. Lawrence indicates that the word refers only to the human female genitalia in English North Country speech: "All animals fuck," Mellors tells Connie, "but only tha hast cunt." The word is usually regarded as a deadly insult when directed at a woman: "You cunt!" the husband shouts at the unfaithful wife in James Baldwin's *Another Country,* as he lunges forward to beat her unconscious. (Compare with the similar use of *you prick.)*

While still too blunt for many tastes, the word *cunt* is increasingly encountered in contemporary speech and letters. Much corny folk humor of the past derives from *not* saying the forbidden word, as in the old jingle where an angry witness tells a dubious judge he saw a couple copulating in the park:

> His you-know-what
> Was you-know-where,
> And if they weren't doing it,
> I wasn't there!

A tearoom functioning as a front for a brothel in a midwestern city reputedly got away for years with running an ad in the local newspaper that included the friendly slogan, "See You When Tea is Ready!" A law-enforcement officer finally said this over to himself enough times and got the message.

The taboo on the word *cunt* has given it a kind of magic or instant triggering effect on the erotic centers, as pornographers well know. Note how often *cunt* is used in only two pages of a hardcore porno novel, *The Incest Contest:*

> First, he rammed his fingers deeper and tighter into both their rectums. This brought their cunts that much closer to his mouth . . . The hottest part of Virginia's cunt was her clitoris . . . A fraction of a second before Virginia's Big O fluids started to stream out, Jason twisted his head towards Joanne's cunt . . . Jason was treated to the rare spectacle of watching the various parts of his wife's cunt vibrate, uncontrollably. The cunt lips, both outer and inner, flew wide apart . . . he watched the first drops of love dew sputter out of the cunt box . . . This deluge of cunt cream hit him from both sides. By now, love juices were streaming uncontrollably out of Virginia's cunt . . . the cunt honey flowing out of both women poured directly between his lips and down his throat . . . When, at last, the flow from both cunts had abated, he sucked and licked each cunt . . . The legs of both women were spread wide apart, and their drenched cunts gaped back at him. Both cunts still looked adorable and edible.

In addition to cunt, which is the best-known of all synonyms for the female genitalia, there are numerous other euphemisms (not listed elsewhere in this dictionary), such as: *fleshy part, commodity, masterpiece, novelty, mark of the beast, mother mark, private property, mother of masons, mother of Saint Patrick, nether eye, towdie, claff, peculiar river, centrique part, bower of bliss, living fountain, carnal trap, contrapunctum, toy, Venus's mark, parts of shame (!), the star over the garter, delicate glutton, mouth of nature, sensible part, the eye that weeps most when most pleased, Cupid's alley, Lapland, bit of meat, oyster, green grocery, Miss Brown, seminary.*

CURSE

The menstrual period; from *the curse of Eve,* arising from a loose reading of Genesis, which does not actually mention this among the curses Jehovah put on Eve.

CUSH

The female genitalia; related to COOCH, both of unknown origin. Maybe a pleasantry brought back from India by English tommies; *khushi* in Hindustani means pleasure.

CUT THE MUSTARD

Virility or potency in males is called cutting the mustard, but this is most often used negatively, as a put-down, as in "You can't even cut the mustard."

DADDY-O

In black slang, any male, with a slight connotation of insult. Much of the banter among black males is semi-insulting, and only tone reveals when real hostility begins (see DOZENS). The insult in *Daddy-0* derives from the reference to SUGAR DADDY, an older man who supports a younger mistress for her sexual favors, or from *daddy,* an aging homosexual seeking very young males.

DAISY CHAIN

Group sexual activity in which each participant gratifies one partner while himself (or herself) being gratified by another. The origin of the expression is not certain, but it may come from *daisy,* a nearly obsolete slang term for a homosexual. A daisy chain, in practice, must be anal and/or oral; unfortunately a genital daisy chain is, given the limitations of human anatomy, impossible – although perhaps nice to contemplate. Gershon Legman has thoughtfully provided a rigorous mathematical demonstration in his book, *Oragenitalism,* that every daisy chain with an odd number of participants must be at least partially homosexual, while an even-numbered daisy chain can be 100% heterosexual; for this contribution science will always be grateful. Thus, for 2x males (x = any number) plus 2x females, there will always be a female between two males; whereas, 2x plus 1 males will lead to SODOMY somewhere on the chain, and 2x plus 1 females will lead to LESBIANISM.

The daisy chain is one extreme of group sex, representing maximum togetherness, so to speak. The opposite extreme is known as "closet sex," in which the participants meet together in one place but pair off and go to separate rooms before the real action begins. In between, there is the traditional orgy with everybody in the same room but not so systematically arranged as in a daisy chain. All these variations are definitely "in" these days, and a large number of personal ads in the underground press are placed by individuals seeking entry to such groups. In fact, a Chicago writer who placed an ad for persons interested in forming a Sunday School for children of unbelievers found himself deluged with letters from people who were convinced this was a new code for some form of group sex activity. Some of them were very persistent and found it hard to believe that the ad meant just what it said. There was also a graffito expressing the philosophy, "Daisies of the world unite, you have nothing to lose but your chains."

The most famous daisy chain in popular lore is one that is not even described if the following joke is told properly: A staid English banker, in Paris on business and shocked at a view from his window, summoned a policeman and indignantly led him to the courtyard where the offense was occurring. The philosophical gendarme, however, merely shrugged his shoulders with Gallic tolerance. "Lucky Pierre," he sighed, "always in ze meedle." Lucky Pierre is almost as widely known as Speedy Gonzales or Hans Carvel. See CARVEL'S RING.

DARK MEAT

Black men and women; a term used by whites to categorize them sexually.

DERBY

Oral copulation, usually a BLOW job, as in "She gave me a derby." The metaphor seems to derive from GIVE HEAD.

DICK (or DICKY)

The penis. This usage is immortalized by the folk poem:

> When the frost is on the punkin'
> That's the time for dicky-dunkin',
> And when the weather's hot and sticky
> That's the time for dunkin' dicky.

Both this meaning and the employment of *dick* to mean detective are of highly obscure origin; as is also *what the dickens* meaning "What the devil." *Dick* and *dickens* are English diminutives of Richard, and evidently some person of that name made himself infamous. *Dick* meaning policeman has some uncomplimentary sexual connotation, and in police slang, Dickless Tracy is a female detective.

DIDDLE

In American slang, either to have intercourse or to MASTURBATE — except in the rural South, where *diddling* means the first short one-inch thrusts before real FUCKING begins. In English slang, a swindle; deriving from Jeremy Diddler, a swindler in an 1803 novel, *Rising the Wind*.

DIESEL DYKE

The more masculine partner in a LESBIAN relationship; the BULL DYKE; from the diesel engine which moves, as Freud himself noted, in a "phallic" manner.

DILDO

An artificial penis used for female MASTURBATION or pretended heterosexual intercourse between LESBIANS. From the Italian *diletto,* delight. In Robert Ruark's *Something of Value,* two Englishwomen hunting lions in Kenya carry about a box bearing a mysterious object which they call "John Thomas." (This was Mellors's name for his penis in Lawrence's *Lady Chatterley's Lover.*)

One of the most famous dildoes in modern fiction is "Steely Dan from Yokahama," described by Burroughs in *Naked Lunch*. About to add a RIM job to a BLOW job, the heroine straps on Steely Dan III, filled with warm milk.

"What happened to Steely Dan I?"

"He was torn in two by a bull dike. Most terrific vaginal grip I ever experienced. She could cave in a lead pipe. It was one of her parlor tricks."

"And Steely Dan II?"

"Chewed to bits by a famished candiru in the Upper Babboonsasshole."

One of the more daring sex scenes to appear on the Hollywood screen was in *Myra Breckinridge,* based on Gore Vidal's CAMPY sex farce, in which Raquel Welch (Myra), wearing a red, white and blue stars-and-stripes bikini, performs a dildo rape on young-STUD Rusty, whom she has seduced.

It is now permissible to advertise these devices in America; here is a typical ad:

LITTLE GEM DANDY

Representative of the male organ. Extremely lifelike. Should adequately fill the needs of any woman requiring satisfactory stimulation. Comes with one-speed vibrator and carrying bag. Lubricate with Vaseline to keep soft and pliable. Size: 1½" X 6". Made of pink rubber. $29.00

Dildoes now come in all sizes, all colors and all shapes. One popular ad boasts of 22 different kinds of dildoes, including the Suction Dinger, Mini-Brute (with vibrator), Double Dong (for two women who want to share everything), Black Bomber (all in black), Thriller (vicious-looking, with thornlike extensions up and down

The Book of Forbidden Words

its shaft), Courageous Destroyer (12 inches long, with attached imitation testicles) and Health Mate (6 inches, with rubbery spikes at the base).

Another use of the word *dildo* was immortalized by the Earl of Rochester in a quite unique poem, "Signor Dildo," concerning an Italian gentleman of that name who introduced London society ladies to a new pleasure. A few sample verses convey the theme of the whole:

> The pattern of Virtue, her Grace of Cleveland,
> Has swallowed more pricks than the nation has land;
> But by rubbing and scrubbing so wide does it grow
> It is fit for nothing but Signor Dildo.
>
> He civilly came to the Cockpit one night
> And proffered his Service to fair Madam Knight.
> Quoth she, I intrigue with Captain Cazzo.
> Your nose in mine Arse, good Signor Dildo!

The English gentlemen form a posse and drive the invader from London:

> Nigh wearied out the Stranger did fly
> And along the Pall Mall they followed full cry.
> The women concerned from every window
> Cry'd for Heaven's sake save Signor Dildo!

Dildoes for anal intercourse have also appeared on the market, as well as artificial vaginas, which were originally designed for married women who were biologically impaired. Vaginas, in one ad, are available in three qualities: a $20 model, filled with warm water; a $25 model made of foam rubber; and the best buy, at $30, one that pulsates and is guaranteed to simulate the real organ.

DINGE QUEEN

A homosexual whose particular fetish is black men; from *dinge,* obsolete slang for blacks.

DINGUS

The penis. This may be one of the few complimentary terms for the male organ in English speech, if one agrees with those scholars who derive it from Latin *dignus,* meaning worth (or dignity). On the other hand, it may simply be a Latinization of the German *ding* or Dutch *dinges,* both meaning thing. In either case, it recently got into a movie title, Frank Sinatra's *Dirty Dingus McGee.* Burroughs, in *Naked Lunch,* describes Steely Dan III as a dingus:

> She puts on a record, metallic cocaine be-bop. She greases the dingus, shoves the boy's legs over his head and works it up his ass with a series of corkscrew movements of her fluid hip. She moves in a slow circle, revolving on the axis of the shaft. She rubs her hard nipples across his chest. She kisses him on neck and chin and eyes. He runs his hands down her back to her buttocks, pulling her into his ass. She revolves faster, faster. His body jerks and writhes in convulsive spasms. "Hurry up, please," she says, "the milk is getting cold." He does not hear. She presses her mouth against his. Their faces run together. His sperm hits her breast with light, hot licks.

DIP THE WICK

To copulate. Another version of this metaphor is *dunk the* DINGUS or *dunk the love-muscle.*

DISCIPLINE

A code word used in personal ads. Those offering "discipline" are sadists seeking masochistic sexual partners. Although no statistics are available, psychiatrists tend to believe that there are many more masochists than there are sadists, so these ads are likely to draw a wide response. See OBEDIENCE.

DO A TUNE

To perform oral sex. See WHISTLING.

DOCTOR

A frequent sex-fantasy figure, especially for women, hence his constant appearance in the role of hero in books, movies and TV shows directed at a female audience. Children also like to "play doctor" as a way of satisfying sexual curiosity and exhibitionism. Among men, however, the M. D. is a figure of contempt more often than not. Hence, to "doctor" a report is to distort it.

In contrast to the superhuman doctors in some books for women, modern fiction has produced a gamut of quacks and "mad doctors" – from Doc Daneeka in *Catch 22* to Dr. Benway in *Naked Lunch,* who cuts the hospital's cocaine with Saniflush to support his own dope habit, accidentally severs a patient's femoral artery while operating and quarreling with his equally mad assistant (who is high on nutmeg and imagines he is back on the farm cleaning a chicken) and ends up performing cut-rate abortions in subway toilets.

A typical joke at the expense of doctors: The new nurse ignorantly asks the meaning of penis. The doctor, wishing to seduce her, opens his FLY, exhibits himself and says, "This is a penis." "Oh," she answers, "it's just like a prick, only smaller!"

And this personal ad shows the advertiser's ardent respect for his doctor: "Help, I need you! Ladies, 30 to 45 in N.E. Ill., Joliet area: 'Doctor's orders!' Must have relationship with the fair sex in order to prevent leg paralysis . . ." See LEG.

DOG

In black slang, usually an old, case-hardened WHORE; in white slang, any unappetizing female.

DOG-FASHION

Intercourse with a woman's vagina while she is in the position for anal intercourse. Legends about old maids and their dogs are widespread, but according to Kinsey only 2.5% of females in his sample actually attempted sex with animals. On the other hand, if Kinsey's figures can be extended to the whole population – as most statisticians believe they can be – this amounts to 4,000,000 women in the United States alone. It makes one wonder about the rich spinsters who leave their fortunes to pet poodles.

DOGHOUSE

The imaginary refuge of men who are denied sexual companionship by their wives for offenses real or imagined, as in "He's been in the doghouse for a week."

DOLL

An underworld term for any woman, popularized by Damon Runyon and by Abe Burrows' musical version of several Runyon stories, *Guys and Dolls*. The implications are rather obvious and are made grossly evident in a *Zap Comix* parody of our technological future: "Nobody will work! All production, distribution and maintenance will be done by computerized robots. People can spend all their time playing, eating or watching TV! . . . Or, they can fuck! Special fucking androids will be available to everyone! Social problems will disappear. Risk of involvement with the opposite sex will be eliminated!"

Similar thoughts seem to motivate the ads for life-size dolls ("anatomically complete!" the copy announces) which appear in some underground papers.

DONG

The penis; perhaps from *dingus*, or from the clapper of a bell. See BELLE.

DORK

The penis. This was used in the title of a celebrated underground movie, *Kansas City Dork*, concerning the fantasies of a veteran who lost both hands in the war.

DOSE

Venereal disease, usually gonorrhea, as in "He came down with a dose."

DOUBLE FEATURE

A *double feature* is when the male reaches orgasm more than once in a short span of time.

DOUBLE-GAITED

Bisexual; from a "double-gaited horse," one which excels at both galloping and trotting.

DOUCHE BAG

An unattractive woman.

DOVE

A term of affection exchanged between lovers, and often associated with sex. This goes back to Babylon and Greece where the sex goddesses Ishtar and Aphrodite were identified with doves. A fresco excavated from the remains of a brothel in Pompeii shows a group of courtesans in a garden surrounded by dovelike flying penises with which the women are engaged in a pretty game of pursuit and capture.

The dove seems to be especially appropriate as an erotic image because of its coloring, as Jack Kerouac indicated in his novel, *Doctor Sax,* in which "come-colored doves" play a significant role in the climax. More timid publishers forced him to change this to "semen-colored doves" when he inserted the same fantasy a second time in *On the Road.*

The exact mechanism by which the Holy Ghost impregnated the Virgin Mary has been a subject of continual speculation and debate among Catholic theologians, including the acute Aquinas; only Thomas Sanchez in his *De sancto Matrimonii Sacramento* has inquired whether Mary had an orgasm on that occasion. (He decided that she didn't.) Modern Catholics are often abashed to discover, in various European cathedrals, that this miracle was interpreted with astonishing literalness by our pious ancestors; many surviving paintings show the Holy Ghost, in the form of a dove, flying from God to the Virgin, carrying the sperm in its beak; others show Mary's virginity being preserved during the act by the Angel Gabriel impregnating her through the ear; in another version she is impregnated by God speaking or blowing through a tube that runs from his mouth across the floor and up under her skirt. These portraits of the miracle are discussed in Rattray Taylor's *Sex in History* and Zilboorg and Henry's *History of Medical Psychology.*

In this connection, Robert Reisner has recorded a bathroom graffito conveying the hot news flash, "God is dead, but don't worry – the Virgin Mary is pregnant again."

DOWN

In black slang, for a PIMP to have a hold over a WHORE ("she can't quit, he downs her"), or for one man to dominate another ("Don't try to down me, man"). The white equivalent is *put down* as in "He really put down that movie" or "She put him down." Also, *put-down,* as in "He took that remark as a real put-down." And in the drug culture, "downers" are barbiturates and other sedatives, as distinguished from "uppers" (amphetamines and other stimulants).

DOZENS

Also known as "Dirty Dozens," a humorous conversational game among black males in which each tries to outdo the other in obscenity and insult. It usually begins with deceptive mildness; "Your mother wears army shoes" is a traditional starting point. Thereafter there is no limit save that of the imagination of the participants. It might go: "Yeah, well she doesn't peddle her ass on the corner like your mammy." "Yeah? Well my mammy doesn't have to pay the men like your ugly old mammy." And so forth, bringing in grandmothers and other female relatives as it goes along. The highlight of a dozens session might be:

> I hate to talk about your mama,
> She's a good old soul.
> She's got a humpbacked pussy
> And a rubber asshole.
> She's got scales on her ass
> That's tight as a drum.
> She's got nipples on her titties
> As big as a plum.
> She's got something 'tween her legs
> Called sweet love jam.
> It smells like shit
> But it's goooood, God damn!

How these routines came to be called the "dozens" is unknown; one suggestion is that this is a corruption of *doesn't* from the refrain, "Yeah, but she doesn't . . ." This phrase was punned on in the title of a war movie, *The Dirty Dozen*.

DRAG

To say "Charles is going out in drag tonight" means that he is going out dressed in women's clothing. A "drag queen" is a male who is sexually aroused by wearing women's clothing (also known as a transvestite or an eonist). There are several night clubs on the East and West coasts which feature transvestites, and a popular stage group called "The Cockettes" recently made a film, *Tricia's Wedding,* a parody of Tricia Nixon's wedding in drag.

DRIPPING FOR IT

Used in reference to a hot-blooded woman, as in "She's dripping for it," with reference to vaginal lubricity.

DROPPING HAIRPINS

Inserting homosexual code terms into a conversation in order to determine if the listener is also GAY; sometimes also called "dropping beads."

DRY FUCK

Imitation intercourse with all the clothes in place, resorted to by young people fearful of being caught. Also called a "dry run," "dry humping" and in the 18th Century a "dry bob." *Young Lust,* a deadpan parody of those romantic comics for girls, by the same merry nihilists who produce *Zap Comix,* once featured a cover with the typical clean-cut WASP hero being looked at by the archtypical teary-eyed WASP heroine, who is thinking, in a large balloon, "Two weeks ago he was dry-humping me in the elevator! And now . . . and now I'm lucky if he remembers my goddamn name!!" See HUMP.

D.S.O.

Army hospital slang used by orderlies to describe one of the least publicized forms of sacrifice that soldiers make for their nation; it stands for *dick shot off.* See DICK.

DUCK-FUCKER

In the past, a Royal Navy expression for the official in charge of the ship's poultry, a man regarded with the same suspicion as a sheep-herder in the American West. This explains the English oaths, *fuck-a-duck, Lord fuck a duck* and (in polite novels) *Lord love a duck.*

DUFF

The ASS, as in "Don't just sit on your duff" or "Get off your duff and give us a hand." Evidently of military origin, and related to *dough* in the World War I term *doughboy (dough* is pronounced "duff" in some English dialects, and means anything that is roughly handled – like an enlisted man's ass).

DUTCH WIFE

An elongated, firm pillow placed in bed, in the tropics, as a kind of primitive air conditioning; it ventilates the man sleeping with it. This is one of a family of terms belittling the puritanical, Calvinistic Dutch, such as: "Dutch kitchen," one that is spotlessly clean; "talking like a Dutch uncle," talking strictly and severely; "in Dutch," in trouble; "Dutch courage," alcoholic bravado; "the Dutch act," suicide; and "Dutch treat," one for which you yourself pay and which is, thus, no treat at all.

EASY RIDER

A PIMP, in southern slang. The popular movie of this title contained ironies which many viewers missed. The heroes, Billy and Wyatt, suggest Wyatt Earp and Billy the Kid, but as dope-pushers, or HUSTLERS, they are of the "easy rider" ilk. The connotation behind the term is that pimps live off their WHORES' earnings. This was used in the old blues song, "Memphis Blues": "Mr. Crump don't allow no easy riders here."

EAT

To perform FELLATIO or CUNNILINGUS. All that is actually eaten, of course, is semen, and that only during fellatio (it is 95% protein and contains an average of 2 calories, if anyone is interested). Nevertheless, the cannibalistic implication of this metaphor is the subject of a play, *Suddenly Last Summer,* by Tennessee Williams, in which the homosexual protagonist, after "eating" (fellating) many of the hungry young denizens of a backward island, is in turn actually eaten by them. And the modern equivalent of the Egyptian goddess Isis restoring her dead husband, Osiris, to life by fellating him is a brutal joke about a widow who asks the undertaker to amputate her husband's penis. "My God, why?" he asks. "For years now I've been eating him the way he wanted," she says. "Now I'm going to eat it the way I want!"

On a less hostile level, "J," authoress of *The Sensuous Woman,* recommends putting whipped cream on a lover's penis before fellatio; Legman, in *Oragenitalism,* describes a long list of similar variations of cunnilingus, starting with the elegance of sprinkling rare champagne into the vulva before the act and ending with the crudity of pouring orange juice from a tin can. A popular French variation involves inserting a banana directly into the vagina; as the man sucks it out and eats it, the woman experiences simultaneously some of the sensations of both cunnilingus and coitus. (The dilemma of whether to FUCK or eat is resolved in this recent graffito: "I'd rather fuck the pizza and eat the waitress. [Underneath] I did. The pizza's better.") A more scientific approach to this "dynamic duo" – simultaneous clitoral and vaginal stimulation – is the Chin Dildo, for sale in Yokahama sex shops, which allows the gentleman to nibble the clitoris while providing artificial copulative motions in the vagina.

Strawberry, champagne and other flavored douches have recently been introduced to the American market; rock composer Ed Sanders has celebrated (or caricatured) this trend in a song titled "Coca-Cola Douche":

> My baby ain't got no money,

> But her snatch it taste like honey,
> Cause she makes that Coca-Cola Douche.

One should also mention the French scientist who invented a formula to "make ze pussy taste like ze orange." When he went to a leading Paris bank he was bluntly turned down. "However," said the bank president, "we will gladly loan you five million francs to find ze formula zat make ze orange taste like ze pussy!"

Finally, the erotic connotation of *eating* inspired the dinner date as a favorite makeout gambit with men; analogously, husband-hunting young women know that "the way to a man's heart is through his stomach" and are eager to demonstrate their home cooking. The same chain of associations inspired two of the trickiest of all limericks:

> There was a young fellow named Skinner
> Who took a young lady to dinner.
> They sat down to dine
> At quarter past nine
> And at quarter past ten it was in her.
> (The dinner, not Skinner –
> Skinner was in her before dinner!)

and the topper:

> There was a young fellow named Tupper
> Who took a young lady to supper.
> They sat down to dine
> At quarter past nine
> And at quarter past ten it was up her.
> (Not Tupper, and not the supper
> – it was some son-of-a-bitch named Skinner!)

ECDYSIAST

A striptease dancer. A new word created by H. L. Mencken at the request of Gypsy Rose Lee, who wanted a polite name for her profession, it derives from Greek *ec,* out of, and *dysia,* clothing or foilage.

ENGLISH CULTURE

Code used in personal ads to mean sadism and/or masochism. An ad saying, "Interested in English, French and Roman Culture" signifies a desire to participate in sadism, bondage, oral sex and orgies. The English, however, refer to sadism as "kink kicks" and play on the words *birch* and *cane* in their personal ads. See KINK.

ENTER

To have intercourse with a woman. John O'Hara used *enter* in this way in his novel, *Ten North Frederick.*

ESKIMO PIE

A frigid woman. Usually used in the phrase "Put a stick in her and she'd be an Eskimo Pie."

EXTRACURRICULAR ACTIVITIES

A joking reference to fornication, used by college boys. Also applied to extramarital sex.

EYE

To *have eyes for* someone generally connotes sexual desire; but *in a pig's eye* is an expurgation of *in a pig's ass. Bung your eye* and *Here's mud in your eye,* those mysterious toasts, suggest some anal symbolism. The Army oath, *In your eye, all six inches of it* is part of the same tradition, and in ancient Egypt *the eye of Hoor* meant the anus. *Eye* is also sometimes used to designate the opening of the urethra in the head of the penis; this metaphor is used in Arabian poetry where the penis is sometimes called "the blind eye that weeps."

FAG (or FAGGOT)

A male homosexual. The origin of this word is obscure; it has something to do with the English public-school system in which younger students act for a time as "fags" (servants) for the older boys and *fagged out* implies being overworked, as is often the case among the "fags" in those schools. Nobody seems to have any notion, however, how this *fag* became elaborated to *faggot* when it came to mean a homosexual. There may be a link to the heresy burnings of the Holy Inquisition, in which the kindling wood was called "faggots." Many of the inquisitors were convinced that all heretics were homosexuals and all homosexuals were heretics (see BUGGER). *Faggot* may come, then, from some lost expression, such as "He's headed for the faggots," meaning he doesn't seem quite orthodox. Homosexual-hunting still occurs in persecutions of the unorthodox; Thomas Foran, prosecutor of the Chicago Seven Conspiracy trial, charged outside the courtroom that they were all "freaking fag revolutionaries."

Fag may also mean a cigarette, both in England and on our East Coast.

FAIRY

A male homosexual. The first use of *fairy* in English was to describe the "little people" living in the hills who were alleged to have magic powers. These creatures were treated mythologically by poets like Spenser and Shakespeare, but modern folklorists and anthropologists have noted that the earliest references to the fairy folk seem to describe a real people who were feared and respected.

Nobody knows for certain how this word came to be applied to homosexuals, but it is no more than a century old and may have derived from touring Shakespearean productions in which directors often cast homosexuals as fairies on the grounds that they had a fey quality that was lacking in ordinary men, a quality which audiences would respond to without quite recognizing.

Which raises the possibility of a link between *fairy* and *fey* or *fay,* meaning magic powers or a person possessing such powers, such as the famous Morgan the Fay in the tales of King Arthur and the Grail. There are two main forms of ceremonial magic both sexual; one involves heterosexual rituals, and the other, homosexual rituals. It is conceivable that during the centuries of their underground existence, these cults could have developed a tradition in which *fey* (or *fay)* was associated with the homosexual rites.

FALL OFF THE APPLE TREE

To surrender one's virginity, usually in the form of a question: "Did she fall off the apple tree yet?" The imagery of falling, like that of flying, is sexual. Note how this imagery pops up in such expressions as *fall in love, head over heels in love, knocked off her pins, he fell for her, a fallen woman.*

In a surprisingly large number of movies and comics, the villain dies by falling from a height, shouting an orgasmic "Arrrrgh" in the comic books. This was the fate of the archetypal erotic brute, King Kong (the wretch had earlier been COPPING A FEEL, in a scene cut before the film was released), who fell from what was at the time the world's highest and most phallic skyscraper.

FALL OFF THE ROOF

A euphemism that has become a joke. *She fell off the roof* means that she has her menstrual period.

FALSIES

Padding used to ostensibly increase the size of the female breasts; from an old witticism implying a commercial motivation, *false advertising*. These gimmicks used to be called "gay deceivers," before GAY took on its modern meaning.

FAMILY JEWELS

The testicles (considered favorably, for once!); also known as "crown jewels." A related witticism is "heirlooms," which has a nice pun in it, if you think about their function in reproduction, ORCHIDS is another favorable term.

FANCY HOUSE

A whorehouse; from the 18th-19th Century use of *fancy* to mean a prostitute. Confusingly, boxers were also called "fancies" in 19th Century English slang; a "fancy Dan" is a sharp dresser, while a "fancy-pants" is a suspected homosexual.

FANNY

The buttocks; usually used appreciatively of a pleasing woman ("Look at the fanny on her"), but occasionally addressed sarcastically by one male to another ("Get off your fanny and help").

FART

To pass wind; from Old English *foertan,* which has the

same meaning and also signifies to explode (the source of standard English *petard,* a type of bomb). Behind both the anal and military usages is Latin *ped,* to break wind.

Modern uses include "old fart," an authoritarian boss or teacher; "fart-face," anybody the speaker wishes to insult; "a fart in a gale of wind," a meaningless speech by a politician or other "windbag"; "farting around," wasting one's time; and in English slang, a "fart-catcher" was a servant because decorum compelled him to walk directly behind his master on the street. In Irish wit, if a person accidentally breaks wind in public, someone asks innocently, "Did an angel speak?"

The pleasure of the release of tension associated with farting is noted by Burroughs in *Naked Lunch.* An actress in a stag movie (SKIN FLICK) is giving a BLOW job, and "as she suck down toward the root of his cock, she tickle his prostate mockingly. He grin and fart."

The most famous use of *fart* nowadays is in the sad scrawl often found inside paytoilets: "Here I sit broken-hearted/ paid a dime and only farted."

FART-LOVER

An insult with obvious implications. Variations: "He farts in the bathtub and bites the bubbles"; "He goes around sniffing the seats of bicycles."

THE FEATHERY FLICK

A technique of cunnilingus which climaxes with the male tongue on the very point of the clitoris, flicking as gently as a feather; popularized by the anonymous author of *The Sensuous Man.*

FEEL
To caress sexually. See COP A FEEL.

FELLATIO (or TO FELLATE)
Stimulation of the penis with the mouth and tongue. See COCKSUCKER, BLOW and EAT.

FEM (or FEMME)
An effeminate homosexual of either sex, in contrast to the BUTCH, who takes the male (dominant) role. In show biz, however, a femme is just a woman, whether she be hetero or homo, as in O'Hara's *Pal Joey:* "He has aired the femme that got him the job," meaning he jilted the lady who got him the engagement to sing at the night club.

FERRY
A prostitute. This is one WHORE's word not yet picked up by homosexuals to pin on one another, but a popular joke has a man ask over the phone, "Do I have the South Street ferry?" and receive the lisping response, "Thpeaking!" Compare this with the magnificent insult in Rodgers and Hammerstein's *Carousel*: "You broken-down old pleasure boat."

FIFTH WHEEL
A heterosexual male who has innocently wandered into a homosexual bar; from the old saying, "I need him like I need a fifth wheel on my car." In general conversation, anything superfluous or undesired, as in "I need government inspectors like I need a fifth wheel on my car."

FIG

The vagina. This can be traced through various languages back to the ancient Romans, and making *the fig* (a hand gesture resembling a fig, or a vagina) is a traditional South European insult meaning "Go fuck yourself." The fig as a visual sexual metaphor was vividly depicted by Alan Bates in the film, *Women in Love,* in which he peels a fig while describing, with heavy sexual overtones, the correct way to peel and eat the fruit. Bates climaxes this scene by popping the juicy fig into his mouth.

FINGER

A hand gesture, middle finger up and others turned down, which is widely understood to mean "Fuck you!" A related expression is "fucked by the fickle finger of fate," said by those whose plans are thwarted; but in the underworld to "finger" somebody is to inform against him to the police.

FINGER-FUCK

To bring a woman to orgasm by manual caresses, either by putting a finger or fingers into the vagina, or playing externally with the clitoris. Also called "playing stinky finger" by teeny boppers, and used in the classic sense in one version of "Frankie and Johnnie":

> Frankie got out at South Clark Street,
> Looked in a window so high,
> And there she saw her Johnnie-man
> Finger-fucking Nellie Blye.
> He was her man, but he done her wrong.

FIRE SHIP

Sailor's slang for a woman with a venereal disease.

A popular sea chant called "The Roving Kind" was commercially recorded in the 1950s and widely played on radio and TV even though it contained the line, "She was nothing but a fire ship rigged up in a disguise." Evidently, the censors of that age were not nautical men. See BURN.

FISH

Derogatory male homosexual slang for women, possibly from the Cockney use of *fishmonger* to mean a prostitute. Both terms are allegedly based on the vaginal aroma of women who are not over-finicky about personal daintiness, as in the old witticism: " 'Hi, girls,' the blind man said, passing the fish market."

FISH QUEEN

Homosexual slang for a very effeminate male.

FIST FUCK

Male MASTURBATION; also called "fucking Rosy Palm and her five sisters."

FLAME

A woman with whom one is having an affair; sometimes, a woman one is engaged to marry.

FLASH

The technique of an exhibitionist who lets his penis hang out of his trousers, closes his overcoat over it and then flashes the coat open when a woman passes.

FLAT-BACKER

Black slang for a WHORE who will only perform straight sexual intercourse and refuses FRENCH JOBS or other exotica.

FLESHPOTS

A 17th Century term that has survived only because of its use in the King James Bible, this usually means a place of sin, such as a whorehouse or night club.

FLIT

A very effeminate male homosexual.

FLOOZY

A prostitute; from *Flossy,* a common name for English country girls, who were often reduced to whoredom after coming to the big cities. This was used by Truman Capote in *The Grass Harp:* "He bought a red racy car and went skidding around with every floozy in town; the only nice girls you ever saw in that car were his sisters."

FLUTE PLAYER

A male homosexual; a visual metaphor about their oral habits. *Playing the skin flute* is a related schoolboy phrase meaning masturbation, and also is derived from the shape of the penis.

FLY

The opening in the front of a man's trousers. The origin of this term is unknown, but according to psychoanalysts, flying is symbolic of copulation; hence, the randy reputation in folklore of airline pilots and, even more, of stewardesses. Beelzebub, "Lord of the Flies," is an early Hebrew name for the devil, and witches were once believed to fly to their sabbaths (magical sex orgies) on broomsticks, symbolic of the erect phallus.

The origin of the trouser fly, incidentally, has more to do with eroticism than with urination, according to Allen Edwardes in *The Cradle of Erotica:*

> The Turks introduced the fly to Europe between the 18th and 19th Century. Its purpose was not only to facilitate urination, but also to facilitate "the active analism, fornication, rape, and mutual fellatio or masturbation so common among them. So-called passives have both an open crotch and a small fold or fly in the rear of their drawers to allow free egress of their own erect penis, which the so-called active clasps and manipulates, as well as free ingress of their partner's phallus per anum.

We were really flying can refer to either an exceptional sex session or a drug trip; *fly-by-night,* now describing a shady business scheme, was originally an insult to an old woman, accusing her of witchcraft; *to take a flyer* is either to have a woman in a great hurry, with risk of interruption, or, more generally, to take a chance on anything hazardous. See CANARY, FALL OFF THE APPLE TREE and FLYING BRAVO.

FLYING BRAVO

A menstruating woman is said to be "flying bravo"; probably deriving from the Spanish bullfighting advertisements which promise *torros bravos* (brave, dangerous bulls), all of whom end up bleeding after facing the *matador.*

FLYING PHILADELPHIA FUCK

Generally considered the supreme sexual experience for a male. Most Americans have heard of this divertissement, but few know what it is precisely. Properly speaking, it is not a FUCK at all, but a variety of oragenitalism, performed with the aid of a kind lady, a rocking chair and a very sturdy curtain rod. The woman sits on the rocking chair, while the man, nude, stands upon its arms, holding on to the curtain rod with both hands. She FELLATES him by rocking herself back and forth, and, at the crucial moment, he lifts his feet off the arms of the chair and hangs from the rod. Allegedly, because every muscle in his body is under maximum tension, his orgastic spasms will be magnified most salubriously. (This is very tricky, because the curtain rod sometimes snaps unexpectedly, or the rocker turns over, and both parties are apt to land on the floor rather abruptly.) *Go take a flying Philadelphia fuck in a rolling donut* is a contemptuous dismissal in the family of *go take a flying fuck at the moon, go jump in the lake, go take a long walk on a short pier, go shit in your hat.* Raymond Chandler once said that his favorite of such expressions was Chicago gangster Dan O'Banion's mild "Be missing," which the novelist enviously pronounced "deadly in its restraint."

The expression *a flying fuck* dates back at least to 1845, when it appeared in a remarkable volume by painter and etcher Thomas Rowlandson, engagingly entitled, *Pretty Little Games for Young Ladies and Gentlemen: With Pictures of Good Old English Sports and Pastimes.* The book consisted of ten ribald etchings, each accompanied by a poem apparently also the work of the artist. The sports celebrated are FELLATIO, CUNNILINGUS and similar diversions. One plate, "New Feats of Horsemanship," shows a young RAKE and his lady fair on horseback, at a gallop, her skirt raised to show her buttocks, and his penis (of heroic dimensions) pushed beneath to enter her vagina; both faces are flushed with passion. The verse reads:

> Well mounted on a mettled steed
> Famed for his strength as well as speed
> Corinna and her favorite buck
> Are pleas'd to have a flying fuck.

Sex in flight is a basic fantasy, not yet extensively explored by science-fiction writers. Anyone who has copulated in an airplane is quick to boast about the achievement to friends and describe the novel sensations in detail, and the possibilities of sex in a free fall are apparently the cause of the enduring popularity of the limerick:

> There once was a man from Lasair
> Who fucked his girl on the stair.
> The banister broke
> And he quickened his stroke
> And finished her off in midair.

Xaviera Hollander has a lyrical passage on airborne sex in her autobiography, *The Happy Hooker:*

> He was such a charming person that, by the time the stewardess removed our trays, I already wanted to go down on him. A lot of acrobatic skill was required to accomplish this feat without being observed. The way we finally did it was to cover me to the tip of my head with a light blanket while I pretended to be getting my vanity bag from under his window seat. Doing it got us so turned on that we wanted to make love all the way . . . As soon as the coast was clear we removed the armrests from the seats, squeezed down

together under the blanket, he facing my back spoon-fashion, and proceeded to make love. We had to be very quiet, and, we soon discovered, very careful, because a couple of times he became overamorous and I almost fell down between the seats.

We made a game of doing it between the stewardesses walking up the aisle to answer call lights and the passengers walking sleepily to the lavatory. The challenge of making love 30,000 feet in the air made it even more exciting.

Copulation at the speed of light will eventually be enjoyed by our descendants, no doubt, but interpreting Einstein, the men will have to be careful to ensure that they keep their penes perpendicular to the direction of motion and never parallel to it, for otherwise the Lorenz contraction would take place and relativity would shrink the erection as fast as passion mounted it. In treating such a case, even Masters and Johnson would need the assistance of a mathematical expert on General Field Theory.

The association of these diversions with Philadelphia is rather odd, considering the otherwise stodgy reputation of that town, which has been immortalized in a million jokes, including W.C. Fields's classic, "I was in Philadelphia once, but it was closed." The latest in this line is a graffito found in Philadelphia itself by Robert Reisner, which said, "Philadelphia is not dull – it just seems so because it is next to exciting Camden, New Jersey." Perhaps Philadelphia just landed in this term through the accident of its alliteration with *flying* and FUCK. See GO DOWN.

FORT BUSHY

The female pubic hair; a variation on BUSH, and in some colleges a "bush patrol" is a heavy PETTING session. *Fort Bushy* has the same implication as such expressions as *He conquered her, She surrendered to him.* An even more graphic illustration of the combative linkage is Norman Mailer's unforgettable "I flung her a fuck the equivalent of a ten-round fight."

THE FOUR Fs

From an old saying "Find them, feel them, fuck them, forget them" – the life script of a successful Lothario. In black slang, *to weave the four Fs around a chick* is to seduce and abandon her. Originally, a pun on *4F,* the draft classification of those not eligible for military service. A much older version was longer and went "Find them, fool them, feed them, feel them, fuck them and forget them." See FUCK and FEEL.

FOUR-LETTER MAN

A contemptible person; a slang expression so obscure that its meaning has changed several times. Originally, it meant a homosexual and referred to the four letters of *homo.* Later, it came to mean PIMP; and Lord only knows what Hemingway had in mind in "The Short Happy Life of Francis Macomber," when – after Macomber has disgraced himself by cowardice – the professional hunter, Wilson, calls him a "four-letter man." (Wilson later decides that Macomber's wife is a "five-letter woman," evidently Hemingway's own invention and probably meaning BITCH.) In the movie version of *Gentlemen Prefer Blondes,* a college athlete who has won four letters in sports tells Marilyn Monroe proudly, "I'm a four-letter man!" – to which she replies, aghast, "Well, I wouldn't brag about it!"

FOX

A good-looking young woman. Black slang, based on the fox's reputation for both treachery and lechery, and possibly from the fact that the fox is one of the worst nuisances in rural life. In one of his explicit fantasies in *Naked Lunch,* Burroughs describes "a horde of lust-mad American women" as "she-foxes":

> Dripping cunts, from farm and dude ranch, factory, brothel, country club, penthouse and suburb; motel and yacht and cocktail bar, strip off riding clothes, ski togs, evening dresses, Levis, tea gowns, print dresses, slacks, bathing suits and kimonos. They scream and yipe and howl, leap on the guests like bitch dogs in heat with rabies. They claw at the hanged boys shrieking "You fairy! You bastard! Fuck me! Fuck me! Fuck me!" The guests flee screaming, dodge among the hanged boys, overturn iron lungs.
>
> A.J.: "Call out my Sweitzers, God damn it! Guard me from these she-foxes!"

FREAK

Somebody whose sexual proclivities are weirder than the speaker's. But the attitudes behind these words are changing, at least in the counterculture; witness two popular buttons, one of which says, LET'S FACE IT: WE'RE ALL QUEER, and the second, BE CREATIVE: INVENT A SEX PERVERSION. See KINK.

FRENCH

To perform oral sex, as in "She frenched me." The expression arose during World War I and memorializes the fact that American soldiers of that period had never encountered this diversion at home. As Lenny Bruce once said, if our troops had been sent to Poland in that conflict, today we would be saying "She polacked me." American astonishment at both this pastime and also the Gallic sporting combat in which opponents kick with the feet but are forbidden to punch with the fists is immortalized in a couplet brought home from that war: "The French, they are a funny race/They fight with their feet and fuck with their face."

French culture (as in the personal add "Frantic Francophile seeks contact with bored housewives with shapely legs. I am an ex-showgirl, white, 28 years, will teach French culture . . .") is code for oragenitalism. The "French disease," in English slang, is syphilis (called "The English malady," curiously, by the French themselves!). *French kiss* is ambiguous; in some parts of our country it means a passionate, open-mouthed kiss with tongues joining (also known as a SOUL KISS), while in other places it means oragenitalism. A "French letter" is a CONDOM, a nearly obsolete witticism that goes back to the time when letter and envelope were the same sheet of paper. A "French tickler" is a condom with a small feather or other device on it, to give the woman an extra thrill.

FRENCH JOB

WHORES' slang for FELLATIO. In many brothels there will be one girl who prefers French jobs to copulation, based on her own notions of ethics, aesthetics and decorum, while others will try to avoid French jobs if they can. According to happy hooker Xaviera Hollander in an interview in *Screw* magazine, many prostitutes look forward to French jobs because "It's easier. It's quicker. They don't get erosion of the vagina."

FRUIT (or FRUITCAKE)

A male homosexual; but *Fruitcake* also means crazy, from the old *nutty as a fruitcake*. Compare this use of *fruit* with "vegetable," a sexless individual, a catatonic or a person with brain damage.

F.T.W.

A slogan of the Hell's Angels, often found scrawled on walls or stitched on their jackets, meaning *fuck the world*. *F.T.N.*, found on subway walls, is more limited in its hostility; it means *fuck the niggers*. The most common of all these expressions of sexual outrage, of course, is the ubiquitous *fuck you*, which is aimed at every individual who happens to see it.

FUCK

To copulate. There is a popular belief that *fuck* derives from f*or* u*nlawful* c*arnal* k*nowledge,* once used in rape trials but this is completely undocumented.

The actual origin of the word has been lost, but the general outline of its history can be traced: German *ficken* means both to strike or hit with the fist and also to have sexual intercourse; Latin *fustis* is a club or cudgel and the probable origin of French *foutre,* fuck. All these suggest a definitely hostile attitude toward the female recipient of such attentions, and even the late Latin *futuere,* to copulate, itself goes back to the brutal *battuere,* to beat.

Fuck is still omitted from almost all dictionaries and superstitiously spelled *f-k* in those which include it. In his translation of the *Arabian Nights,* Sir Richard Burton tried to get around its negative associations by coining his own pseudo-Gallic variation, *futter.* This has been picked up by a few other writers, including translators of Rabelais, but has never been incorporated into actual Anglo-American speech. *Fuck* first appeared in literature in Joyce's *Ulysses:* "I'll break the fucking neck of any fucking bugger who says a word against my king," Private Carr shouts drunkenly. Nearly 200 pages later, with even greater boldness, Joyce employs it in its true meaning, as Molly Bloom thinks of confessing her ADULTERY defiantly to Leopold ("I'll tell him yes your wife has been fucked and damn well fucked"). The censorship problems Joyce confronted intimidated other writers (except D.H. and T.E. Lawrence) for several decades thereafter, and Norman Mailer, trying to convey both the crude poetry and the monotony of Army speech in *The Naked and the Dead,* prudently compromised with the spellings *fug* and *fugging,* the latter being accurate for some American dialects. Allegedly, Tallulah Bankhead said to Mailer at their first meeting, "You're the man who doesn't know how to spell *fuck.*" Mailer later claimed that it was her press agent who had said it to his press agent.

A few years later, James Jones smashed the taboo to shreds in *From Here to Eternity,* in which his soldiers use *fucking* in nearly every speech and Sergeant Warden, when accusing his mistress of infidelity, tells her bluntly, "He says he fucked you." Jones also recorded many genuine bits of G.I. poetry, including:

> We're the men of Schofield Barracks,
> We are riders of the night,
> We are dirty sons of bitches,
> And we'd rather fuck than fight.

Since Jones didn't go to jail, other writers (and their publishers) grew bolder. In John O'Hara's *Ten North Frederick,* when one character makes a long speech justifying the double standard (that adultery is permissible in males, but not in females), the hero tells him, "You're a fucking hypocrite – and I mean that literally." By 1958, Allen Ginsberg was able to use this real and vivid language in a homosexual context (in his poem, "Howl," one line of which describes those who "let themselves be fucked in the ass by saintly motorcyclists, and screamed with joy"). Attempts by authorities to ban the poem in San Francisco were stopped after a brief trial.

The use of *fucking* as an all-purpose adjective has increased so much in recent decades that it is the target of a joke about a sailor who returns from shore leave to recount his exploits to his shipmates: "First I went to a fucking bar and had a few fucking drinks. Then I picked up a fucking broad on the fucking street and we went to a fucking hotel and rented a fucking room. Then we had intercourse."

And as a noun: A short man sidles up to a tall, statuesque blonde at a party. "What would you say to a nice little fuck?" he asks boldly. Magnificently bored, she stares down at him and drawls, "Hi, nice little fuck."

Another popular joke about the omnipresent syllable: A male school teacher, an ex-Marine, asks his class to name the best thing in life. "The love of your mother," says the star pupil. "Very good," responds the teacher, beaming. "Love of your country," shouts another future politician. "Even better," beams the teacher. Then the class delinquent speaks up. "Fucking," says he. The teacher goes into a fury and demands that this little wretch bring a letter from his father the next day explaining such disruptive behavior. The following morning he demands to know if the boy has the note. "No," is the answer. "My father says fucking *is* the best thing in life an' the only guys who don't think so are cocksuckers an' he doesn't correspond with *them.*"

W. C. Fields immortalized the word when he allegedly commented that he never drank water because fish fuck in it. The word is now so acceptable that Paul Newman got away with rapping about the varieties of fucking in a PLAYBOY interview: There was "sport fucking"; there was "mercy fucking," which would be reserved for spinsters and librarians; there was the "hate fuck," the "prestige fuck" and the "medicinal fuck," which is, "Feel better now, sweetie?" A few short years ago such a conversation, if published, could have killed an actor's career.

The most famous and witty usage of *fuck* in modern times is attributed to authoress Dorothy Parker, when somebody from the *New Yorker* magazine called her home and said that editor Harold Ross wanted to know when she'd come into the office and do some of her work. "Tell Mr. Ross," said Dotty, "that I'm too fucking busy, and *vice versa.* "

Finally, a mimeographed sheet currently circulating is a good example of recent folk humor and current attitudes toward this once most forbidden of all taboo words. Praising its versatility, it lists *fuck's* various applications besides the sexual one:

>Fraud I got fucked at the used car lot.
>
>Dismay Oh, fuck it.
>
>Trouble I guess I'm fucked now.
>
>Aggression Fuck you.
>
>Difficulty I can't understand this fucking job.
>
>Displeasure What the fuck is going on here?
>
>Incompetence He's a big fuck off.

I know that you can think of many more uses and with all these uses, how can anybody be offended when you say FUCK?

We say, use this unique word more often in your daily speech. It adds to your prestige. Say it loud and proud, "FUCK YOU."

Many people have preferred not to say it at all, let alone loud and proud, and hence the euphemisms for *fuck,* if anybody could ever tabulate all of them, might fill another book. Among those mentioned by Peter Fryer in his *Mrs. Grundy: Studies in English Prudery are:* to *know* (before 1200); to *have carnal knowledge* (1686); to *do one's kind* (before 1230); to *ride* (1250); *love-work* (1250); *fornification* (1300); *meddle* (1340); *copulation* (1483); *enjoy* (1598); *Venerean mirth* (1611); *commerce* (1624); *intimacy* (1676). The poets have contributed *come aloft* (Spenser*); do the act of darkness, make the beast with two backs, plough, pluck* and *trim* (Shakespeare); *go bed-pressing* and *go vaulting* (Marston); *do the divine work of fatherhood* (Whitman). Others too archaic or obscure for inclusion as separate entries in this dictionary are*: pizzle; plug; strop one's beak; get one's kettle mended; do a bit of front-door work; feed the dummy; get Jack in the orchard; tumble; go stargazing; do it.* And this is only a selection – there are at least several hundred words that mean fuck.

FUCK BOOK

Southern slang for a pornographic novel. *Screw* magazine uses "Fuck Books" as the name of its book review column.

FUCKED AND FAR FROM HOME

Confused, frightened, in desperate straits; in other words, feeling like a young girl who has been seduced and abandoned. This is almost always metaphoric, as in "When the I.R.S. was through auditing my return, I was fucked and far from home."

FULL HOUSE

Said of an unfortunate person who has two or more venereal diseases at the same time, "He has a full house."

FUNK

A state of fear, depression or embarrassment, as in "I was in a funk," or "I was in a blue funk." This is an English term often thought to be obscene by Americans, probably because it's seldom heard and resembles FUCK. It comes from the Old English root meaning to smoke, and cartoonists often show smoke coming out of one's ears during tension.

The American black usage of *funky* derives from an older, rural southern use and as an adjective is ambiguous; it can mean bad, as in "That was some funky shit she handed me, man," or groovy, as in "Brother, those are really funky clothes you've got on," or may describe a fine kind of music: "He plays a funky guitar." Only context and intonation convey the exact sense intended. In the late Sixties, a popular dance was the "Funky Chicken"; and recently the white counterculture has picked up the uses of the word which in the past were exclusive to blacks.

FURBURGER

The female genitalia; usually used in reference

to CUNNILINGUS: "He's smiling like he just ate the furburger." This is from *hamburger*, of course, and it parodies such restaurantese as "oliveburger," "cheeseburger," "pizzaburger." See EAT.

FUZZ

The police; from Cockney *fuzzies,* which now means police, but originally applied to anyone that the speaker disliked. This may derive from *fuzzy-wuzzies,* an insulting term for the Sudanese tribesmen who fought against England in the Boer War; or from *don't fuck around* and its polite alternatives, *don't fuss around* and *don't futz around,* the police being regarded as people who are paid to FUCK around, fuss around and futz around in what others regard as their own private business. An "F.L.," in New York underworld and drug-culture slang, is an untrustworthy individual, a possible informer. The original was *fuzz-lover,* but the abbreviation is a play on the Yiddish *T.L. (tochus leker),* meaning Ass-kisser.

GADGET

The penis. This is what Lewis Carroll's celebrated semanticist, Humpty-Dumpty, called a "portmanteau" word; it combines *gauge* and *gasket* and originally meant any tool for which the speaker can't remember the correct name, as in "Hand me that gadget." Thus, when *tool* came to mean penis, so did *gadget,* as in the limerick:

> The Reverend Hedley van Smedley
> Pulled on his tool very steadily.
> It grew fourteen inches
> And now in the clinches
> He rams home a gadget most deadly.

GADZOOKS

This mysterious oath, which keeps popping up in historical novels and movies, is an abbreviation of *God's hooks* – the nails with which Jesus was crucified. Similarly, *God blind me* became *gorblimey; God* sometimes becomes *gosh; Jesus* masquerades as *gee* or *geez;* SHIT becomes *pshaw* or *sugar; oh* FUCK becomes *oh fudge;* and *up your* ASS becomes the vaguer *up yours.*

GAFF

A house of prostitution; probably deriving from two sources: early French *gaffer,* a spear, by phallic metaphor, and the nautical *gaff,* a fish hook. "Don't take any of his gaff" means "don't be intimidated by his boasting," and relates to "Don't be a sucker" and "Don't swallow the bait." The use of *gaff* for a brothel, therefore, may refer to customers frequently having the impression that they were "hooked" (somehow parted from more money than they consciously remember spending). See HOOKER.

GALLOP THE ANTELOPE

To MASTURBATE; similar terms are *flog the dolphin, beat the bishop* and *flub the dub.* This strange metaphor probably dates back to early settlers of the West, who must have been amazed by the onanistic behavior of the animal in question, which obtains an erection and ejaculation by rubbing its horns against the ground rhythmically. In the mating season, male antelopes who have failed to capture a harem may masturbate in this fashion as often as three or more times each morning.

GALORE

All you could want; more than enough. An English adaptation of the Irish *go leor*, plenty, immortalized in the name of one of Ian Fleming's heroines, Pussy Galore. See PUSSY.

GAME

Young whores hardly broken to the profession, in recent Cockney; in 18th Century slang, the dupe or gull of a swindle. To "die game" is to die at the gallows. "What game are you playing on me?" or "What's your game?" are questions asked when somebody suspects a confidence trick.

GAMS

A woman's legs; used admiringly by tabloids or press agents of the Thirties and Forties. In 18th Century slang, however, this was insulting and meant crooked or ugly legs. The origin is from the French *jambes*, legs.

GANG BANG

Group sex in which several men take turns copulating with one woman, with or without her consent. The term is similarly used by homosexuals to designate sequential BUGGERING, with or without the consent of the star performer.

Many women are naturally multiorgasmic, some of them intensely so, like the señorita in the limerick:

> There was a young lady from Spain
> Who liked it again and again
> And again and again
> And again and again
> And again and again and again.

In some religious cults, multiple orgasm is thought necessary to create the proper "astral" vibrations, and hence the prominent role of group sex rites, or orgies, in those religions. The story that Cleopatra FELLATED 1oo men in a single night may demonstrate not RANDINESS, but that she practiced some such form of magic.

Religion aside, some ladies just happen to dig that sort of thing, as in another limerick:

> There was a young lady named Gloria
> Who was had by Sir Geoffrey du Maurier,
> Then six other men,
> Then Sir Geoffrey again,
> Then the band at the Waldorf Astoria.

GARDEN

The female genitalia, especially the pubic hair. The classic Persian work of erotica, translated by Sir Richard Burton, is called *The Perfumed Garden,* and gardeners frequently appear as seducers in Boccaccio and other masterpieces as well as in run-of-the-mill pornography.

GASH

The vulva and/or vagina; a sadistic metaphor, from early English *garsh,* to carve, and modern English *gash,* a wound. This is exemplified in the joke about the boy who sees his mother menstruating as she emerges from the tub. "What's the matter?" he cries, disturbed. "Oh, nothing," she answers, embarrassed. *"Nothing,"* he exclaims, "why, somebody cut your prick off!" See PRICK.

GAY

Homosexual, as in "He's gay" or "She's gay." The "gay

world" is homosexual society; "gay bars," bars catering to homosexuals. In the 19th Century, Cockney "gays" were young WHORES.

Until recently, homosexual and bisexual writers used *gay* as a code word that heterosexuals would not recognize, but now it is widely known. Examples of the code usage: Aleister Crowley, in *Little Essays Toward Truth,* in an essay on "Chastity," urges the reader to "let no day pass without a gay deed of bold daring"; Truman Capote in his first novel, *Other Voices, Other Rooms:* "A gay breeze tossled his hair queerly" (a double-barreled *double entendre).* See QUEER.

GAZOOK

A young boy used for anal intercourse by adult homosexuals; probably a distortion of *gadzooks,* but there seems to be some connection with the "geek" or "gazeek" who once appeared in carnivals, a performer who pretended to be an ape man or other subhuman and gave proof of his animal status by such acts as eating live chickens.

GELD

An old verb meaning to castrate. A gelding is a horse which has been castrated and also, in rural wit, a man accused of lacking virility.

The original of *geld* was Old Norse *geldr,* a castrated horse; the unrelated *gelt* (money) is via Yiddish *geld* (gold, or money in general) and Old High German *gielt,* interest, usury – the source of the Modern English *yield* and old *geld* meaning a crown tax. Perhaps buried somewhere in this process is a metaphor about usury and taxation being methods of clipping or castrating their victims.

GEOGRAPHY

The female genitalia, as in "I'd like to explore her geography." See AROUND THE WORLD.

GEORGIAED

WHORE's slang for being swindled by a customer who escapes without paying, as in "The sonofabitch georgiaed me and went out the window." This evidently derives from some such incident in Georgia, or involving somebody from Georgia, or a woman named Georgia.

GET

One's children, in rural and deliberately offensive slang: "I want you and your get off this land by sundown." From recent English *get,* the offspring of animals, a shortening of *beget.*

Get in means to have intercourse, as does *get into her panties; get it off* or *get your rocks off* is to achieve orgasm; *get it up,* to have an erection. The question, *Did you get some?* generally means "Did you screw?" Freud commented on the sexual symbolism of horseback riding and *get up, git up* and *giddap,* addressed to a horse, may have sexual connotations. The oft-repeated masculine wish to be "hung like a horse" (have a horse-sized penis) reinforces this. Compare Robinson Jeffers's interesting erotic poem, "Roan Stallion," in which the heroine's admiration for a gigantic steed gradually turns into lust and she finally attempts to copulate with him. See also FLYING PHILADELPHIA FUCK.

GIG

The female genitalia, in some parts of the United States, but in other places it means a job. Chaucer uses *gigg* to mean a wanton or promiscuous woman, and Francis

Grose defines it as either the nose or the vagina. *Gig* is derived from *jig,* to dance, from Middle French *giguer,* a lively and sensuous dance of that period. From this root comes French *gigolette,* a prostitute, and Italian *gigolo,* a male prostitute or at least a man who lives on gifts from women. *Gig* as a job, then, has the same connotation of prostitution as *hustle* does. See HUSTLER.

GINCH

The female genitalia, in cyclists' slang. This is often used as a collective noun, as in "Any ginch here?" or "Any new ginch on the scene?" but a new woman may be known as "the new ginch" until a better name is found for her. Hunter Thompson uses this quite nicely in his book, *Hell's Angels:* "Many had left their own women behind, fearing trouble, but now that the trouble was dissipated, there was not going to be any strange ginch either."

GINGER

A prostitute who robs, or "rolls," her customers. *Ginger man* is Dublin slang for a fellow who can't be downed or defeated – the Irish equivalent of our ghettos' BADASS CAT or BADASS MOTHERFUCKER.

GIVE HEAD

To perform FELLATIO; originally, this was a witticism or perhaps a euphemism. Among high-school boys, it is still regarded as droll to ask another, quite innocently, if he ever "took it in his head to make money." If he gullibly answers yes, this information is shouted loudly several times – "He took it in his head to make money!" There is general hilarity until the victim realizes that he has, in effect, confessed to homosexual prostitution.

Conception and birth through the head is an old folklore theme; for instance, Athene sprang from the brow of Zeus, Rabelais's Gargantua was delivered through his mother's ear, and, in a modern joke, a homosexual who develops goiter immediately begins knitting baby booties.

Head also means toilet in the Navy.

GLORY HOLE

Homosexual slang for a hole in the partition between two toilets in a public lavatory, which is used for FELLATIO. The participants are in two separate but adjacent cubicles, hoping by this means to evade police detection. A "Judas window" is a hole drilled by the Vice Squad to spy on homosexuals from the next room.

GOALIE

The clitoris; a simple metaphor from ice hockey.

GO ALL THE WAY

To copulate, as distinguished from merely NECKING, groping, PETTING, FEELING UP and other quasi-monkish monkeyshines. It is only used in reference to women ("She'll go all the way"); society wisely takes this for granted about males.

GOBBLE

To FELLATE. A "gobble-prick," 18th Century slang, is a hot-blooded woman. Ed Sanders is the author of a book of verse entitled *Gobble Poems,* a title that did not shock those familiar with his earlier publications, such as *Bugger, Fuck You, The Dick* and *Fuck God Up The Ass.* See BUGGER, FUCK, DICK.

GODDAM (or GODDAMN)

Contractions of *God damn* or *God-damned. God damn you* was the strongest oath possible when religion was taken seriously, and this led to various prudent substitutions, some of which still linger; for example: *blast you, gosh darn you, gol-darn you, tarnation take you. Damn and blast* survives in England; *damn, blast and thunder* is also heard on occasion. The popularity of the use of *goddamn* in the English Army once led to English soldiers being called "goddams" by the French.

No comment on *goddam* would be complete without quoting the anonymous ballad, two centuries old and still popular, "Sam Hall":

> Oh, my name is Samuel Hall, Samuel Hall,
> Yes, my name is Samuel Hall,
> And I hate you one and all,
> You're a gang of fuckers all,
> Damn your eyes, damn your eyes,
> Goddamn your eyes!

Sam goes on that way for several colorful stanzas and is finally hanged, after quite a sensational trial:

> Oh, the jury they did stare, they did stare,
> Yes, the jury they did stare,
> For to hear me curse and swear,
> And the judge I did not spare,
> Damn his eyes, damn his eyes,
> Goddamn his eyes.

God was a subject of great terror and apprehension in the past, but nowadays he is more often a figure of fun. There is the story, for instance, of the psychiatrist summoned to heaven to treat the Lord. "What's the problem?" he asks Saint Peter before being ushered into the presence. "For two weeks now, he's been convinced he's Norman Mailer," is the answer.

Or: A man dies on the operating table and is miraculously revived through a heart transplant. On awakening, he announces that he has seen heaven. "What was God like?" he is asked by eager reporters. "Well," he says, "first of all, *she's* black . . ." The same idea is expressed more explicitly in the graffito, "God is a whore and what's more, she's black."

Or, again: A priest and a bishop are playing golf. Each time the priest muffs his swing, he screams, "Goddam it, missed again!" – and then profusely apologizes for his bad temper. Finally, not mollified by the apologies, the bishop orders the priest to show more control, whereupon, in shame, the priest calls upon God to strike him dead if he utters another blasphemy that day. At the very next hole, however, he swings wild again, and before he can catch himself he has shouted, "Goddam it, missed again!" He and the bishop stare at each other in apprehension as the skies darken, thunder rolls dramatically and a bolt of lightning flashes downward – and kills the bishop. From above, a petulant voice delivers the punch line: "Goddam it, missed again!"

GO DOWN

On the East and West coasts, this almost always means to perform oral sex; for example, "She went down on his cock" or "She went down on him." Confusingly, in the Midwest it often means intercourse, and saying "She went down for him" is often misunderstood.

GOING DOWN LIKE A SUBMARINE

This is said of a girl who shows great enthusiasm for FELLATIO: "She goes down like a submarine." See GO DOWN.

GOLDEN SHOWERS

To be urinated upon, a delight enjoyed by those whom psychiatrists describe as urolagnic. This term is seldom heard in speech, but is frequently seen in personal ads: "Interested in bondage, discipline and golden showers" means that the advertiser devoutly desires to be tied up in ropes, whipped soundly, and pissed upon. The people who answer these ads must be quite as remarkable as the people who place them. See also BOSTON TEA PARTY and WATER SPORTS.

GOOSE

A gesture (or the act of making the gesture), allegedly humorous, in which an unwary person is startled by either a finger between the buttocks or a squeeze upon the testicles. Considered good, clean fun; conventioneers have been known to goose passing girls with long poles having electrical shockers on the end. Goosing is never compared to the activities of COCKSUCKERS, toe queens or bondage-and-boot maniacs. However, there are storm clouds on the horizon; the *Village Voice,* during April 1971, featured some lively debate about goosing, women's liberationists claiming it was a male vice as bad as murder, and various others arguing that men, after all, are the victims more often than women. Several psychiatrists have observed that the practice is most common in all-male institutions, such as the Army and various schools. William Menninger's *Psychiatry in Wartime* treats it as the least harmful of all outlets for repressed homosexuality.

At one time, goosing was a fad in Hollywood, according to H. Allen Smith's *The Compleat Practical Joker,* and Douglas Fairbanks, Sr. became so addicted to the pastime that other actors complained and he was reprimanded by the studios. He later took to operating long-distance, with a fishing pole, while hiding behind the sets, and it was his special pleasure to ruin a whole scene by striking at the moment of a dramatic climax. Lexicographers are puzzled about the origin of this expression, which goes back to Rabelais, but agree that it probably has something to do with the goose, the common fowl with the long neck. H.L. Mencken notes that the goose is a "most pugnacious bird," often given to nipping the buttocks of humans who offend it, and suggests this may be the origin. Others trace the derivation through English slang, *silly goose,* a fool or inept joker. A well-known incident relates that Senator Thomas Hart Benton, a great wit and controversialist, was hissed during a speech and shouted back at the heckler, "Only two animals hiss – a snake and a goose. Stand up so we can see which you are!"

GORILLA PIMP

Black slang for the most vicious type of procurer, the implication being that he is all muscle and no brains. The origin is *gorilla,* not the animal but a burly criminal of similar comparatively low intelligence employed by criminal gangs as an enforcer or "muscle." A group of such characters is known as a "wrecking crew." The sense of humor of these types is often primitive, and Senator Robert Kennedy, when investigating this field, unearthed the story of a California businessman who resisted the mob's efforts to move in on him. He was kidnapped, knocked out, returned home and found that a banana had been forced up his rectum. The next day he received a phone call saying, "Next time it'll be a watermelon." When publisher Bob Harrison offended the mob, two gorillas came up to his office, on the 16th floor, and held him out the window by his ankles for five minutes. When they left they said, "Next time we'll let go."

GRANDMA

An elderly male homosexual; perhaps from the well-known line in "Little Red Riding Hood": "What big eyes you have, Grandma!" See EYE.

GRAPEFRUITS

Large female breasts. According to H. Allen Smith, this term originated in the brassiere industry and was used by workers to describe the largest standard size. Special models, of even greater dimension, were known as "watermelons."

GREEK CULTURE

Code in personal ads, meaning homosexual anal intercourse. Prostitutes use the expression *Greek trade* to mean men who desire heterosexual anal intercourse. Due to Plato's high and idealistic praise for male SODOMY in his *Symposium,* Europeans have long regarded Greeks as being especially devoted to this practice; Greeks, in turn, regard it as a peculiarly Turkish invention and are convinced that there is no man in Turkey not addicted to it. (Oddly, Shakespeare calls homosexuality "the Italian habit" in *Richard III.*) Sex historians point out that even in classical times many Greeks despised homosexuality, and, thus, Plato was not speaking for his nation but only for a small circle of friends. The use of *Greek culture* to mean anal sex, like the similar employment of *French culture* to designate oral sex, is a historical accident or misunderstanding.

There are some real cultural differences among homosexuals, however. European homosexuals are much more inclined to anality than American homosexuals, who are more interested in oral gratifications. Some sexologists think this is also discernible in the sexual preferences of European and American heterosexuals. And sadism deserves the code designation of "English culture," since it appears in more English pornography than in that of any Continental country and – judging from personal ads – is more sought-after by Englishmen than by others. One French historian, noting this salient fact, has tried to prove that De Sade was actually of English descent!

GREEN SICKNESS

In English slang, any nonspecific disease of young girls, humorously attributed to a lack of sex. (The male equivalent is BLUE BALLS.) A "green girl," in both England and New England, is a virgin; "greenhead" and "greenhand" are inexperienced young men; but a "greenhorn" is either a new employee or an immigrant. The latter metaphor seems to include a reference to the first horns sprouted by bulls at puberty.

GROCERIES

The penis and testicles, in homosexual slang; probably a shortening of *grocery basket*. See BASKET, BOX LUNCH, SEAFOOD.

GROOVY GUY

A male homosexual, usually used in a coded conversation to mislead outsiders – as GAY was once used until it became too well known.

GROPE

To fondle the genitalia, sometimes awkwardly or without consent. Groping is less hostile than GOOSING, but not much better than PAWING or COPPING A FEEL – real elegance demands more tact than any of these terms convey. Ed

Sanders once dedicated an issue of his magazine, *Fuck You,* to "All those groped in the silent halls of Congress by J. Edgar Hoover." A "group grope" is a party that is beginning to show symptoms of developing into an orgy.

GROWL

The female genitalia. To call a man a "growl-biter" is an insult in New York, accusing him of practicing CUNNILINGUS, with the implication that this is a rare, demeaning and perverted habit. See BITE, BEARD, CAT, WOLF, FOX, VIXEN, EAT.

GUN

The penis. The Marine Corps has an interesting punishment for recruits who mistakenly call a rifle a "gun." The offender must walk all over the base holding his rifle in one hand and his penis in the other, greeting every person he meets by reciting:

> This is my rifle;
> This is my gun.
> This is for shooting;
> This is for fun.

The Terry Southern-Stanley Kubrick movie, *Dr. Strangelove or How I learned to Stop Worrying and Love the Bomb,* was a more artistic and less naive exploration of the same gun-sex theme. The name Strangelove suggests sexual abnormality; another character is named Bat Guano (batshit); General Jack D. Ripper is portrayed as a latent homosexual who can't keep his hands off Captain Mandrake (a mandrake is a plant shaped like a penis and is often believed to be an aphrodisiac) and has a typically anal obsession concerning the "purity of essence" of our drinking water, as well as fearing that heterosexual intercourse

154   The Book of Forbidden Words

will deplete his "precious bodily fluids." Bat Guano is equally paranoid and suspects everybody else of homosexuality (or "preversion," as he calls it). The bomb is finally dropped by Captain "King" Kong, who falls to earth with it, tucking it between his thighs like a giant phallus (see FALL OFF THE APPLE TREE). The few survivors go to live under the earth (according to psychoanalysts, in the unconscious, anything under the earth equals hell equals the anus). This is "strange love" indeed!

Our language constantly perverts words that have anything to do with sex; it is almost impossible for a man to say that he would like to copulate with a woman without using words that imply that he wants to soil her, degrade her and beat her into oblivion – "boff" her, "bang" her, "screw" her, "give her the business" – and this is where the natural imagistic association between penis and gun becomes compulsive and sinister.

In Arthur Penn's 1966 film, *The Chase,* a neurotically promiscuous woman offers suggestive praise for Marlon Brando's pistol, and he replies, poker-faced, "Ma'am, I don't think you've got room for any more pistols." Penn's next film, *Bonnie and Clyde,* made the connection between guns and sex even more explicit, and a contemporary SKIN FLICK, *The Minx,* actually had a scene in which an actress MASTURBATES with a gun. In Hitchcock's *To Catch a Thief,* the rapid cut from Cary Grant seducing Grace Kelly to a rising skyrocket evoked knowing laughter in some theaters, as did the similar cut from a sexual flirtation to a rising and firing cannon in *Don't Go Near the Water.* The same identification pops up in Mae West's famous line: "Is that a gun in your pocket or are you just happy to see me?"

John Dillinger, the most famous gunman and bank robber of the 1930s, was reputed to have a 23-inch penis, which was prominently featured in some of the porno comic books of the period. This legend did not die with Dillinger; folklore claims the fabulous organ is pickled in a jar at the Smithsonian Institute and shown to certain select visitors. It is almost 40 years since Big John's death, but Smithsonian officials recently confirmed that they receive at least one phone call a week asking if this yarn is true.

John Lennon and Paul McCartney seem to be playing on this ambiguous symbolism rather deliberately in their song, "Happiness is a Warm Gun," which concludes with the memorable lines:

> I need a fix 'cause I'm going down,
> Down to the bits that I left uptown.
> I need a fix 'cause I'm going down.
> Mother Superior jump the gun.
> Mother Superior jump the gun.
> Mother Superior jump the gun.
> Mother Superior jump the gun.
> Happiness is a warm gun.
> Happiness is a warm gun.
> When I hold you in my arms
> And I feel my finger on your trigger,
> I know no one can do me no harm,
> Because happiness is a warm gun.

HAIR PIE

The female genitalia, usually with a reference to CUNNILINGUS, as in "He ate hair pie last night and his wife's been smiling all day."

HAIRY

This word has several meanings, depending on context. "The conversation's getting hairy," in the South, is a polite request for less bawdiness and more decorum; a "hairy question" is a hard one to answer; a "hairy situation" is a dangerous or threatening one.

Hair itself is a powerful sexual symbol, both positive and negative. The Puritans introduced the modern short haircut (the Cavaliers called them "roundheads"). In many primitive tales collected by Sir James Frazer, the loss of a man's hair means either the loss of virility or loss of magical powers (the Biblical yarn about Samson and Delilah is an example), and today many men suffer acute shame at the onset of baldness. Any kind of conspicuous extra hair is regarded as a stigmata of wildness, animality and sexual irregularity, as in the folk rhyme:

> Those mountaineers with hairy ears,
> They care not for mere trifles;
> They hang their balls upon the walls
> And shoot at them with rifles.
> In times of war they heal each sore
> Without the aid of stitches;
> When tail is rare, they'll rape a bear,
> Those rugged sons of bitches!

A secondary meaning set in during the post-Puritan centuries when only women had long hair; due to Oscar Wilde and a few other flamboyant homosexuals, long hair on men became identified with homosexuality rather than with heterosexual virility. Both associations now co-exist in different generations.

HALF AND HALF

This is what prostitutes call a "specialty"; it consists of COCKSUCKING until "relief is only seconds away," and then switching to a coital position for the climax. The name, like that of the popular pipe tobacco, is taken from a traditional English drink consisting of 50 percent beer and 50 percent ale (or stout). An old Cockney joke tells of a man who wakes the pub-keeper in the wee hours, pounding on the door and shouting, "I wants me 'Arf-n-'Arf!" The tavern owner empties the chamberpot out the window on him, saying, "Take that – it's 'arf mine and 'arf me old lady's!"

HALF-MAST

An incomplete erection, as in "The best she could do, he was still at half-mast." See POLE.

HAMMER

The penis. This was punned on, probably deliberately, in the name of Mickey Spillane's famous private detective, Mike Hammer.

HAMMOCKS

Female breasts, as in "She was a beautiful dish with hammocks like Mussolini's balcony."

HAND JOB

MASTURBATION, usually when performed by another. A "hand queen," or "candy maker," in homosexual slang, refuses to give BLOW jobs. "It's handmade," said disparagingly of a large penis, means that the proud owner achieved it through masturbation (a myth without any grounds); this is usually remarked by men who are not so formidable in that department themselves.

HARD LEG

An old, unattractive WHORE. See LEG.

HARD-ON

An erection, as used by Saul Bellow in *Seize the Day:* "one of those subway things . . . like having a hard-on at random." To suggest greater passion, some will say a "purple hard-on." Kurt Vonnegut puns on this in the first line of *God Bless You, Mr. Rosewater:* "The Second World War was over and there I was at high noon, crossing Times Square with a Purple Heart on."

HARD UP

Sexually frustrated; but this expression can also mean short of funds. It is unwise to say, "I've been hard up for a month," unless you know which meaning is customary in the place you happen to be.

HARLOT

A WHORE; but originally a RANDY young man.

HARRIDAN

Nowadays, any bad-tempered old woman; but originally, an aged and unattractive prostitute. The source is French *haridelle,* a worn-out horse. By similar metaphor, *nag* is used for either an old mare or a scolding wife.

HAT

The female genitalia; dating back at least to the 18th Century when Grose defined it and explained the origin as a popular pun, "It is frequently felt." See FEEL.

HATCH

The vagina; celebrated in the limerick:

> There was a young lady named Scratch

Who had a rectangular hatch,
So she practiced coition
With a mathematician
Who had a square root to match.

HAVE

To copulate with, as in "I've had her and she's good in the hay." (Curiously, women seldom say, "I had him.") The most noteworthy use is in the joke about Joe and Moe who regularly attend the burlesque show together. Every time Joe enthuses about a particular stripper, Moe replies casually, "I've had her and she's good." Joe, suspecting that this is empty boasting, is annoyed. One night the M.C. announces that the next performer, Princess Irene, is a famous Egyptian belly-dancer who has never appeared in the United States before. As she begins her act, Joe says acidly, "I suppose you've had her, too." Moe replies anxiously, "Quiet, you fool – I'm having her right now!"

HEAD JOB

Bikers' slang for FELLATIO or, as it is more generally called, a "BLOW JOB." See GIVE HEAD.

HEADLIGHTS

Large female breasts; a visual metaphor from the automobile, which Marshall McLuhan curiously overlooked in his famous study of the sexual symbolism in automobile advertising, *The Mechanical Bride*. There is also a famous poem by e.e. cummings, "seeing she was brand-new," which can be read, line by line, either as the trial run of a new car or as the seduction of a timid girl.

The first use of modern psychology as an advertising

tool occurred in 1941 when Dr. Ernest Dichter wrote a study for Pontiac explaining the sexual symbolism of the automobile and indicating how subliminal use of this could be used to increase sales. Pontiac followed this advice, and sales skyrocketed. Since then the head-doctors have been all over the shop in advertising, and our TV commercials are even more Freudian than our dreams.

Psychoanalysts suggest that the auto became a sex symbol because of the phallic movements of its pistons. More plausible is the sociological theory that the "bedroom on wheels" (as Philip Wylie once called it) was imbued with erotic connotations because it allowed young people to get away from the prying eyes of their elders. In either case, the car is the scene of an ever-increasing number of bawdy stories. A popular one concerns the policeman who bragged that he could seduce an attractive but stern-looking young policewoman who had all the other bulls IN HEAT. To prove his boast, he arranged the assignation in his police car with the shortwave radio on "Transmit" so the men at the station house could hear the details. As he and she were getting cozy, she accidentally knocked his lunch on the floor, and he picked it up to brush it off. "You're not going to eat it when it's that dirty, are you?" she asked. "Say sandwich!" he screamed. "Say sandwich!" See EAT.

HECK

An obvious substitution for *hell*. According to comedian Fred Allen, *heck* was invented by CBS: "When a bad CBS vice-president dies, he goes to heck. When a good one dies, he goes to the Rainbow Room." *Heck* is a contraction of *hector*, a bully, 17th Century slang based on the bravery of Hector in Homer's *Iliad*. This gave birth to the superlative *since Hector was a pup,* meaning for a long time, and to *by Hector* and *by heck,* which became polite substitutes for *by hell.*

HEDGE WHORE

The lowest class of prostitutes; a rival of the Cockney *threepenny upright.* In Brooklyn they are dubbed "two-bit Sadies"; elsewhere they are known as "heavy cruisers," "town bikes" or simply "tanks."

HELL

The inferno; from Old Norse, *Hel,* the goddess of the dead. Aleister Crowley has proposed that it is from Old English *hele,* to conceal, hell being the place where God buries his mistakes. Partridge makes a similar observation, tracing *hell* back to Indo-European *kel,* to hide.

Hell has had more offspring than any oath in English, including such variations and elaborations as *hellfire; hell-for-leather; what the hell; what the rambling hell; what the ring-tailed rambling hell; hellcat; hell-hound; where the hell; why the hell; what the hell; who the hell; give him hell; go to hell; hell-hole; hellbox* (a printer's depository for used-up type); *from hell to breakfast; like a bat out of hell; they're moving hell* (said of any rapidly speeding vehicle); *hell and high water; hell and damnation; go to hell and bake biscuits; a hell of a note; 'till hell freezes over.* Mencken describes *hell* as a general intensifier, meaning that it will fit into a sentence almost anywhere and add vividness to the thought.

HELL FIRE CLUB

An organization founded in England in the 1760s by Sir Francis Dashwood, and which claimed Benjamin Franklin as a member. It was officially known as the

Order of Saint Francis, but was not named after Saint Francis of Assisi but after Dashwood himself. The meetings were held at an old deserted abbey which Dashwood had bought cheaply and redecorated to his own tastes; the saints, for instance, were honored with stained-glass windows, but some of them bore distinctly impious expressions, while others were engaged in such labors as are not usually associated with holy men of the Christian religion: copulation, BUGGERY, FELLATIO, CUNNILINGUS – that sort of thing.

Years later, it was discovered that even the GARDENS around the abbey had been shaped by Sir Francis's strange cast of mind; viewed from the highest tower, the hedges formed a distinctly feminine outline, and where the thighs met was a fountain that gushed forth profuse waters in a most indelicate way.

The club meetings fell midway between the authentic Black Mass and the proceedings of a society of very learned whoremongers. Much poetry of a RANDY nature was read, for instance, and papers were also sometimes presented on the more scatological implications of various Christian dogma. The principal business, however, was mostly drinking and wenching. Dashwood, with the help of Benjamin Franklin, actually put together the modern form of the Anglican *Book of Common Prayer* in this setting.

The Order of Saint Francis came to an abrupt end. John Wilkes, one of the members, annoyed the Earl of Sandwich, another member, by siding with the American colonists when the Revolution began. To make matters worse, Wilkes smuggled a live orangutan, painted weird colors, into the abbey and released it while the earl was conducting a bogus Black Mass to terrify a new initiate. It not only terrified the earl himself, but also bit him, painfully, on the shoulder. A few days thereafter, the earl rose in the House of Lords and demanded Wilkes's expulsion and arrest, charging that he was the author of an obscene book. Wilkes had to flee to France to escape prison; but his friends mounted a counterattack, and it was soon well known that the Earl of Sandwich was himself a member of the Hell Fire Club. In the subsequent hullabaloo, Sir Francis Dashwood himself had to flee for a while to Spain, and the abbey was demolished by the forces of Law and Order.

Later, Dashwood was admitted back into England and surreptitiously revived the Order of Saint Francis in a new location, which was not discovered until a century later. Wilkes, for his support of American interests, has the honor of having Wilkes-Barre, Pennsylvania, and Wilkesboro, North Carolina, named after him.

Wilkes's book was entitled *An Essay on Woman* and was a parody of Alexander Pope's famous "Essay on Man." It was dedicated to Fanny Murray, a famous courtesan of the period, gave the author's name as "Pego Borewell" (PEGO was current slang for the penis) and had as its frontispiece an erect phallus with a Greek inscription calling it the "Savior of the World." There were copious and scholarly footnotes, some signed by "Rogerus Cunaeus" (See ROGER and CUNT).

The theme of the poem is the hedonistic philosophy of "gather ye rosebuds while ye may," expressed with pungent directness:

> ... (since life can little more supply
> Than just a few good fucks, and then we die)
> But fuck the Cunt at hand, and God adore.
> What future fucks He gives thee not to know
> But gives that cunt to be thy blessing now.

HIDDEN TREASURE

The female genitalia. A New York joke uses a variation of this metaphor: A "pirate girl" is defined as one "with a sunken chest and a box everybody's been into." See BOX.

HIP PEDDLER

A low-class, street-walking prostitute. This is probably an expurgation of ASS *peddler*.

HOLE IN ONE

To have intercourse with a woman on the first date; a metaphor borrowed from golf. See SCORE.

HOLY WEEK

A wife's menstrual period, when many Jews and Christians have an aversion to intercourse due to the Biblical taboo.

HONEY

A LESBIAN who will engage in homosexual activities only if such activities are initiated by someone else, as in "She can be a honey if the right girl approaches her."

HONEY FUCK

To copulate with a very young girl, or, in some parts of the country, a long and leisurely FUCK, whatever the ages of the people involved. An expurgated version of this term appeared in Philip Wylie's *Finnley Wren* (1934): "He was keenly aware of the mysterious pains and penalties attached to 'honeyfuggling.' " As a term of affection, *honey* is probably as widely used as *dear* or *darling*. *Honeymoon,* which now means a trip taken after the marriage, originally referred to the phases of the moon and was a cynical joke implying that pleasures of marriage wane steadily from this point onward. A "honeypot" is the vagina, as Teeny Marie says in *Blue Movie*: "Who wants to dip into my fabulous honeypot?!?" In the Army, the "honey-wagon" is, ironically, the truck that cleans out the latrines. See CHERRY PICKER and CRADLE ROBBER.

HOOKER

A prostitute of any class; deriving, however, from recent English *hooker,* a thief, and Old English *hok,* an implement for grabbing. *Hock,* meaning to steal by shoplifting, is Midwestern slang, evidently from the old pronunciation of *hook.* The *hock* in *hockshop* (pawnshop) and the *huck* in *huckster* (peddler) evidently come from the same root, as does HUSTLER. The label was pinned on prostitutes seemingly because some combine thievery with their profession.

HORNY

Sexually aroused or desirous of sex. The association is with the old horned gods, Pan and Dionysus, who symbolized fertility. A "horned man," however, is a cuckold, and an unfaithful wife "puts the horns" on her husband; he is then "hornified" or even "capricornified" in recent English slang. The origin of this metaphor is most likely *hormad,* blind with rage.

HOT NUTS

Male passion; the male equivalent of *hot pants,* as in "He has hot nuts for that chick." The neuter term, for people of either sex, is *the hots,* as in "Everybody at this hotel has the hots for somebody else." Someone who always has the hots is a "hotcha," as in Raymond

Chandler's *The Big Sleep:* ". . . Sternwood's younger daughter, the hotcha one . . . " And in the Sixties there was a group called *Doug Clark and the Hot Nuts,* which specialized in bawdy songs.

HOT PANTS

It used to be said of a wanton or promiscuous woman, "She has hot pants," implying that she is DRIPPING FOR IT, but, recently, the fashion industry used the term *hot pants* for short shorts, and thus the old meaning has become blurred.

HOT TO TROT

Cyclists' slang meaning passionate or eager for sex, as in "That chick was really hot to trot with the whole gang."

HOWITZER

The penis. See GUN.

HUM JOB

A specialized form of FELLATIO, allegedly of Arabic origin, in which the lady hums while GOBBLING the man's TOOL. In the most elegant and excruciating variety, the humming alone – without any other lip, tongue or head movements – eventually produces the orgasm, after a few hours or so.

HUMP

To copulate; a term that has endured for centuries.

A popular rhyme which may have contributed to the popularity of *hump* as a sex word is:

   The sexual life of the camel

Is stranger than anyone thinks:
One night a horny old camel
Attempted to bugger the sphinx.
Alas, the ass of the statue
Was filled with the sand of the Nile,
Which explains the hump on the camel
And the sphinx's inscrutable smile.

Some people are sexually aroused by humpbacks, or hunchbacks (the underground press frequently has personal ads from men seeking hunchbacked women), and Victor Hugo's "hunchback of Notre Dame," Quasimodo, is a favorite figure for many people's masochistic projections. Conversely, Guy Endore has a sexual horror novel (whose title has changed with each edition, from *Methinks the Lady* to *The Furies in Her Body* to *Nightmare*) in which the schizophrenic heroine is monumentally tortured (or imagines she is) by an incredibly sadistic hunchback. And Terry Southern's bestseller, *Candy*, has a sequence in which the heroine – a "Christian humanist," he calls her – is so possessed by pity for a passing hunchback that she drags him into her bed, but, at the crucial moment, rejects his penis, crying, "Your hump! Give me your hump!" When he obliges, she reaches a frenzy in which all repressed elements burst forth and her verbal taboos crumble (usually she says nothing stronger than "Good grief," like the kids in *Peanuts*); she howls maniacally, "Fuck! Shit! Piss! Cunt! Cock! Crap! Prick! Kike! Nigger! Wop! Hump! HUMP!"

HUNG

To be endowed with a large penis, as in "He's hung like a horse" or "He's well hung."

The fantasy of the giant penis has always haunted male psychology, hetero as well as homo; the earliest religious carvings are "ithyphallic"; that is, the statues in question showed gods with gigantic WANGS on them.

In the magic of secret groups like the Ordo Templi Orientis, one achieves the mystic trance by copulating while envisioning one's penis growing ever larger and gradually reaching heaven, all the while mentally chanting a magic formula. While this rite requires more concentration than most men can manage during sex, the same ithyphallic religious tradition appears in our folklore; for example, in the story of the man walking down the street who sees a weeping woman and asks what's the matter. "Moe Blotzstein is dead," she wails. Walking on, and wondering who Moe Blotzstein was, the man encounters another weeping woman, and another, and another, until it seems that every woman in town is mourning the mysterious Blotzstein. Finally, the man passes a funeral parlor, where dozens of women are gathered weeping for Moe Blotzstein. Curious, the man creeps into the parlor after it is closed and looks at the dead man. A suspicious bulge attracts his attention, and he examines further, discovering that the corpse has the biggest penis he has ever seen. A foul scheme crosses his mind, and he amputates the gigantic organ, intending to seek a plastic surgeon who can graft it onto himself. When he arrives home, with the miracle wang wrapped in brown paper under his arm, his wife asks him what he is carrying. "A salami," he says evasively. "Oh, good," she says, "I've been wanting some." And before he can protest, she has grabbed the package and opened it. Immediately, she pales and sinks into a chair. "My God," she says, "Moe Blotzstein is dead!"

The myriad possibilities afforded those who are well hung are partially explored in this limerick:

> There once was a man from Nantucket
> Whose prick was so long he could suck it.
> Said he with a grin,
> As he wiped off his chin,
> "If my ear was a cunt, I could fuck it!"

The ultimate in male fantasy is a well-known underground pornographic novel, *Skirts,* by "Akbar del Piombo" (pen name of a rather famous novelist). In this unique work, the hero's penis grows larger each time he has intercourse. The end has him being fellated by a woman, his now incredible tool running through her intestinal tract, out her bottom and into a second, a third and finally an endless series of beauties, *en brochette.*

James Jones has even written a whole novel, *Go to the Widow-Maker,* based on the thesis that all male rivalry is derived from this "Mine is bigger than yours" competition, which is, in fact, rather keen and quite conscious among many adolescent and preadolescent boys. There are even various quack gimmicks for sale in the underground press, claiming to enlarge penile size; and the mistaken belief that this miracle can actually be performed through incessant MASTURBATION is widespread in high-school locker rooms. In the New York area, there is even a legend that "it's all in the rhythm" and that the feat can be accomplished by chanting, in time to one's strokes, "Make-my-prick-grow," a prayer that will be answered eventually, it is claimed, if one persists long enough.

The ingenious Hindus have actually developed a kind of secondary caste system based on penile size, as described by Allen Edwardes in *The Jewel in the Lotus:*

> *Shushah* (hare man), the beau ideal of manhood. He is lithe and strong . . . his

penis corresponds in erection with the *yoni* [vagina]. It is small (two or three inches), and proportionately thin.

Mrigah (buck man), the perfection of warriors. He is fleet and graceful . . . his penis is slightly thicker and longer, four or five inches.

Vrishubha (bull man), the tough, muscular artisan type . . . his penis is (for a merchant) from six to seven inches in length, or (for an agriculturalist) from seven to eight.

Ushvah (stallion man), the most coarse and vulgar of the group. He is worthless and indolent save for propagating his kind . . . he has adorning his body a nine-to-ten-inch, wrist-thick tassel; and his seminal water flows like the Ganges in flood.

HUNK

A very muscular man, assumed to be sexually powerful as well; from *hunky,* a Hungarian, which also gave us the black term *honky,* any white man. The word was first popularized by 20th Century Fox in the 1940s in publicizing actor Victor Mature: "What a Hunk of Man!" the ads said. It took Mature about 20 years to convince people that he could also act.

HUSTLER

A prostitute. The immediate source of the word is *pool-hustler,* a term coined around the turn of the century, describing a cheat who pretends to be incompetent at billiards until the stakes are high enough – and then wins "by accident."

Hustle, meaning to work at any job, is recent black slang, conveying the cynical view that our whole society is corrupt and that any way of earning money involves victimizing somebody. Lenny Bruce reflected this outlook when he said, "Any clergyman who has two suits while children are starving is a hustler."

IMPUDENCE

The penis, as in "I'd like to give her my impudence." One of Norman Mailer's characters, even more insolently, calls it "the Avenger" and uses it to conquer a young lady who has offended him by liking the poetry of T.S. Eliot. ("The Avenger" immediately responds to her presumption and he wants "to prong her right there on the floor.")

IN HEAT

To be in a state of acute sexual passion. The origin is rural and was first used to refer to the period when animals could mate: "This is the month when the cows are in heat."

IN LIKE FLYNN

A reference to Hollywood actor Errol Flynn, *in like Flynn* is a colloquialism meaning to seduce a woman quickly, as in "Five minutes after we got to her pad I was in like Flynn." An "Errol Flynn" in recent slang is a type of pastry sold in long, thick cylinders, also called JELLY ROLL. It is also rumored that the exuberant Flynn originally wanted to title his autobiography *In Like Me,* but was persuaded to use the more decorous title, *My Wicked, Wicked Ways.*

IN THE ALTOGETHER

In the nude. The term is so obviously quaint and archaic that virtually nobody regards it as obscene. Thus, some years ago Danny Kaye recorded "The King's New Clothes," based on the Hans Christian Andersen fable, which was not banned from radio even though it had the refrain:

> The king is in the altogether,
> The altogether, the altogether,
> And it's altogether too chilly a morn!

IN THE RAW

Naked, without a stitch; used by Budd Shulberg in *What Makes Sammy Run:* "They went swimming in the raw."

IRISH TOOTHACHE

Pregnancy, as in "She's got the Irish toothache again." Related terms include *Irish confetti,* the semen after ejaculation, or bricks and stones thrown around in a street-fight; *Irish dip,* intercourse; *Irish marathon,* a full night of love, a multiple NUMBERS GAME; *Irish draperies,* large female breasts; *Irish evidence,* perjury; *Irish clubhouse,* a brothel.

ITCH

Sexual desire, as in "Have you got the itch again?" American juvenile lore holds that the only cure for itching testicles is to "go out and get laid." The title of George Axelrod's play and movie, *The Seven Year Itch,* refers to a married man's desire for extramarital sex, which according to folklore strikes most strongly in the seventh year of marriage.

I.U.D.

An intra-uterine device for contraception; sometimes also called a "pussy butterfly."

JAB

Any woman; probably from Irish *gob,* the mouth, via English *gabble,* to talk constantly; or else from Middle English *jabben,* to peck, by a similar metaphor to *henpecking.*

JACKET

A CONDOM; from standard English *jacket,* a short coat. *Jack* means any man – from the prevalence of Johns, Juans, Jacques and Ivans all over Europe – and, hence, the male of many animal species is designated by the prefix *jack* – , *jackass, jackrabbit, jackdaw.* Related terms include *jack-of-all trades; jack-in-the-box* (the clitoris); *jack's house* (the privy, later *Jake's house* or *Jake's*); *jackknife.*

Other associations include *jack whore,* a BULL DYKE or BUTCH LESBIAN; *jack,* money or cash; *jack-a-napes,* an ugly man, perhaps originally *Jack of apes; Jack of legs,* legendary English giant who, Robin Hood fashion, robbed from the rich and gave to the poor. His grave, with headstone and footstone fourteen feet apart, still exists.

JACK OFF

To MASTURBATE, usually applied only to males. (The female counterpart is RUB off.) One plausible suggestion about the origin of the term is that it is a schoolboy distortion of *ejaculate.* The phrase is nicely played on in a popular folk song (with emphasis on puns supplied for the reader's convenience):

I saw her *snatch* her briefcase from the window.
I held her *but(t)* a moment in the rain.
She went racing in a taxi to the depot
Just to see her brother *Jack off* on the train.
Jack – off – on – the – train.

Portnoy's Complaint, the most famous of all masturbation comedies, contains such variations as WHACKING OFF, *firing my wad, dropping my load, squirting my seed,* JERKING OFF and *pulling my* PUTZ.

JAILBAIT

A girl below the legal "age of consent," which differs from state to state; from the fact that intercourse with her is statutory rape (even if she instigates it) and can result in a prison sentence.

JAM

Black slang meaning to SCREW, as in "I'd like to jam that chick," or "Go away, you mammy-jammer." The implication is that the penis is so large it can only be forced (jammed) into the vagina, and is comparable to the Elizabethan *yard,* which literally meant a long stick.

JAM SESSION

A bout of sexual intercourse; from musicians' slang in which a "jam session" is an impromptu jazz concert by a group of musicians playing only for one another or for a small group of friends.

JASPER

Black slang for a LESBIAN; from *jasper* meaning a pious

or prudish person, which in turn derives from the Reverend John Jasper, a famous black clergyman. In white slang, for some reason, a "jasper" is a country boy, as H. Birney wrote in the *New York Times Book Review:* "A western . . . needs something more than two jaspers with a grudge . . ."

JAW ARTIST

Homosexual slang for a skillful FELLATOR; sometimes also used by swinging heterosexuals to refer to a superior COCKSUCKER, of whom it may also be said, "She can do more tricks on six inches of dick than three monkeys on a twenty-foot tree." See DICK.

JAZZ

To copulate, as in "I'd like to jazz her." H. L. Mencken tells of an Englishman who, knowing only the English meaning (to dance), innocently asked an American girl, "Would you like to jazz?" and got an indignant reaction. *Jazz* was a term popular in the 1940s and 1950s and has African roots (*chass, yass*) meaning dance. The contemporary equivalent is BALL. *Jaxy,* the vagina, does not come from these African roots, but from 18th Century English *jaxy,* a WIG. See also MERKIN, MUFF, RUG.

JELLY ROLL

Originally, the penis, in turn-of-the-century New Orleans slang; later, either the penis or the vagina, depending on context; now, sex generally. The original idea was a visual metaphor for a type of pastry sold in long, thick cylinders, and a man with a jelly roll was sweet to the ladies. This is the origin of the nickname of the great jazz musician, Jelly Roll Morton.

JERK (or JERK-OFF)

A jerk or jerk-off is a fool, and to jerk off is to MASTURBATE; evidently from the old belief that it destroys the mind. *Jerk the gherkin* is an elaboration on *jerk off* and also means to masturbate.

JIG-JAG

To SCREW, as in "I'd like to jig-jag that doll."

JINGLE-JANGLE

Copulation. This is punned on in the folk song, "The Tinker," in which the hero consoles lonely housewives as he repairs their plumbing; the chorus is "With my jingle-jang-jingle-jang-O!" *Jing-jang,* in parts of the South, is the vagina; and *Yankee Doodle* may have had a similar meaning once. (Note the chorus "Yankee Doodle, keep it up/And with the girls be handy"; *doodle* still means penis in the Ohio Valley.)

And then there's the deathless joke about the Swede who hides in the closet when the husband of his paramour returns unexpectedly. Hanging up his coat, the husband sees the Swede's BALLS between two other garments. "What are those?" he asks. "Christmas bells," the wife improvises quickly. "Let's hear their peal," says the suspicious spouse, giving them a terrific blow. Whereupon a strained voice gasps: "*Yingle-yangle,* you son of a bitch!"

JISM

Semen; a distortion of *jetsom,* ballast thrown overboard from a ship. Burroughs has a free-form fantasy about jism in *Naked Lunch:*

Ever make sex in no gravity? Your jism just

floats out in the air like lovely ectoplasm, and female guests are subject to immaculate or at least indirect conception . . . Reminds me of an old friend of mine, one of the handsomest men I have ever known and one of the maddest and absolutely ruined by wealth. He used to go about with a water pistol shooting jism up career women at parties. Won all his paternity suits hands down. Never used his own jism you understand.

JOCK

An athlete, also called a "jockstrap"; usually intended contemptuously when used by nonathletes, especially in the Army or in schools where athletes are given special privileges. The origin is Elizabethan *to jock,* meaning to copulate, via 17th-18th Century *jock,* the penis, and modern *jockstrap,* an elasticized groin support sold under the name "athletic supporter."

Jocker is a male homosexual in England; *jock,* a sailor; *jockey,* a LESBIAN; *jockey club,* a male homosexual club. *Jockey,* a professional horse-racer, seems to derive from *Jock* or *Jack* meaning any man, with the diminutive "ey" signifying smallness.

JOHN

In whore's argot, any of her clients; in ordinary slang, a public toilet. Both usages probably derive from *John Doe,* a convenient legal fiction for an unknown party in a law case, or from *John Hancock,* meaning anyone's name, as in "Just put your John Hancock right here," which, of course, developed out of the first, largest and most clearly legible of the signatures on the U.S. Declaration of Independence.

Johnnie is also occasionally heard to mean the penis, either from the above chain of associations, or from *Lady Chatterley's Lover,* in which Mellors fondly calls his organ "John Thomas" and even engages in dialogues with it. Among the blue-collar class, the "johnnie" is sometimes the lady's bathroom, as distinguished from the "john," the men's room.

JOINT

Either the penis or a marijuana cigarette. The double meaning is especially interesting in the light of the origin of the word, the Sanskrit *yoga,* union, from which comes the "yoga" method of mental and physical training and the "yogis" who practice it. Several forms of yoga involve sexual energies (called "Kundalini"), which popular books on the subject for Anglo-American readers generally avoid discussing, and the Shivite sect uses marijuana in their variety of yoga; thus the modern "joint" is, in both senses, a yogic device.

JONES

Black slang with two meanings: sometimes the penis, as in "She was hot for his Jones"; sometimes a hard-drug habit, as in "His Jones is up to 50 bucks a day" (namely, it costs him $50 per day to buy as much heroin as he needs). William S. Burroughs, a white author who was addicted for 15 years, sometimes refers to "Opium Jones, the spirit of Death and Addiction," who haunted him in those days, and Burroughs played the role of "Opium Jones" in *Chappaqua,* the film autobiography of another ex-addict, Conrad Rooks. Other terms for a drug habit are *the monkey* and *the Chinaman,* as in "He's got a monkey on his back," or "He's got a Chinaman on his back."

JOY STICK

The penis; one of the few complimentary and nonhostile names for this organ in English. A "joyboy" is a young male homosexual; Evelyn Waugh wrote a "Mr. Joyboy" into his novel, *The Loved One.*

JUMBUCKS

The testicles; a humorous boast, based on the famous Jumbo, a gigantic elephant kept in the London Zoo around the turn of this century. In Australia, however, "jumbucks" are young cattle, as in the ballad, "Waltzing Matilda": "Down came a jumbuck to drink beside the billybahn."

KEPT WOMAN

A mistress; a woman whose bills are paid by a man not her legal husband, for which she, in turn, grants him sexual favors. This is often abbreviated to *keptie,* as in *New York Confidential* by Jack Lait and Lee Mortimer: "Park Avenue is the place to keep your keptie."

KEY TO THE STREET

To be denied sexual communion by one's wife is to be given the key to the street (in other words, to be locked out). A milder more ambiguous metaphor is *in the* DOGHOUSE.

The marriage of Scarlett O'Hara and Rhett Butler in Margaret Mitchell's *Gone With the Wind* has fascinated readers and movie-goers for two generations now, particularly in relation to the long years during which Scarlett gives Rhett the "key to the street" and the dramatic climax when he finally rapes her. This fantasy continues to haunt the psychology of many, as Terry Southern indicated in his *Blue Movie,* concerning a

Hollywood producer who likes to act out his fantasies, together with real actors. The producer (C.D.) plays a swashbuckling Yankee soldier, who, Errol Flynn style, bursts into a room where "mom" (Louise) and her "immaculate white pantalooned daughter," Scarlett O'Hara (Angela), await:

> *"I'm going to fuck you, Scarlett O'Hara,"* said C.D. tersely, pushing her onto the bed, *"I'm going to fuck you hard and long!"*
>
> "Oh please, suh," Louise beseeched, "that little girl is a *vuhgin!*"
>
> "Use the *name,* damn it," snapped C.D. in a sharp aside, "keep using the *name!*"
>
> "Sorry," said Louise quickly in her normal voice, then resumed: "Ah beg of you, suh, please don't do it to my little Scarlett! Scarlett is a *vuhgin!*"
>
> Meanwhile, C.D. had pulled down the lacy top of the bodice, exposing her breasts.
>
> "Oh please, suh . . ."
>
> "All right, tell your mother what I'm – what this Yankee soldier is doing."
>
> "Oh Momma . . . the Yankee soljuh is . . . kissing my breast."
>
> "Not *kissing,"* C.D. fairly hissed.
>
> "Oh Momma, he's . . . this Yankee soljuh is . . . *sucking* my breast!"

"Suh, ah beg of you . . . cried Louise very convincingly. C. D. tore at the pantaloons, not pulling them down, but ripping them open at the crotch, its seam having previously been weakened by snipping a few threads inside.

"Oh Momma, he's . . . he's got it in me . . . he's doing it, Momma . . . the Yankee soljuh . . . *he's fucking me!*"

"Oh suh, ah beg of you . . ."

"Okay," said C. D. urgently, "*now, now!*"

"Oh Momma," Angela wailed, "he's making me come . . . the Yankee soljuh is making me come . . . ah'm going to faint . . . oh Momma, *he's fucking me half to death!*"

Louise came in precisely on cue, grand old trooper that she was:

"Oh suh, how *could* you do that to my Scarlett! Ah shall report it to youh captain – "

"*Say* it, Louise," urged C.D., "quick, *say* it!"

" – and tell him," she hurried, "how you *fucked Scarlett O'Hara! And made her come!*"

And as C.D. strove into a frenetic spasm, shouting, "*I'm fucking you, Scarlett! I'm fucking you, Scarlett!*" Louise picked up a Polaroid flash camera from the dresser and popped a pic.

KING

A very masculine LESBIAN; a BULL DYKE.

KINK

A sexual deviate; a freak. Usually applied to sadomasochists, people with fish or foot fetishes, enema-lovers, and others weirder than you or I. *He's bent* is English and American underworld slang meaning he's a sadist.

KISS MY ASS

Literally, a request for ANALINGUS; but as an insult, it is meant to degrade, as in "Bitch, get on your knees and kiss my ass!" The Celts more elegantly express the same thought by saying, "Kiss my royal Irish arse," or, in more polite company, by merely saying the initials, "K.M.R.I.A."

The origin seems to be Cockney; women of that class, when leaving an unsatisfactory mate, have been known to raise their skirts in the back and say, "Kiss it goodbye, Bertie – you'll never see it again."

KNICKKNACKS

A term sometimes used to mean the female breasts; derived from *Nick,* the devil. One of the most infamous Nicks in literature is in Chaucer's "The Miller's Tale," in which young Nicholas seduces his landlord's wife and is happy abed with her when another suitor, named Absalon, comes singing at her door. When Absalon begs for a kiss, the lady maliciously sticks her ARSE out the darkened window. He kisses it, but goes away sore confused:

> He knew quite well a woman has no beard

But something rough and hairy appeared.

Finally deciding that he has been gulled, Absalon goes to the blacksmith, heats up a poker and returns, singing more songs and demanding more kisses. This time Nicholas decides to play the joke and sticks his own butt out the window. Chaucer concludes piously:

> And Nicholas is branded on the BUM
> And God bring us all to Kingdom Come.

KNIGHT

A male homosexual. This is just about the only flattering term in English for homosexuals, and is probably a disguised witticism since 16th-19th Century English slang was full of humorous knights, such as *knight of the open road*, a highway robber; *knight of the thimble*, a tailor; *knights of the post*, rogues who lounge outside court, willing to swear anything if a barrister pays them enough.

Knight and *king* (see KING) are from the same root according to Partridge; a popular riddle asks, "What's the difference between a king and a knight?" Answer: "Once a king, always a king; but once a night is enough."

KNOCKERS

In contemporary American speech, the female breasts. "A pair of knockers you could hang your hat on" are the most admirable variety, although close rivals may be "a pair of knockers that would drive a bishop to kick a hole in a stained-glass window," or even a pair of which is said "She has knockers like Rockefeller has money."

Knockers meaning breasts probably comes from *door-knockers,* which hang about breast-high and, on old houses, are often quite large.

KNOCK UP

To make a woman pregnant is to "knock her up." This was simply "knock her" in the 18th Century; NOCK, meaning the male organ, appears around Shakespeare's time.

LABANZA

The buttocks; a misunderstanding of Italian *la banza,* the stomach.

LACE, LACY

In homosexual slang, a "lacy" is a homosexual and "lace curtains" is the foreskin of the uncircumcised penis. "Laced mutton," in 18th Century slang, was a prostitute, and "cold mutton," in the 19th Century, an unsatisfactory prostitute.

Lacing meaning a beating is still occasionally heard; this comes down from the 16th Century when it was a fashionable form of threat to say "I'll lace your jacket handsomely." The "lace-curtain Irish," finally, are not homosexual but merely prosperous and are so called by those who are, in turn, dubbed the "shanty Irish." The "cut-glass Irish" look down on both of these groups.

LAKANUKI

Army slang, especially in the Pacific, meaning lack of sex and used to explain any psychosomatic illness or general irritability. This fanciful disease, despite its Oriental name, is a distortion of standard American *lack of nookie.* See BLUE BALLS.

LAVENDER

Heterosexual slang for a homosexual, as in "He's a bit

on the lavender side." This probably derives from the late 19th Century, when lavender became identified with modernism in art and the latter with homosexuality; for instance, when Oscar Wilde wore lavender trousers, flaunted his great love for Lord Alfred Douglas and various young men, and preached the doctrine of Art for Art's Sake. He paid for it.

LAY

To copulate with, as in "I'd like to lay her," from Middle English *lien*, to be prostrate. In current slang, if the man is full-blooded, the lady is not only laid but "laid, relayed and parlayed." A common expression among males is "She's a good lay."

When Stokely Carmichael responded to the new feminism by saying that "the proper position of women in the Movement is prone," many were confused, some thinking he had meant to say supine, and others assuming that he was professing a personal predilection for Turkish pastimes.

Then there is the tender ballad, popular with high-school boys:

> Tara-ra-ra-boom-de-ay!
> I finally got a lay!
> I got it yesterday
> From the girl across the way!
> Tara-ra-ra-boom-de-ay!
> I'm goin back today!

Belle Kaufmann's novel, *Up the Down Staircase*, points out that any high-school English teacher who gives a lesson on *lay* and *lie* is looking for trouble.

LEAD IN THE PENCIL

Virility; a good erection, as in "He has lead in his pencil." Freud regarded the pencil as a phallic symbol, and actually the words *pencil* and *penis* are etymologically related.

LEATHER

Unlike many words in personal advertisements in the underground press, this is not a code. Some people get their kicks by making love to a partner wearing a garment of this material.

LEG

Black slang for the vagina; compare MIDDLE LEG, white slang for the penis. "She broke her leg" in the past meant that she bore a bastard, and this may have been the source of the show-biz expression, *"Break a leg,"* said to an actor on opening night because it is thought that wishing an actor well will bring him bad luck. See BROKE HER ANKLE.

LESBIAN (or LEZ, LES, LESSIE)

A female homosexual; from Sappho of Lesbos, the most famous female homosexual poet in history. (Actually, Sappho was bisexual, as was Oscar Wilde, but in both cases the simple legend has long since permanently replaced the complex fact.)

Many men have a strange fascination with lesbian sex, and producers of porno books and movies are always careful to include at least one such scene. There is a popular pattern in a large number of these tales: The heroine later discovers that heterosexuality is actually more satisfying.

Behind this male fantasy there appears to be a male wish to enjoy a totally female orgasm, even if only vicariously. Curiously, several modern novelists have explored this and found it sinister. Hemingway, in a short story called "A Sea Change," describes a young man whose lady wants his permission to go off for a lesbian weekend. He refuses angrily at first, but gives his consent when she promises to tell him all about it afterwards. His face then alters in a frightening way. Similarly, in Norman Mailer's *The Deer Park,* the blacklisted movie director, Eitel, keeps his integrity despite great pressure until his mistress lures him into a bisexual orgy. His decline thereafter is swift. In James Jones's *The Merry Month of May,* the hero has harbored a fantasy all his life of having a private orgy with two bisexual women. At 50, he finally does it, with tragic results.

Bafflement at how homo-hetero-bi trios are possible is recorded in two of the world's best-known limericks:

> There once was a fairy named Bloom
> Who went up to a lesbian's room.
> But they argued all night
> About who had the right
> To do what, and with which, and to whom.

> J. Caesar was really a guy –
> He was hetero, homo and bi.
> He could have or be had
> By a lass or a lad,
> Or even by both when he'd try.

LET THE HAIR DOWN

To confess homosexuality; usually used by one male homosexual to a suspected other: "Let your hair down and admit you're one of the girls."

LIE IN STATE

To have two or more women in bed with you.

LIGHT

"Do you have a light?" is a code used by homosexuals to discover if another male is also GAY, and is similar to "Do you like seafood?" See SEAFOOD.

LILY-WHITE

Homosexual slang used to describe an effeminate male. Curiously, in 19th Century Cockney the same word was ironically used for a chimney sweep, and is sometimes used satirically nowadays to describe a segregated neighborhood or a political conservative.

LINE

A seductive speech, as in "He gave her his line until she was dripping for it"; but in English speech from the 14th Century right on until the 19th, *line* was a verb for the copulation of dogs.

LINGUIST

A practitioner of oral sex; a rare term used only in personal ads and punned upon in this one: "White male, 36, cunning linguist, desires to practice his French on plump women (over 225 pounds), 28-45. Dominant and/or lesbian OK . . ." See CUNNILINGUS.

LITTLE BROTHER

The penis.

LITTLE BROWN EYEBALL

The anus. A related Irish witticism is "I'll give him a kick where it won't blind him."

LITTLE SISTER

The vagina. Raymond Chandler used this as the title of a novel about Hollywood.

LOB

The penis; from English *lob,* a lugworm, and Middle Low German *lobbe,* a plump or overweight person. Like the Elizabethan *yard,* this actually implies a penis of formidable size.

LOBSTER TAILS

One of the venereal diseases. A variation appears in this ballad about the black folklore hero, Shine (discussed in greater detail under MOTHERFUCKER):

> Shine had two cents in his pocket.
> He went to a place called "Dewdrop Inn."
> He asked the broads to give him cock for a lousy fin.
> She took Shine upstairs and she gave him a fuck, and all this pats.
> He came out with the syphs, the crabs, lobstertoes, and a hell of a case of the claps.
> He went to the doctor. Said, "Doctor, doctor, can't you 'stand,
> Please remember I'm a fucked-up man."
> Doctor got his bag, rips in his tools.
> He says, "Sit here on my three-legged stool."
> He starts hammering and cutting, breaking and sawing.

Shine said, "Doc, is that the best you can do?"

He said, "Quiet, motherfucker, 'cause your nuts go too."

See CRABS and CLAP.

LOCAL

An art midway between prostitution and Swedish massage. The customer, in a massage parlor known to provide this service, merely remarks that he would like to have "a local," and the masseuse, after the price is agreed upon, MASTURBATES him. The same parlors, for a higher price, will usually also provide a BLOW JOB if that is requested.

LOLLIPOP

Homosexual slang for the penis.

LOO

A public lavatory; English upper-class speech, perhaps from the Cockney use of *loo* to mean the whole community gathered together. However, an alternate derivation, equally plausible, traces *loo* to the French *l'eau,* water.

L.S.

Code in personal ads, meaning "love slave," generally with masochistic overtones. An example: "Stunning topless dancer, am 32, deliciously stacked (40-24-38), crazy about younger men. Will be an absolute 'L.S' to an extremently handsome, strong-willed, well-built youth, 18-21. All desires everything . . ."

LUCK (or GOOD LUCK)

Catchphrases used in the South – "Luck!" "Good luck!" – whenever somebody steps in dogshit on the street; based on the old superstition that such an accident will bring one good fortune. A racist variation is that sleeping with a black woman will provoke the same change in one's fate. See CHANGE ONE'S LUCK.

MACK

A pimp; from the Parisian *mec,** with perhaps some influence via the character of MacHeath in John Gay's *Beggar's Opera* and MacHeath's modern counterpart, Mac the Knife *(Mackie Messer),* in Berthold Brecht's adaptation, *Theepenny Opera.* Mac's song, "This Bordello Where We Ply Our Trade," nicely captures the irony of the pimp's life, half victim and half victimizer. The same ambivalence is also expressed in the story of the pimp in bed with his tart when a customer knocks. It is winter, but the mack climbs out on the fire escape in his jockeys. While he waits, the JOHN enjoys a leisurely BLOW job, then sends out for wine and food, dines sumptuously in bed with the lady, smokes an expensive cigar and then BALLS her before finally leaving. She rushes to the window and helps her man in, rubbing his blue hands and cuddling his shivering body. "Is the s-s-s-sucker gone?" he chatters weakly.

~•~

In French, '*un mec*' is 'a guy', and if the origin of the word seems unclear, some have suggested that *mec* might have been derived from "*maquereau*", which means mackerel, like in English both the fish and a pimp. So, rather than having *mack* coming from the French *mec*, I suspect that both words may have simply historically evolved in parallel, originating from the same root. – *our French Editor*

~•~

MADAM

The manager of a whorehouse; originally, of course, this was meant to be as ironic as calling a basketball player "Shorty." In the 1700s, Hyde Park in London was called "the market of Madams," and this polite title for an impolite profession is, of course, punned upon deliberately in the title of the Ethel Merman musical, *Call Me Madam.*

The most publicized recent madam is Xaviera Hollander, who was ordered to leave the United States. She quipped in a newspaper article, "Now that I'm making all this money they're going to deport me and I won't have a chance to spend it here." The article goes on to say, "Xaviera Hollander, the New York brothel-manager who wrote *The Happy Hooker* . . . was ordered to return to her native Holland. She entered the United States in 1969 as a Dutch government employee. She later changed jobs."

MADGE

The female genitalia; from Scottish *madge,* any woman, which evidently derives from the ubiquity of Madge as a female name. In the 18th Century, "madge culls" were male homosexuals, *cull* being roughly equivalent to our *guy.*

MAIDENHEAD

The hymen; a metaphor based on Old English *maigdenhad,* equivalent to our *maidenhood,* the state or condition of being a virgin.

MAIN PIECE

Black slang for a promiscuous man's favorite lady, the one who has his emotional if not sexual fidelity; also called his "main squeeze."

MAKE

To seduce a woman, as in "Did you make her?" or, sometimes, "Did you make out with her?" In nurseryese, *make* means to urinate or have a bowel movement, as in "Now sit on the potty and make, dear." (Compare the *make* in "This will make you or break you," said of any hazardous experience, and which implies retaining or achieving bodily and mental health.) A "make-out artist" is a Don Juan, a cocksman, a master of the FOUR FS.

MAKE LOVE

To copulate; the most popular euphemism for FUCK in modern American. A celebrated underground editor, devoutly opposed to hypocrisy, once told of losing his current girlfriend because when she used the expression *making love,* he ungallantly replied, "You're making love; I'm fucking." The expression is also used humorously in a cynical ballad that emerged from New York Puerto Rican slums a few years ago:

> My mother makes two kinds of whiskey,
> My father makes two kinds of gin,
> My sister makes love for a living –
> My God, how the money rolls in!

MAMA

One of the three categories of women associated with the Hell's Angels: "Girl friends," who just hang around with the gang and haven't been more specifically defined by the group yet; an "old lady" (of any age), one who is married to, or otherwise totally committed to, one Angel and can't be balled by the others without a fight; and "mamas," who belong to everybody and may even be tattooed, traditionally on the buttocks, with "Property of Hell's Angels."

MAMMY-SUCKER

In black slang, an insult that is felt to be even more offensive than MOTHERFUCKER. Folk singer Arlo Guthrie has also coined the memorable *father-raper* in his talking blues, "Alice's Restaurant," but this hasn't caught on.

MARGE

The passive partner in a LESBIAN relationship, as distinguished from the dominant or masculine BUTCH partner or BULL DYKE.

MARY

A passive male homosexual; evidently from the universality of Mary as a female name, or perhaps a joke at the expense of the Virgin Mary. See QUUIIN.

MASON

A lesbian who prefers the BUTCH or male role; from the fact that membership in the Masonic orders is restricted to men only.

MASTURBATION

Manual self-stimulation or manual stimulation of one's sexual partner; in either case, a helping hand in times of need. Some derive this directly from *manes,* hand, plus *tubare,* to agitate, but Partridge reasonably suggests *mas,* semen, plus *tubare.* Both derivations come directly from Low Latin, *masturbari.* The practice is well-nigh universal, and so are the guilt feelings of its practitioners. Mark Twain wrote a charmingly humorous essay on the subject, "Notes on the Science of Onanism," but his family suppressed this essay for over 50 years. The whole bizarre story of the Victorian masturbation hysteria (which persisted until the 20th Century) is told in *The Manufacture of Madness,* by Thomas Szasz, M.D., who emphasizes that the leading medical authorities of the time endorsed the myth that this pastime can lead to insanity, loss of ambition, school failure and serious physical ailments.

One of Joyce's achievements in *Ulysses* was to reduce this terror to a series of jokes. (For example, "A Honeymoon in the Hand," or "Every Man His Own Wife.") When people are able to laugh, they are less afraid. Even so, other novelists continued for a long time to avoid the subject or else to treat it nervously. James T. Farrell's *Studs Lonigan* trilogy, often praised for its "brutal realism," uses very oblique language when it gingerly touches on this (while being quite explicit, for its period, about the hero's whorehouse adventures), and scientific writers, fearful of sounding too permissive about this so-called vice, repeated endlessly that "masturbation is harmless, except in excess." The last three words, always undefined, left boys and young men (almost all of whom masturbate at times) and young women (about half of whom, according to Kinsey, also masturbate) with the same old anxieties. Masters and Johnson pointed out that almost every subject they interviewed thought his or her own rate – once a day, once a week, or once a month – was close to the "dangerous" level of "excess," which, of course, does not exist; when you have too many orgasms, you get tired and stop having orgasms – and that's *all* that happens.

Finally came *Portnoy's Complaint,* by Philip Roth – the *Iliad* of onanism, the "Beethoven's Fifth" of masturbation, the *Crime and Punishment* of the bathroom orgasm ("the Raskolnikov of whacking off," the hero mournfully calls himself) – In 195 pages of hyperbolic prose, Roth minutely and hilariously explores every ounce of terror that loving parents can load onto a teen-age boy. ("The sticky evidence is everywhere! Is it on my cuffs too? in my *hair?* my *ear?*")

MATINEE

Sex in the afternoon; from theatrical usage and a 1930s recipe for an ideal marriage: "Once a day, plus matinee." A Chicago man accused of raping several women during the day was dubbed the Matinee Rapist by newspapers.

MATRIMONIAL PEACEMAKER

The penis, a witticism several centuries old but still popular.

MEAT

The penis; as in BEAT THE MEAT

MEMBER

The penis; from the Latin *membrum virile.* Usually, this was given as *privy member* in 13th-16th Century usage, and *carnal member* or just plain *member* thereafter. Robert Burns characteristically refers to it as the "dearest member."

MERKIN

A pubic wig or imitation pubic hair. These were in wide use from 1600 to 1800 due to frequent loss of body hair as a side effect of the smallpox epidemics of those days. One of the earliest uses is in a 17th Century anonymous ballad, "The Puritan," in which a good divine of the church and a "holy sister" sit down together to study a religious text, but eventually get distracted:

> He laid her on the ground.
> His spirits fell a ferking.
> Her zeal was in a sound.
> He edified her merkin
> Upside down.

The word is still heard occasionally, now meaning the CUNT itself, and was punned on in the film title, *Can Heironymus Merkin Ever Forget Mercy Humppe and Find True Happiness?* and in the name of the president in *Dr. Strangelove,* which was Merkin Muffley. See MUFF.

MICKEY
The penis.

MIDDLE LEG
The penis. Joyce recorded it as 1904 Dublinese in *Ulysses:* "How's your middle leg? Come here till I straighten it," a WHORE cries.

MISSIONARY POSITION
The coital position most favored in our society, with the woman supine and the man above her; the name derives from the Polynesians, who were astonished when told that other positions were regarded as sinful. Also known as the "Mama-Papa position," because of its orthodoxy.

MISS LAYCOCK
The vagina; a Cockney witticism.

MOLL

A prostitute; evidently from the prevalence of Molly as a lower-class English and Irish name, and no doubt influenced greatly by the enduring popularity of Defoe's *Moll Flanders*. In the 19th Century, *moll* was defined as "the female companion of low thieves," but in current American she would be called a "gun moll" (from *gun* meaning thief, not *gun* meaning firearm; the origin is Yiddish *gonef,* thief, which also gave us the underworld *cannon,* a pickpocket) or "gangster moll." In tramp slang, any woman, whether or not she prostitutes herself or associates with criminals, is still a moll. The occasionally heard use of *molly* to mean a male homosexual is from *Miss Molly,* an 18th Century term referring to homosexuals.

MONEY

The vagina; usually employed only in addressing small children, as in "Mary, pull your dress down before everybody sees your money." This was recorded as early as the 18th Century, and 19th Century slang dictionaries also list *money-box,* possibly the origin of our modern BOX.

A lady I know was once invited by a prostitute to join that profession, with the words: "You're sitting on a fortune, honey – cash in on it." See also HIDDEN TREASURE and SPEND.

THE MONOSYLLABLE

The female genitalia; an elegant euphemism for CUNT, first used in 1714. In the 19th Century *the article* was sometimes substituted, evidently because *the monosyllable* had come to be regarded as obscene!

MOON SHOT

Anal intercourse; a space-age term, obviously, but with a reference to the older *mooning* (anal exhibitionism) discussed in our entry under RED EYE. In police slang, all sexual deviates are called "mooners," from the old belief that these persons are especially active, like werewolves, when the moon is full.

The popular comic-strip hero, Moon Mullins, does not derive his name from such predilections – although, ironically, he becomes the victim of a "moon shot" by no less than Popeye himself in a famous old eight-pager (discussed in ASHES HAULED) – but from the older *moon-head* (compare with *lunatic*), which means one whose mind has been stolen by the magnetism of the moon.

MOOSE

A prostitute. A term of very obscure origin, the sexual meaning may derive from the usually tall, husky girls (also called "dinosaurs" or "battle-axes") employed in some brothels to handle customers who seem drunk and unpredictable, just as "Moose," among men, is a nickname given to abnormally large or burly individuals. One such character is Moose Malloy in Raymond Chandler's ultrahard-boiled thriller with the ironic title, *Farewell, My Lovely*. Moose is described as "tall, but no more than six foot six" and "no broader than a beer-truck" and generally "as inconspicuous as a tarantula on a piece of angel food cake."

MOSES

To "stand Moses" in recent English slang meant to have an illegitimate child fathered on your wife by another man; a metaphor probably deriving from the Bible story of Moses being found in the bulrushes and raised by Pharaoh's daughter. There is a joke about the two Baptist churches in a very small town: A traveler asks what doctrinal difference separates them and is told that the first holds that Pharaoh's daughter really found Moses in the bulrushes, and the second holds that that's just what she said.

MOSSYFACE

The vulva; a joke that's been around since 1800.

MOTHER

A MADAM or brothel-keeper. The homosexual dope-pusher in the play and movie, *A Hatful of Rain,* is called Mother, either from this usage or by abbreviation from MOTHERFUCKER.

MOTHERFUCKER

Literally, one who copulates with his mother. The most insulting obscenity in modern English, this has given birth to various timid, euphemistic or quasi-humorous variations, such as *mother-jumper; mother-ferrier; mo'-fo'; mammy-jammer* (see JAM); *futher-mucker;* the truncated adjective, *mothering;* and, most popular of all, the *mother* used in middle-class speech. Ordering a second martini in the film, *The Apartment,* Jack Lemmon said, "Give me another of those mothers," and this passed the censors even in 1960.

Motherfucker is usually thought to be of black origin, but seemingly appeared first among poor southern whites. It appears quite prominently in many classic pieces of black folklore; for instance, the ballad of Stackerlee (also spelled Stagolee), which has numerous variations and is known in almost every black community, contains the unforgettable boast:

> I've got a tombstone disposition and a
> graveyard mind
> I'm a mean motherfucker and I don't mind
> dyin'.

This is in the tradition of the boasts of the Homeric heroes, the Norse *Eddas* and the orations of Davy Crockett (who once claimed to be "half horse and half alligator"). Stackerlee is the sort of man known in the ghetto as a "mean motherfucker" or sometimes a "baaaad motherfucker"; these terms are complimentary or at least respectful, and signify the virtue which Mexicans call *cojones* (balls) or *machismo* (hypermasculinity). A "baaaad motherfucker" might be someone frightening and certainly unethical by ordinary standards, but you would much rather have him on your side than against you; he is hard as nails and would rather die than crawl. Bobby Seale, Chairman of the Black Panther Party, named his son Malik Nkrumah Stagolee Seale. Seale explains in his introduction to *Seize the Time:* "One of my son's names derives from the lumpen proletariat politically unaware brothers in the streets. Stagolee fought his brothers and sisters, and he shouldn't have. The Stagolees of today should take on the messages of Malcom X as Huey Newton did, to oppose this racist, capitalist oppression our people and other peoples are subjected to."

Another black epic gives further dimension to the motherfucker mystique. Shine, the cook on the Titanic, leaps overboard after the collision and starts swimming. The captain's daughter comes up on deck and pleads with him to save her. His answer is unsympathetic –

> There's pussy on the land and pussy on the sea,
> But pussy on the land is the pussy for me

– and he swims on. A shark attempts to devour him,

but he again refuses to be deflected from his purpose, saying:

> You're the king of the ocean, the king of the sea,
> But you gotta be a swimming motherfucker to out swim me.

Shine is standing on a corner in Harlem two hours before the news of the sinking of the Titanic reaches New York. Shine may not be a "baaad motherfucker" in the full meaning of that title, but he is in the vicinity, since he has the willpower to postpone sexual gratification, can outswim a shark and beats the wireless telegraph across the Atlantic. However, there is another kind of motherfucker who is distinctly less admirable, and he is usually known as a "signifying motherfucker." Such a person has all the surface attributes of a really baaad motherfucker, but caves in under attack; he is mere bluff. *(Signifying* means using words without the will or intent to back them; most U.S. government promises are regarded as "signifying" in the black ghetto.) The classic example is the Signifying Monkey in a legend so old and so Uncle-Remuslike that some folklorists suspect it goes back to Africa. It is worth quoting at some length:

> Deep down in the jungle, near a dried-up creek,
> The signifying monkey hadn't slept for a week.
> Every night when he was ready for a piece,
> Brother Lion came by a-roaring like police.

The monkey decides to down the lion, but being only a signifier he doesn't attempt a frontal assault; instead he uses the old let's-you-and-him-fight gambit, telling Lion that Brother Elephant has been "calling him out of his name," to wit:

> He says he fucked your mammy and your auntie, too,
> And if you ain't careful, he's gonna fuck you.

This puts Brother Lion in a proper rage and he charges off to face the elephant down:

> He ran through water, he ran through mud,
> He came to a bar called the Bucket of Blood.
> There sat Elephant, two whores upon his knee,
> He was drinking boiler-makers and smoking tea.
> Lion walk up and spit right in his eye,
> Say, "Rise, motherfucker, you're gonna die!"

Elephant majestically delivers one powerful kick, and Lion crawls away "more dead than alive." As he totters toward his den he passes the monkey, who laughs and tells him:

> The sky is blue and the grass is green
> And you're the dumbest motherfucker this jungle's ever seen.

Alas, the monkey laughs too loud and loses his balance. Lion is on him with "all four feet" as soon as he hits the ground. With "tears in his eyes," the monkey offers an apology and a ringing declaration to reform and mend his ways. The gullible lion spares him – whereat he scrambles up the tree again and, laughing, declaims:

> The sky is still blue and the grass still green
> And you're still the dumbest motherfucker this jungle's ever seen.

The monkey laughs so hard that again he falls out of the tree, and the legend ends with:

> Deep down in the jungle near a dried-up creek,
> Nobody's seen that monkey for more than a week.
> But there's a new tombstone and here's what it say:
> "Here's where a signifying motherfucker lay!"

The black meaning of *motherfucker*, then, is far from simple, and a "baaaaad motherfucker" is admirable or at least awe-inspiring, whereas a "signifying motherfucker" is merely a contemptible four-flusher.

When *motherfucker* journeyed down town and entered white speech, it lost this ambiguity and became merely the "roughest" word around. At one time it was sport in the Navy to use it on new recruits from middle-class backgrounds, then duck – they almost always started throwing punches. As the word became better established, it naturally became less shocking; among some whites it is now used as casually and cordially as *son of a bitch*. It can still get a rise out of those who have led sheltered lives, however, including policemen; in New Jersey a Black Panther Party organizer was arrested for disorderly conduct for saying to a white traffic cop, "Just a minute, motherfucker." The attorney for the defense argued that *motherfucker* is not always an insult or threat in ghetto speech, but the judge evidently felt that it could not really have been intended cordially coming from a Panther to a policeman. The accused was fined.

Inherent in the term *motherfucker* is the charge of mother-son incest, a taboo that is close to being universal, anthropologists agree, and which, unlike other sexual restrictions, is almost universally obeyed, too.

Kinsey and his associates, for instance, investigated a record 1500 sex offenders in American prisons and found that although a large percentage of them were sentenced for incest, not one in the 1500 had committed mother-son incest. Father-daughter incest, paradoxically, turned out to be far more common than was realized before this study. Hence, the word *motherfucker* may have forced its way into our culture but the deed itself has not.

MOTHER OF ALL SAINTS

The female genitalia, in Cockney and Dublinese and occasionally in America, as in "Then she lets her bathrobe accidentally-on-purpose fall open a bit and I see the Mother of all Saints."

MOTHER SUPERIOR

A MADAM or brothel-keeper (note its interesting usage in the Lennon-McCartney song under GUN). Parker Tyler in his book, *Screening the Sexes,* has dubbed Mae West "Mother Superior of the Faggots," based on her own admission in her autobiography that she "knew that female impersonators imitated her," and that she wrote a play about homosexuals called *The Drag.* See DRAG.

MOUNT THE RED FLAG

To have intercourse with a woman during her menstrual period. This vivid visual metaphor should be compared with POLE and HALE-MAST.

MOUSETRAP

The vagina; evidently from an 18th Century joke calling it "the parson's mousetrap" because it can lead one to matrimony. The play, movie and song called *The Tender*

Trap was in general about love, but seemed to be playing on this meaning also. See also CAT.

MOWED LAWN
A shaved vulva, sometimes found in models or in women after childbirth.

MUFF
The female genitalia; recorded as early as 1785. In New York, a "muff-diver" is one who performs CUNNILINGUS.

MUFFINS
Small breasts, as distinguished from *watermelons*, HAMMOCKS and GRAPEFRUITS.

MUSCLE
The penis; sometimes also called the "love muscle."

MUTTON
The female genitalia, with an obviously oral connotation. *Mutton-monger* was 18th Century wit for a Don Juan, and *cold mutton* a 19th Century insult for an unsatisfactory WHORE. Compare the connotation of *mutton* with the much more acceptable *lamby-pie,* a common term of endearment. Terry Southern in *Blue Movie* has a scene where Teeny Marie, a hairless, breastless, one-legged, one-eyed woman, makes the offer, *"Who wants a taste of my lamb-pit?!?" Mutton-headed* means stupid or inept, probably from the low intelligence of the sheep. *Mutt,* nowadays a dog, was originally a fool, by contraction from *mutton-head,* and this is the inspiration for the name of Augustus T. Mutt in *Mutt and Jeff.*

The most amazing motive for murder in modern times

was that of a San Francisco man who heard his beloved dog called a "fussy mutt." This animal-lover brooded over the insult for two hours, then got his pistol and went back and shot the offender dead. This is recounted in S.I. Hayakawa's *Language in Thought and Action.*

NAKED LUNCH

This is the title of a William S. Burroughs novel which was the subject of a censorship trial in Boston. The prosecutor alleged that the words *naked lunch* referred to what he called "an unnatural sex act," but poet Allen Ginsberg, testifying for the defense, insisted that the expression reflected the "cannibalism" of modern society. Burroughs states his own intent clearly in the Introduction to the Grove Press edition: "The title means exactly what the words say: NAKED lunch – a frozen moment when everyone sees what is on the end of every fork . . . If civilized countries want to return to Druid Hanging Rites in the Sacred Grove or to drink blood with the Aztecs and feed their Gods with blood of human sacrifices, let them see what they actually eat and drink. Let them see what is on the end of that long newspaper spoon."

NANCE (or NANCY)

A male homosexual; the origins are *Nancy* and *Nanny,* children's distortions of *Ann. Nancy* became a name in its own right and then a nickname for prostitutes, after which it got into homosexual slang. *Nanny* became a maidservant, but by the old association with *Nancy,* a "nannyhouse" was a brothel in 16th-18th Century slang.

NARCISSISM

Self-love; from the Greek legend of the youth,

Narcissus, who fell in love with his own image in a pool and drowned trying to embrace it. Popularizers of psychoanalysis often seem to regard the myth as an allegory against MASTURBATION; more probably it is a warning against compulsive drug abuse. *Narcotic* and related words are sometimes said to derive from *Narcissus,* the soporific flower which grows beside pools and inspired the legend.

NATURAL

Nowadays this means a person of inborn talent – a natural, a born winner – but in 14th-19th Century English, it was a contraction of *natural child,* a bastard. The state of nature, according to some English political philosophers, means anarchy, and John Adams alarmed the delegates at the first Continental Congress by saying bluntly, after the Declaration was signed, "Now we are in the state of nature." According to this way of thinking, the natural is the evil, and the function of reason is to transcend it. *(Behaving like an animal* or having *barnyard morality* are two other catchphrases of this antinature philosophy.) And yet we tell someone who feels awkward and timid, "try to act natural."

A "crime against nature," in American and English law, is any form of nonprocreative sex; this goes back to medieval Catholic doctrine in which the church's sexual rules were considered "natural" and any departure from them "against nature." Contraception is against nature according to Catholics. In this framework, nature is always right and violating nature's norms is evil.

The "natural" is also a black hairstyle where the hair is allowed to grow out without the straightening process many blacks used to prefer. There is a lack of consensus about what clothing or hairstyle is actually "natural," and *Mohammed Speaks,* organ of the Nation of Islam (the Black Muslims), is convinced that many so-called natural styles are actually white and crusades against them with the fervor of the antiwhite-sugar people in the food-fad field. Black poet Don L. Lee offers another interesting comment in a poem titled "Contradiction in Essence":

> I
> met
> a
> part
> time
> re
> vo
> lu
> tion
> ary
> (natural hair, African dressed)
> (always angry, in a hurry etc.)
> talk
> ing
> black
> &
> sleep
> ing
> whi
> te

NECK

To "neck" is to engage in sexual foreplay but not carry through to coitus. The results for the male can be found under BLUE BALLS and for the female under GREEN SICKNESS. It used to be held that "necking" was above the neck and PETTING below, but the distinction has become blurred.

"Neck weed" in 18th Century Cockney was Indian hemp,

then used in hangmen's nooses, now more commonly known as the source of marijuana. The "neck verse," in 16th-18th Century English slang, was a way of escaping hanging; if a felon could recite a single verse from the Bible in Latin, he obtained "privilege of clergy" and was branded instead of suffering the extreme penalty. The rare Ben Jonson avoided the gallows this way after killing a man in a duel.

NO MONEY IN THE PURSE

Said of a man who is temporarily impotent, "He has no money in the purse."

NOOKIE

The female genitalia; or the woman herself when regarded as merely a sex object; or even the sexual act. The word comes from *nook,* a private place away from prying eyes, and is also the source of NECK.

In the 18th Century, "noozed" meant either married or hanged, depending on the context, while "nub" curiously meant both the neck and intercourse.

NOTCH

The female genitalia; probably a visual metaphor.

NUMBER ONE and NUMBER TWO

Number One is nurseryese for urination, as in "Now make number one, Johnnie." This is also used to mean oneself, in the proverb "Take care of number one," which means, roughly, look out for yourself and to hell with everybody else. Then there's the limerick which inspired Tennessee Williams's title, *Night of the Iguana:*

There was a young gaucho named Bruno
Who said, "About sex there's one thing I do know:
Women are fine,
And sheep are divine,
But the iguana is numero uno!

Number Two is nurseryese for defecation. A New York joke has two Bronx women discussing culture: "And then I went to Carnegie Hall," says one, "and heard Beethoven's Symphony, you should excuse the expression, Number Two."

NUMBERS GAME

A session of BALLING in which the emphasis is on variety and endurance. The implication is the participants pass through the "69" (mutual oragenitalism); the "34½" (FELLATIO or CUNNILINGUS – a witticism created by dividing 69 in half); the "79" (the "69" with all ten fingers in her rump) and the "99" (anal intercourse).

NUNNERY

A brothel; a slang term that has been around since about 1600 and is still heard occasionally.

This is another of the family of anticlerical jibes, and there *is* a question of how much celibacy actually existed in convents and monasteries. One view, as presented in 1837 in the celebrated book, *Awful Disclosures of Maria Monk,* concerned the author's experiences in a Canadian convent. Among the charges she made was that the nunneries practiced infanticide to conceal the sexual activities of the nuns. In 1873, William Hogan of Albany, New York, a former priest who had become an attorney, published *Auricular Confession and Nunneries,* in which he alleged that in his years in the priesthood he had never met a nun "who has not been debauched by her own confessor." Some of the results of clerical celibacy (when it *is* practiced) are treated in Aldous Huxley's historical novel, *The Devils of Loudun,* and the recent movie version of it, *The Devils,* concerning a nun who is literally driven mad by sexual frustration. Further results were one innocent man burned at the stake and a whole town driven to hysteria, all of which really occurred in Loudun circa 1640.

NUTS

The testicles; evidently directly from the Roman fertility ritual of throwing nuts at the bride and groom after a wedding. The nuts represented the testicles, as the rice, at a modern wedding, symbolizes semen.

NYMPHO

A highly-sexed woman; a contraction (and misunderstanding) of the medical term *nymphomania,* which describes a pathology in which a female seeks incessant copulation out of an inability to achieve orgasm. The joke claiming that the ideal wife is "a rich nymphomaniac whose father owns a liquor store" is based on ignorance of men, women, nymphomania and the anti-aphrodisiac effects of alcohol.

OATS (or WILD OATS)

Semen, as in the expression *to sow his oats,* or *his wild oats,* meaning to engage in a period of sexual promiscuity before "settling down" to marriage.

OBEDIENCE

A code word used in personal ads. Those offering "obedience" are masochists seeking sadistic sexual partners. See DISCIPLINE.

OCCUPY

To have sexual intercourse with a woman. Now rarely used, this is a variation of the more common *to possess*.

OLD BLIND BOB

The penis. Note the parallel with the Persian use of *the blind eye that weeps* as a poetic metaphor for the penis, or, more specifically, the urethra hole, and *blind* meaning uncircumcised in homosexual slang.

OLD DIRT ROAD

The anus; to go up the old dirt road (or up the mustard road) is to have anal intercourse.

OLD JOE

Venereal disease of any kind. The origin is completely unknown; one can only suggest that somewhere, some time, there was a guy named Joe who became rather notorious for having one FULL HOUSE after another.

OLD LADY

Hippie slang for a woman living with a man in a fairly monogamous manner with or without a marriage ceremony. "She's my old lady" could mean she's either a steady girlfriend or a wife.

OLD MAN

Slang for a man living with a woman on a regular basis with or without the blessings of either church or state. In blue-collar slang an "old man" is usually the speaker's father, as in Damon Runyan's book about his father, *My Old Man*. This can lead to confusion on the rare occasions when hippies and blue-collar workers talk to each other. Also, in U.S. Army usage, "the old man" is the company commander.

OLD TOM

A LESBIAN; from *tomboy*, which traditionally meant a girl who likes boy's games, but is now used by lesbians to mean a woman who plays the male role.

ONE-EYED MONSTER

The penis; a reference to the urethral hole. Compare POLYPHEMUS, also meaning the penis but named after the one-eyed giant cannibal in Homer's *Odyssey*. See also OLD BLIND BOB.

ONE-MAN BAND

CUNNILINGUS performed with attention to the following details: The tongue stimulates the clitoris and its environs only, while the vagina is excited by the man's thumb, and his middle finger stimulates her anus. Devotees claim that this is the most intense sexual experience a woman can have, and it is highly valued among many occultists who call it the Rite of Shiva.

The term *one-man band* comes from an old vaudeville stunt in which the performer would play several instruments simultaneously, using his mouth to hop back and forth on horns and harmonicas, while both hands and both feet were busy with percussion instruments.

ONE THAT BITES

A woman who can do the CLEOPATRA is said to have "one that bites." See SNAPPER and BITE.

ONE-WAY BABY

Homosexual slang for a heterosexual; sometimes varied to *one-way* CAT.

ON THE MAKE

Actively looking for a sexual partner. The slang use of *on the* allows any concept to be brought into speech easily: for example, "on the nod" is asleep or in a drowsy state induced by drugs; "on the Q.T." is on the quiet, quietly; "on the donicker" (underworld) is riding a train without paying, also called "on the bill" or "on the hype"; "on a trip," the LSD experience. See MAKE.

OOMPH

Sex appeal, as in "She has oomph." This was coined by Walter Winchell decades ago to describe actress Ann Sheridan.

OPERATOR

A man who practices the FOUR FS, a conscienceless seducer; but also an unscrupulous businessman.

ORCHIDS

The testicles. Interestingly, this is direct from the Greek *orchis,* a testicle, from which *orchid,* the flower, derives its name because of similarity in appearance. Some prudish or uptight people have been known to complain that orchids are ugly or unpleasant-looking, usually not fully aware of what has disturbed them.

And some readers have wondered if Rex Stout is being consciously Freudian in his Nero Wolfe detective stories; Wolfe, a super-brain with controlled paranoid tendencies (he is afraid to leave his house) has all the earmarks of a repressed (*very* repressed) homosexual and is, incidentally, fanatically devoted to his hobby – orchid-growing.

OVER THE HILL

Past one's prime. An aged man, suspected of impotence, is said to be "over the hill." In the Army, however, to go over the hill is to desert.

OWLSHIT

Anything tedious or distressing, as in "The boss just dropped another load of owlshit on my desk." This was also used in Norman Mailer's *The Naked and the Dead* when a soldier complains about the food and wants to know what it is: "Owlshit," says the cook tersely. See also CHICKENSHIT, BULLSHIT and WHALESHIT.

PAD

In current American slang, either a bed or an apartment. In 1920s junky (heroin addict) argot, a pad was a place where people gathered to smoke opium together, probably from the use of *pad* to mean cushion, and the use of very plush cushions in Chinese opium dens. In the 18th Century, a pad was a highway, "pad borrowers" were horse thieves, "footpads" were highwaymen and a "high pad" was a highway robber.

"Padded" brassieres for women have been around since the 1800s in England (they were made of wax then) and were revived in the 1930s in America, and a padded jockstrap for men recently came on the market – "to give you that traffic-stopping look," the ads say coyly. The former were once called "gay deceivers," but the latter probably deserves the label more. See GAY.

PADDLE THE PICKLE

Male MASTURBATION. The sexual symbolism of the pickle is fairly obvious, and there's an old loggers' tale about the new worker who asks, after a few weeks in the woods, what to do when he's HORNY. "Go stick your dick in the hole in the pickle barrel," the foreman instructs him. "It's better than you'd think." He tries it, and finds perfect gratification. Returning to the foreman, he enthuses, "I'm going to use that every day from now on." "Except every second Wednesday," the foreman says. "Why not second Wednesdays?" our hero asks. "Because from now on, that's your day in the barrel!" (The heterosexual equivalent is the widely quoted fantasy of "diving head-first into a barrel of tits.")

PANDER

A PIMP or procurer; from Pandaros in Chaucer's *Troilus and Cressida* who procures Cressida for Troilus.

PANSY

A male homosexual; from the flower, which was a symbol of free thought and revolution in 18th Century France. *Pansy* can also mean pretentious or affected, as in H. W. Seaman writing in the *American Mercury* in 1937: "American stage and screen voices in recent years have become so pansy that it is difficult to distinguish an American from an English actor."

PARAMOUR

An "illicit" lover. Two unmarried people living together,

or having a prolonged affair, are said to be "paramours." The root is Old French and Middle English *par amour,* with love.

PARLOR HOUSE

A whorehouse; from French *parlez,* to speak. Perhaps another joke at the clergy's expense, since the "parlor" was a room in a convent – the chamber where nuns could talk to visitors – before it came to be a room in an ordinary house. See NUNNERY.

PARTY

An orgy; but the same word is sometimes used, among respectable middle-class women, to mean an ordinary session of conventional two-person sex, as in the coy, "Do you want a party tonight, lover?" "Party" records contain bawdy songs like "Roll Me Over In The Clover" or sustained double entendres like "Please Mr. Duff Keep Your Hands Off My Muff." PLAYBOY'S "party jokes" are ribald; a "party girl" may be a prostitute or a SWINGER. Peggy Lee's popular recording, "The Party's Over," uses this double meaning for pathos rather than humor – it means the AFFAIR is over.

PASTIES

Tiny pieces of decorative cloth that are pasted over the nipples by female erotic dancers in cities where the rest of the breast can be shown but where the sight of a bare nipple can lead to arrest and trial.

PAW

To roughly fondle the genitalia or breasts of a woman without first obtaining at least tacit permission. A man addicted to pawing is said by women to have "Roman hands and Russian fingers" (roamin' and rushin'), or is called an "octopus."

PEARL-DIVER

Homosexual slang for an individual who prefers to FELLATE others rather than be fellated. The origin of this phrase seems to be a combination of FAMILY JEWELS and MUFF DIVER. To save the reader unnecessary (and possibly painful) misunderstandings, it is imperative to add immediately that in restaurant slang a "pearl diver" is not a homosexual of any sort, but merely a dishwasher.

PEASANTS

Homosexual slang for heterosexuals; based on the old (and inaccurate) notion that homosexuality is an upper-class predilection only.

PECKER

The penis; from Middle Low German *pecken,* to pierce. An amusing play upon the word occurs in the folk rhyme:

> The woodpecker pecked on the outhouse door.
> He pecked and he pecked till his pecker was sore.

And, even more ingeniously, in a folk song:

> I stuck my pecker in the woodpecker's hole.
> The woodpecker said, "Well, bless my soul! Remove it!"
>
> I removed my pecker from the woodpecker's hole.
> The woodpecker said, "Well, bless my soul! Reinsert it!"

> I returned my pecker to the woodpecker's hole
> The woodpecker said, "Well, bless my soul! Rotate it!"
> I rotated my pecker in the woodpecker's hole.
> The woodpecker said, "Well, bless my soul! Accelerate it!"

Roger Abrahams cites this interesting piece from the streets of Philadelphia about a man "looking for a motherfucking job." He meets "a pretty little whore" who invites him to:

> "Come on and sit down over here."
>
> I said, "Well, would you tell me what this here job be?"
> She said, "Well, you got to get down on your knees
> And eat this pussy like a rat eating cheese.
>
> You got to get way down in it and blow it like Louis blow his horn.
>
> You got to peck all around, like a rooster pecking corn."
>
> I said, "Hold it! Wait a minute, bitch, you're talking too fast.
>
> The next thing you know, you'll have my foot in your ass."
>
> I said, "I'm not a rooster, so I can't peck corn and I ain't Louis, so go blow your own horn."

In the Army, a "pecker-checker" is a medical officer, so called because of the frequent examinations for venereal disease among Army men. Other names for this functionary are "cock corpsman," "dick doc" and "pricksmith." The English phrase *keep your pecker up* originally had no sexual connotation; it referred to the pecker (head) of a rooster in a cock fight. The female equivalent is found under CANOE INSPECTION.

PECKER TRACKS

Dried drops of semen found in an incriminating place. (It is standard police procedure to seek such telltale evidence in all crimes of violence, since many seemingly nonsexual assaults actually do have a sexual element.) Gershon Legman in *Oragenitalism* tells an ugly little story about a man-hating woman whose pleasure it was to seduce married men, fellate them, and then spit the semen back on their trousers, saying, "Now, explain *that* to your wife, you rat!" One gentleman, a university professor, hearing of this, allowed himself to appear to fall into her trap and then, smiling, removed the trousers, took a fresh pair from his briefcase, put them on, tipped his hat and left. See FELLATIO.

PEEPING TOM

A voyeur; from the old legend that one man, a tailor named Tom, did not look away when Lady Godiva took her famous naked ride through Coventry as a protest against high taxes. He supposedly was miraculously struck blind by a just God for this human weakness. This was put into verse by Tennyson.

Related terms are *peek freak,* also a voyeur; *peepers,* the eyes; *peeper* (underworld slang) for a private investigator or undercover detective; *peeper* (Cockney), a spyglass; *single peeper,* a one-eyed man.

PEGO

The penis; from *peg,* a wooden stump, as in Long John Silver's famous "peg-leg." A "peg-boy" is a young male who prostitutes himself to homosexuals; "peg-house," a homosexual brothel. There is an unsubstantiated story that boys in East Indian peg-houses were required to sit on pegs between customers, giving them permanently dilated anuses.

PETER

The penis; evidently by the same process that turned *God* to *gosh* and *Jesus* to *gee*. A "peter-eater" is a homosexual, but a "peter-blower," in underworld slang, is not a *cocksucker* but a safe-cracker, from the English gypsy use of *peter* to mean strongbox. "Robbing Peter to pay Paul," also known as "maneuvering the apostles," is borrowing from one friend to pay back another. A "Peter Gunner" is an unsuccessful hunter, and probably the creators of the TV series, *Peter Gunn,* chose the name just to pack two phallic puns into a single name. A "peter-heater" is a jockstrap, and "peter meter," a mythical device for measuring sexual passion and also a movie-rating formula used by *Screw* magazine:

$$\text{Heat of meet} = \frac{\text{angle of dangle}}{\text{mass of ass}} \times \text{thrust of bust}$$

PETTING

Sexual foreplay that stops short of intercourse but not necessarily short of orgasm. The term *heavy petting* is sometimes heard, meaning the same as Kinsey's more technical term *petting to climax,* and can include almost anything, including DRY FUCKING (also called "dry humping"), in which copulative motions are imitated without the penis actually entering the vagina.

The motives for this curious practice are generally fear of pregnancy, the wish to maintain virginity, or a belief that orgasm without intercourse is more acceptable than GOING ALL THE WAY. In fact, however, in terms of pregnancy, FELLATIO and CUNNILINGUS are safer in the absence of contraception than this practice, since even if the sperm is discharged outside but in the vicinity of the vagina, it can seep in and cause pregnancy. Nevertheless, Kinsey found that 28 percent of his male sample and 39 per cent of his female sample had employed petting to climax as their chief outlet in their youth.

"Light petting," which stops short of orgasm, may be as mild as NECKING, or may progress to the point where both partners are left with unpleasant physical sensations (see BLUE BALLS and GREEN SICKNESS). The traditional folk remedies are, for the male, either a cold shower or a quick visit to a whore, and, for the female, a cold shower, period. Since these remedies are imperfect or impractical in many cases, the usual remedy has been masturbation, as D.H. Lawrence sardonically noted in a famous essay on obscenity and censorship. Light petting not carried to the point of painful frustration is, however, both harmless and delightful when practiced occasionally by couples who are having intercourse regularly.

PHILADELPHIA LAWYERS

A woman's legs; so called from the old reputation of Philadelphia lawyers, who were believed capable of clouding any jury's judgment. An old Texas joke: A man who shot a fellow in a cardroom dispute wired to Philadelphia for one of these lawyers to defend him and received the answer: ARRIVING BY TRAIN TOMORROW. BRINGING TWO EYEWITNESSES.

PICCADILLY COMMAND
Londonese for the large band of prostitutes who gather in Piccadilly Circus in the evening.

PICCOLO PLAYER
A homosexual. See SKIN FLUTE.

PICKUP
A female companion who is acquired casually, without benefit of formal introduction, and is hence expected to be sexually permissive; deriving apparently from the drug world, where a "pickup" was once a package of heroin dropped on the sidewalk by a careful pusher, after receiving payment, so as to give no clear evidence of an actual sale if police were watching.

PICNIC
Homosexual slang for FELLATIO, as in "While the straights were watching the movie, he had a picnic in the second balcony." Hollywood moguls may be aware of this usage; when the movie version of William Inge's play, *Picnic,* opened in New York, it was advertised with a photo of William Holden, the star, wearing nothing above the waist. This, allegedly, was to turn on (sexually arouse) female customers, but the GAY set got the message and the theater's men's room temporarily became as popular for CRUISING as Central Park West. Compare with LUNCH BOX and SEAFOOD.

PIDDLE
To urinate; a child's term since at least the 18th Century and probably a distortion of piss. *Piddling* also means trivial, unworthy of notice, as in "Don't bother me with

those piddling details." According to Harry Bennett's biography of the late Henry Ford, *We Never Called Him Henry* (the original title was *S.O.B. Detroit*, but the publishers were persuaded by the Ford family to restrain author Bennett's wit), the automobile magnate would quiet executives whose words he didn't wish to hear by saying, "Stop piddling in my ear."

PIECE (or PIECE OF ASS, PIECE OF TAIL)

A woman when considered as a mere sex object. This expression has been condensed to *piece* for at least two centuries, and in England, at least in rural areas, a man's "piece" is his sweetheart, with no insult implied. *Piece of ass* and *piece of tail* are sometimes used to designate intercourse itself, as in "She gave me a damned good piece of ass."

There is another *piece,* used in the underworld and the ghetto, which means a gun, as in "Don't mess with him, he's packing a piece." This is probably a false shortening of 19th Century *peacemaker,* a pistol, but the new spelling suggests that somebody along the way discerned Freudian implications. See GUN and MAIN PIECE.

PIG

An offensive individual, accused (by this term) of "filthy" proclivities. *Pig* is a powerful insult, and has been for centuries. Policemen are called "pigs," as are other figures of authority – school administrators, government officials, military officers, capitalists and Women's Liberation has dubbed men who consider women inferior beings "male chauvinist pigs." (Interestingly, the "modern" use of *pig* for policeman was recorded as Irish-American slang in 1870.) In 1968, the Youth International Party ("Yippies") ran a pig (a real one) for president in sardonic commentary on the other candidates, and George Orwell, the great predictor of political trends, made the pigs symbols of oppression in his novel, *Animal Farm*.

Expressions like "the open sewer of pornography," "wallowing in filth," "sexual swinishness" are all frequently used by censors, illustrating the anal connotation of *pig*. This animal, as is well known, literally wallows in muck, which is proper and healthy for it but rather revolting to human observers. Pigs have long been tabooed by Jews and Moslems and regarded with contempt by Christians. Robert Graves tells, for instance, of overhearing a group of lower-class English children in one of those contests in which the participants try to outdo each other in verbally breaking cultural taboos (its American equivalent is the DIRTY DOZENS). The winner among Graves's Cockney children was one who glared up at the sky and screamed, "Piggy God!"

All of these associations come together in the most emphatic term of refutation in American English: "In a pig's ass!" The speaker conveys not only that he doubts what he has heard, but that he rejects it as vehemently as our language can reject anything. This is much more hostile, and much more likely to provoke a fight, than the simple exclamations, "Bullshit!" or "Horseshit!" (a popular underground humor magazine even calls itself *Horseshit),* because the anal pig has none of the redeeming genital symbolism of the bull and the stallion. The radical young understand this and have rejected the latter terms as too mild, characterizing all official government pronouncements as "pigshit."

"Pig-sticking" is sodomy, or anal intercourse. "Pig meat," an expression of total sexual disdain, as in "I wouldn't touch that pig meat with a ten-foot pole." A "pigwidgeon," in rural English, is a simpleton, from *pig* plus *pigeon,* the dupe of a swindle. To "cold-pig" someone is to awaken him by removing all the bedclothes in one startling yank. To buy "a pig in a poke" is to be swindled.

Perhaps at this point we should say a word in defense of the harmless quadruped upon whom all this libel has been imposed. Ambrose Bierce, in his sardonic *Devil's Dictionary,* provides the antidote:

> PIG, n., an animal *(porcus omnivorus)* closely allied to the human race by the splendor and vivacity of its appetite, which, however, is inferior in scope, for it sticks at pig.

PILLARS OF THE TEMPLE

A woman's legs; from the older slang phrase *temple of Venus* meaning the vulva.

PILLOW BOOKS

A type of illustrated sex manual very popular in Japan and falling somewhere between the educational/informational and the pornographic. Many are beautifully and tastefully printed. The term is a direct translation from the Japanese.

PILLOW POLO

A jocular name for copulation. A similar jest, not so widespread, is "bedroom baseball."

PIMP

A procurer or whoremonger; standard English since 1607, the origin is somewhere among Middle French *pimper,* to dress in the height of fashion, Old French *piper,* to seduce, and Latin *pipere,* to coo like a bird, to peep. *Pimp whiskin'* was 17th-18th Century Londonese for the top pimp in town. A related insult is "He's only a pimple on a real pimp's ass," similar to Budd Shulberg's offering in *Waterfront.* "You're a pimple on the ass of progress. Disappear."

PING GIRL

Carole Landis – named thusly because she was so busty that her buttons went "ping," according to her publicity agent.

PISS

To urinate. *Piss* was acceptable English until around 1760, and was then abruptly considered taboo. There is an old Cockney joke about the man who tells his doctor, "I can't tell you my problem – I don't speak Latin." During that period, a great many homey old Saxon words suddenly became taboo.

Related terms are: *piss-proud,* having an erection but losing it at an inopportune moment; *a pissing while,* a short time. "He will piss when he can't whistle" is a glum forecast that the man in question will end on the gallows. *Pissing down his back* means flattering him; *pissing pins and needles,* the unpleasant discovery (via painful urination) that you have gonorrhea; *piss prophet,* a scornful term for a doctor since 1625, referring to the diagnosis of illness through urine specimens; *piss-elegant,* pretentious; *piss-a-bed,* a lazy fellow, one who pisses in bed because he's too lethargic to walk to the JOHN. (A topper to this insult is "You'd shit in bed and kick it out with your feet.")

PISSATORIUM

A jocular name for the bathroom or public lavatory; from PISS (to urinate) with the Latin suffix *-orium,* meaning a place for or thing used for – hence, a place for pissing. This is of the family of lower-class words coined to caricature the "elegant" speech of the wealthy; for example, *rambunctious* (looking for a fight) and *bodaceous* (pretentious), both bastardizations of slang words coupled with authentic Latin suffixes. The former is of white New England origin, and the second is southern black.

A similar sport among intellectuals is the coining of fake Latin proverbs, of which the most famous are *Non illegitimati carborundum* (Don't let the bastards grind you down), attributed to General Joseph ("Vinegar Joe") Stilwell; *Via ovicephalas dura est* (The way of the egghead is hard), by Adlai Stevenson; and *Penis erectus non compis mentis* (A stiff prick has no conscience), of unknown authorship.

PISS HARD-ON

An erection upon awakening in the morning, which often subsides after urination. This is not actually caused by the presence of urine in the bladder, as the expression suggests, but is somehow related to dreaming: All males experience partial or total erection while dreaming, but the reason is not yet understood, since this occurs even when the dream is totally without sexual content. Kinsey also found that very young males, around the onset of puberty, experience erections from nonsexual stimuli, such as riding in cars, hearing music, being startled by sudden noises, taking school examinations.

PLASTER-CASTERS

A special class of "groupies," who are, in turn, a special group among "celebrity-fuckers." A celebrity-fucker (the word was coined by writer-editor John Wilcock) is a young woman who will FUCK anybody as long as he's famous; the groupies fuck only Rock superstars; and the plaster-casters, after nabbing a Rock hero, will not let him escape until they have made a plaster cast of his penis. Literally.

WR – Mysteries of the Organism, a movie about psychiatrist Wilhelm Reich, shows Jim Buckley, publisher of *Screw* magazine, being plaster-casted – in vivid detail.

The plaster-casters were first discussed in print by the underground magazine, *The Realist,* and Rock star and poet Ed Sanders has made a record about his embarrassment when he appeared before the American Legion and realized bits of plaster were still clinging to his trouser FLY.

PLAYING CHECKERS

Homosexual slang for a technique of CRUISING in a movie theater by changing seats constantly in search of a possible sex partner. There is, of course, a Freudian interpretation of chess and checkers, written by Reuben Fine, a psychoanalyst who also holds Grandmaster rank in international chess; he believes that the enemy king is a symbol of one's father's penis.

PLAYING CHOPSTICKS

Mutual MASTURBATION; from the crossing of hands while playing "Chopsticks" on the piano.

PLAYING SOLITAIRE

MASTURBATION.

PLAYING THE MURPHY

A confidence game, or swindle, in which a young lady and a hotel clerk conspire to defraud horny men. The girl pretends to be a prostitute and lures a man to a room in the hotel, whereupon she strips naked but demands payment before climbing into bed. Slipping the money into her purse, she goes into the bathroom, allegedly to wash up and affix a diaphragm; since she is nude except for the purse, the man has no suspicions. The bathroom, however, adjoins a room which is empty, and the purse contains a dress. When the mark (victim) gets wise, she is far away, and, of course, nobody in the hotel knows anything about a nude girl running through the halls. The expression itself, *playing the murphy,* may come from the old fold-up "murphy bed," which disappeared into a wall. Among engineering students, the Murphy factor is a term included in an equation, after the fact, to make the answer come out right and deceive the teacher. Murphy's Law, among engineers, holds that if anything can go wrong, it will.

POCKET POOL

MASTURBATION in a theater or other public place by reaching through the trouser pocket. There is a persistent legend that a TV quiz show once incautiously asked a contestant, "What has six pockets and contains balls?" and he, instead of guessing correctly (a pool table), blurted out, "A man's trousers" – after which the show was cut off the air and a half hour of Bach substituted. It's nice to believe there was a half hour of Bach on TV once, but this legend is as fictitious as the dead man in the Coca-Cola vat, the alligators in New York's sewers and Dillinger's 23-inch penis. See BALLS.

POKE

Coitus; probably from standard English *poke,* to strike, and Middle English *poken,* also to strike. This was used in Robert Ruark's *Something of Value* when the heroine, searching for a polite word in her own mind, wonders how it would sound to ask a man, "Could you give me a poke?"

POLE

The penis; a typical exaggeration. *Up your hole with a ten-foot pole* is a taunt among New York schoolboys, and another adolescent joke asks, "Why doesn't Santa Claus have children?" Answer: "Because his pole is frozen." An alternate or topper is: "Because he shoots up the chimney." On Madison Avenue the line "Let's run it up the pole and see if anybody salutes it" became cliche years ago and was replaced by "Let's rub it awhile and see if it firms up."

POLISH HIS KNOB

For a woman to FELLATE a man, as in "And then she polished my knob." This sounds like it might be of Cockney origin, since it could be rhyming slang for BLOW *job.*

POLYPHEMUS

The penis; either rhyming slang, in which case it is of Cockney origin, like *bit of strife* (wife), *go to Bristol* (get a pistol), *briney marlin* (darlin'), or a visual metaphor, the giant Polyphemus in Homer's *Odyssey* having only one eye. See EYE and ONE-EYED MONSTER.

POONTANG

Sexual intercourse, as in "Could I ever use some poontang tonight." It can also mean the vagina in heterosexual slang, or the male genitalia in homosexual slang. The word is partially based on circa-1940 slang for an erection, *boing!* and also perhaps from French *putain,* a WHORE. Thomas Wolfe used it in *Look Homeward, Angel* ("A fellow's got to have a little Poon Tang"), and Jack Paar once smuggled it into his TV show backwards, mentioning a fictitious "Tangpoon" tribe in Africa.

POPE

The toilet bowl. Related phrases are: *the pope's nose,* the rump of a chicken or turkey (called "the protestant's nose" by Irish Catholics); *what a pope of a thing,* what a hell of a thing; *as drunk as a pope; he knows no more than the pope.* In England *pope* is a verb, meaning to go out on November 5 in a Guy Fawkes costume, commemorating the allegedly popish Gunpowder Plot to blow up Parliament.

Protestants have no authority figure comparable to the Pope of Rome, Robert Graves has noted, describing a religious argument between an Englishman and a Frenchman: "To hell with the Pope!" the Englishman said finally. "And to hell with the – the Archbishop of Canterbury!" the Frenchman shouted back. The Englishman merely laughed.

POP THE COOKIES

To have an orgasm, as in "Man, did she pop my cookies."

POP THE ROCKS

To have an orgasm, especially after a period of deprivation, as in "Then I found a chick and really popped my rocks."

POSITION

Nobody knows how many sexual positions there are; the old yarn that there are 69 is merely a pun on the famous position, SIXTY NINE. Tuli Kupferberg quotes 192 real ones amid the many put-ons in his *One Thousand and One Ways to Make Love,* but 192 is certainly not the limit; Gershon Legman has calculated, in *Oragenitalism,* that there are several hundred thousand variations on oral copulation alone, not counting genital and anal permutations.

In current speech, only lower-class workers have jobs; those of the middle class have "positions." This is satirized in the story of the husband who arrives home shouting joyously, "Good news! I've found a new position!" – to which his wife responds crossly, "Never mind that, you lazy bum. Get a job."

An ad recently appeared in many underground newspapers asserting that "Through centurys [sic] men have experimented with different sexual habits. For a detailed picture & written diagram of the Possible Original Method of Sex send $1.00." *Original* can mean the first and primordial, in which case these people are sending out either the typical mammalian mounting posture (called dog-fashion in current slang), or else an amoeba splitting – depending on how literal-minded they are. *Original* can also mean something new, in which case this ad is probably a fraud.

POT

Marijuana; probably from the southern use of *pot* to mean bootleg whiskey made at home. The origin, Old English *pott,* a drinking vessel, remains in *pothouse,* a saloon; from the same root are *chamberpot* and *cooking pot. Pot valiant* is having the courage that comes from strong liquor, a "potboiler" is a book written in a hurry to make money and "pot converts" are derelicts who will join any church or mission that hands out free food. *Potshot* comes from the older *pot-hunter,* one who hunts for sport rather than food, assumed by country folk to be therefore a careless shot. *The pot calls the kettle black* is expurgated; the 18th Century original was *the pot calls the kettle black-arse.*

Another derivation of *pot* meaning marijuana traces it to *shitpot* (see SHIT); and a third, accepted by Michael Aldrich, Ph.D., the leading authority on marijuana's role in history, traces it to Portuguese *potiguaya,* intoxicated.

The use of marijuana as an enhancer of sex has led to much debate about whether or not this herb is an aphrodisiac. In this connection, Youssef El Masry says, in *Daughters of Sin: The Sexual Tragedy of Arab Women,* that most Arabs who use the weed do so only because they think it is an aphrodisiac. He quotes an interesting old legend about three men who arrive at a city after the gates are closed: The first of the three is an alcoholic, the second an opium addict, the third a marijuana smoker. The violent alcoholic says without hesitation, "Let's break open the gates!" The indolent opium addict suggests, "Let's sleep here till morning . . ." The elated marijuana smoker puts forward what he believes to be a brilliant idea: "Let's go in through the keyhole!" And one graffito names the four best things in life: "pot, peace, pussy, perversion."

Most scientific authorities agree that marijuana does not

function as a true aphrodisiac; that is, it cannot create sexual desire or potency where these are absent; it can only enhance and exaggerate those qualities where they already exist. In this connection, and as an example of the ambiguous attitudes of pot-heads (marijuana users), we quote another passage from Terry Southern's *Blue Movie,* in which a writer meets an actress made up to look like an eight-year-old girl, who is "twisting up hash-bombers [marijuana cigarettes] big as cigars." His friend Boris asks: "But did you get laid?"

> "No, man, but dig . . . at one point I asked if there was anything to *drink* and she said 'No, baby, I don't drink,' and she smiles and says, 'How about if I cop your joint instead?' Eight years old right? So I give her a big dumb *'Huh? What'd you say?'* And she runs it down for me: 'Well, you know, give you some head, blow you, suck your cock, that sort of thing.' Well, I'll tell you, B., it tore me up – I mean, I doubt if I've ever turned down a blow-job in my life, *but eight years old,* wow . . . I don't know, maybe I'm old fashioned . . . thirteen, twelve, terrific . . . maybe even eleven . . . or ten, for Chris- sake, if she's got any knockers – I mean, *any breast at all* . . . but the idea of making it with a pre-knocker . . . I mean, wow, who wants to fuck a chick with no tits? It must be a *fag*-trip, right? I mean, it's got to be like fucking a young *boy,* right?"
>
> "But she just wanted to give you some head," Boris reminded him, "the no-knocker thing wouldn't have mattered there, would it?"
>
> Tony clucked and sighed and covered his face with his hand, wagging his head in despair. "I

know, I know, I've been thinking about that – it was the fucking *hash,* B., I swear to God – it fucked me up . . . I didn't know what I was *doing,* for Chrissake . . ."

Boris, ultimate funster that he was, did a big-eyed soap-opera elevation of eyebrow, combo of surprise and indignation: "Oh?"

But it was completely wasted, natch, on Tone the stone – who grimaced as one in pain misunderstood, shutting eyes tight, gritting teeth, shaking head, tolerance at an end: "Man . . . don't you dig – that fucking *dope* fucked up my whole *motherfucking sense of values!'*

POUNDING THE PUD
MASTURBATING. See PULL THE PUDDING.

PRATT
The buttocks, as in the burlesque "prattfall."

PRICK
The penis; from Old English *prica,* a dot or any mark made by a pointed instrument.

The earliest use of *prick* in the genital sense is found in 1592. Three years later, in 1595, Shakespeare punned on it in *Romeo and Juliet* ("the bawdy hand of the dial is now upon the prick of noon"). *All prick and no pence*: English and Irish slang for a man who COPS A FEEL or enjoys other small pleasures from a WHORE before being forced to admit he has no money.

"Witch-prickers" were men who claimed to be able to

detect witches by sticking pins in the suspects, the theory then being that Satan's servitors had one spot on their bodies (the Devil's Mark) where they were immune to pain.

Another *prick,* meaning to ride, derives from the same root via the imagery of spurring the horse. This produced the unintentionally startling opening line of Spenser's *Faerie Queene*: "A gentle Knight was pricking on the plaine." See also BEEF INJECTION.

PRIDE OF THE MORNING

An erection upon awakening, also called a PISS HARD-ON.

PRIVATES

The genitalia of either sex; from the old euphemism *private parts.*

PRO

A WHORE; abbreviated either from *prostitute* or from *professional. Prostitute* itself is from Latin, Greek and Indo-European roots meaning to stand, via the Latin *prostituere,* to stand forward, to show one's self, and is therefore imagistically linked with such English expressions as *a forward young lady.*

PROMISED LAND

The female genitalia, as in "Then she let me into the Promised Land"; from the Old Testament, where Moses and the Hebrews wander 40 years in search of the Promised Land.

PRONG

As a noun, the penis, as in "He had a King Kong prong." As a verb, to copulate, as in "I'd like to prong that babe right now."

PUD

The penis; perhaps from *pudding* in PULL THE PUDDING, or a contraction of the Latin *pudendum*, that which is shameful, often applied to the penis by some uptight Roman stylists.

PULLING THE TRAIN

West Coast slang for sequential BALLING of a single woman by a group of men; a GANG BANG.

PULL OUT

To practice contraception by the method of *coitus interruptus* – withdrawing the penis from the vagina before ejaculation.

Medically, there is no doubt that this practice causes various pains in the groin and, sometimes, the legs; psychiatrically, there is some evidence that chronic resort to this tactic inclines the male toward abnormal and hostile mental states, similar to paranoia. Added to the frustration and pain of this practice is the fact that it is not a 100-percent foolproof method of contraception either. During periods of sexual excitation and *prior to* ejaculation, the penis exudes small quantities of a thin liquid containing a few live sperm, which are fully capable of fertilization.

PULL THE PUDDING

To MASTURBATE, as in "They can spy on us all day to see if we're pulling our puddings and if we're working good or doing our 'athletics,' but they can't make an X-ray of our guts to find out what we're telling ourselves," from Alan Sillitoe's *The Loneliness of the Long Distance Runner*. The origin is unknown, but there may very well be a link to the popular old nursery rhyme:

> Little Jack Horner Sat in the corner
> Eating his Christmas pie.
> He put in his thumb
> And pulled out a plum
> And said, "What a good boy am I!"

PUNK

A passive young male forced into the feminine role in prison homosexuality, in American underworld slang; or, outside prison, a young homosexual. *Punk* meaning prostitute appeared in the 16th Century, as did *punchable wench,* a woman worth bedding. The use of *punk* to mean a petty criminal is due to author Dashiell Hammett, a former Pinkerton detective who wrote about crime more realistically than anybody before or since. Among other things, he included references to the bizarre sexual patterns often found among professional criminals, but most of this material was nervously edited out by his publishers. It was through the book and Bogart movie, *The Maltese Falcon,* where Sam Spade uses *punk* whenever he speaks to young Wilmer, that the word reached a large audience.

The persistence of *punk* owes something to the American Indian *punk,* rotten wood, which smells foul when burning. Thus, in New England, "punk" is still anything foul-smelling. Meanwhile, the relations between the punk and the tougher criminal who uses him as a substitute wife are the central theme in the fiction of ex-jailbird Jean Genet and the subject of the controversial play and movie, *Fortune and Men's Eyes.*

PUSH-PUSH

Copulation; an echoic term.

PUSSY

The vulva. A "pussy butterfly" is an intrauterine contraceptive, so called because of its winged shape. *Pussy* is a favorite word among adolescents, and pops up more often in graffiti than any other word. "John eats pussy!" is frequently seen on buildings and in bathrooms, often followed by "Cunnilingus is next to godliness." An especially clever graffito recorded by Robert Reisner is:

> HAPPINESS IS A WARM PUPPY.
> (Underneath) NO, IT'S A WARM PUSSY.

Other graffiti declare, "Pussy is good for man and boy," and "When I am old and still have hope, I'll wash my pussy with Ivory soap." See CAT.

PUT OUT

To be promiscuous, as in "She puts out." (It is never used of males, since promiscuity is taken for granted in their case; "He puts out" would sound absurd.) The term is more sexually explicit than appears on the surface and relates not to modern *put,* to place, but to the archaic *put,* to thrust forcibly, suggesting vigorous copulative movements and/or a suggestive and inviting body stance.

The desirability of a woman's aggressive participation is illustrated in an old joke about a WHORE who has three prices, $25, $50 and $75, explained as follows: "For $25, I let you; for $50, I help; for $75, you just hang on!" A similar reference to unrestrained female eroticism appears in Shakespeare's name for Falstaff's paramour,

Doll Tearsheet, and in the old Cockney name for a brothel, "pushing academy."

PUT THE BLOCKS TO HER

To copulate with, as in "I'd like to put the blocks to that chick." The metaphor is from logging, where blocks are affixed to the tree before it is felled.

PUTZ

The penis; from Yiddish. The word is also used metaphorically to mean a fool, as in "Look out – it's loaded, you putz."

QUAIL

Any young woman; from *quail-pipe,* a 16th-18th Century jest for a woman's tongue. The origin is *quail,* the bird, from Old French *quaille,* so named in echoic fashion from its shrill call. A "San Quentin quail," in Los Angeles, is a girl below the legal age of consent, sometimes abbreviated to "S.Q.Q." Peggy LaRue Satterlee, who charged actor Errol Flynn with rape in 1942, mentioned during her testimony that Flynn had called her "J.B." (JAILBAIT) and "S.Q.Q." before the alleged attack took place. The jury believed Flynn's denial and acquitted him.

QUEEN (or QUEAN)

A male homosexual. The origin is complex: Old English *ewen,* a woman, became *queue,* the ruling woman and hence modern *queen;* while the same root, spelled *quean,* came to mean a WHORE; or prostitute. The link pops up in poker-player's slang where queens are often called whores – "Three whores, gentlemen; can anybody beat that?" To "play the quean" is to act in a brazen or whorish manner.

He lives on Queen Street, also an English idiom, does not relate to homosexuality but means he is henpecked by his wife. "Mother, pin a rose on me, for I'm to be Queen of the May" is said by Irish wits when a suspected homosexual leaves the room; this oddly identifies sexual inversion with the Virgin Mary, who is the Queen of the May in Catholic liturgy. A variation is "Wake me early, Mother, for I am the Queen of the May." This is similar to the French blasphemy of calling a homosexual *petit Jesus,* "little Jesus."

QUEER

Used either as a noun or an adjective, homosexual; from 16th Century Scottish, where it meant questionable or dubious.

Related phrases are: *queer as a three dollar bill,* homosexual; *queer bit-makers,* 18th Century counterfeiters; *queer,* 20th Century underworld slang meaning counterfeit; *queer ken,* a prison. To "queer the deal" is to inadvertently reveal a swindle and warn the victim away. "Queer plungers" are persons who pretend suicide by jumping into a river, expecting a monetary contribution toward their rehabilitation from whoever dives in to rescue them; the great W. C. Fields engaged in this practice, as well as pool-hustling, when he was young and poor.

Recall the famous joke about Old Terwilliger: Two Englishmen meet on a ship and while conversing discover that they have both lived in the same province of India. "Then you must know old Terwilliger," says the first, who had lived there first. "Yes," says the other, shaking his head, "a sad case, old Terwilliger." "A sad case?" the first exclaims, "Why, what happened? We all looked up to Terwilliger as the very model of a colonial administrator." "Too bad," says the other, "too bad.

They caught him in the woods, attempting to copulate with a mongoose." "A mongoose? Old Terwilliger?" the first exclaims, "I can't believe it. Lord, it was a female mongoose, I trust?" "Oh, yes, a female mongoose." "Well, there! Nothing queer about old Terwilliger!"

QUICKIE

Sexual intercourse in a hurry, with one eye on the clock. The archetypal incident is recorded in a two-liner:

> "Hurry, I hear somebody coming."
> "Sorry, baby, that was *me* you heard coming." See COME.

QUIFF (or QUIM)

Two long-lived words for the vagina; like CUNT they both derive from Middle English *queynte*.

RABBIT HABIT

Promiscuity, as in "He has the rabbit habit" and "She fucks like a bunny." Compare the old joke about the rabbit who hops around BAITING every female rabbit he meets and saying "Wham! Bam! Thank you, ma'am!" He finally encounters a stone rabbit on a lawn, with a resulting: "Wham! Bam! God-*damn!!*" (Alternate ending: a case of mistaken identity, with the punch line: "Wham! Bam! *Sorry, Sam!*") The RANDINESS of the rabbit is the reason he is associated with Easter eggs, eggs having been a pagan fertility symbol before they became associated with Christianity.

RAG

A sanitary napkin. *On the rag* means menstruating. A "human rag" is a student who never misses classes, based on the explanation that he's there for every period.

George M. Cohan wrote a popular song that began, "It's a grand old rag/It's a high-flying flag." Public reaction forced him to revise this to the redundant, "It's a grand old *flag*/It's a high-flying flag."

RAINCOAT

A CONDOM (male prophylactic); probably based on an old objection to condoms, which went, "You don't go in swimming with a raincoat on, do you?"

RAKE

A hedonist, a promiscuous man; from Middle English *rakel,* reckless.

RANDY

Sexually excited or sexually exciting. The former can be a temporary condition, as in "She has me randy," or chronic, as in "You randy old muff-diver." The origin is Old French *a random,* rapidly, and English *at random,* unpredictable. *Rantum-scrantum,* from the same roots, was slang for fornication in the 17th and 18th Centuries.

RATTLESNAKE CANYON

The vagina; from the identification of the penis with a SNAKE.

REAM

To perform anal intercourse; also, for an employer or superior officer in the armed forces to deliver a prolonged and angry diatribe against a person (employee or military inferior) who dares not answer back.

RED EYE

A game popular since 1910, also called "mooning" or "throwing a gotcha," or a "flying I Gotcha," much beloved by drunken and rowdy teenagers. It consists of sticking one's bare backside out the window of a speeding car and shouting, "Red Eye!" (or "Gotcha!") to a startled passerby. Like GOOSING, this is a vanishing amusement, especially since police cars acquired two-way shortwave radios. In the West, oddly, "red eye" is also a shot of whiskey, straight. See EYE and compare the joke about the man with the glass eye who drops it in his whiskey glass while drunk and accidentally drinks it. Not remembering this in the morning, he buys a new artificial eye, but in a few weeks has pains in the upper colon. He goes to a doctor who gives him a proctological examination, but as the proctoscope enters the anus and the doctor bends to peer in, the man hears a gasp of astonishment. "What is it?" he asks nervously. The doctor stands up, grabs the patient's shoulders, turns him around and says sternly, "Listen, I can't help you if you don't trust me."

Compare also the story of the man describing such an examination: "He had his right hand on my shoulder and worked the machine with his left . . . No, he had his left hand on my shoulder . . . Come to think of it, the son of a bitch had both hands on my shoulders!"

Writing about the filming of *The Godfather, Time* magazine indicated that "mooning" has not entirely died out in America:

Brando gave and took advice freely, and encouraged backstage pranks that kept the atmosphere relaxed. A favorite was "Mooning," the infantile practice of dropping one's trousers to show bare buttocks. "My best moon was on Second Avenue," recalls James Caan. "Bob Duvall and I were in one car and Brando was in another, so we drove up beside him and I pulled down my pants and stuck my ass out the window. Brando fell down in the car with laughter."

See ASS.

RED-HOT MAMA

A "screaming" FAGGOT or "piss-elegant" faggot, the "campiest" homosexual in a crowd; a mocking use of the show-biz term for an aging actress or singer with continuing sex appeal. See CAMP.

RED-LIGHT DISTRICT

The section of town where brothels and/or streetwalking prostitutes are most common; from the old custom of keeping a red light outside a brothel as an advertisement, red being the traditional color of passion or impetuosity. See RED-HOT MAMA.

RELIGIOUS OBSERVANCES

Orgasms; usually used in the witticism explaining an irritable person: "He hasn't made his religious observances for the month."

RHINOCEROS

A "rhinoceros" is a man who is HUNG. "Rhino," in hobo slang, is money, and "rhinoceros horn" is a powder allegedly made from the phallic horn of this animal, which is sold to the gullible as the world's most powerful aphrodisiac (which it is not).

Prostitutes hold that men most enjoy FELLATIO when the woman times herself to the rhythm of the silent chant, "One big rhinoceros, two big rhinoceroses, three big rhinoceroses," and so on, each rhinoceros being a full insertion.

RIDING SAINT GEORGE

Intercourse with the woman on top; evidently part of some lost witticism about Saint George and the Dragon. (*Making a bishop* was the 18th Century term for the same art, and it is also sometimes called "the Roman position.")

Riding is always sexual, and Kinsey estimated that a large number of young boys have their first erection while riding in a car, bus or other fast vehicle; in earlier centuries, they probably experienced it first on horseback. *Diligence de Lyon* (literally, stagecoach to Lyon) is French WHORE's slang for CUNNILINGUS with the woman kneeling above the head of a supine man, which some males find more exciting than the more ordinary cunnilingus with the woman supine; the stagecoach, like Riding Saint George, suggests unconscious identification with those passive early-adolescent erections recorded by Kinsey. There is also a popular legend (*a la* the New York sewer alligators or the Second Oswald living in Zurich) about a man who persuaded his ladylove to FELLATE him while he drove his car at top speed. There was an accident, after which the doctors couldn't find his penis until they thought to look in her mouth. Ask five people and you'll find one who knew somebody who knew somebody who was at the scene of this accident, but you'll never find one who actually claims to have personally witnessed this fabled scene.

To "ride" a woman, from Shakespeare to the present, is an occasional metaphor for copulation, but to ride a man is to hound, nag, persecute and oppress him. The customary jokes about cowboys and their favorite mounts is not based on actuality (horses are very seldom chosen for SODOMY, according to Kinsey and his associates) but on the erotic sensations most people experience when horseback riding. This also accounts for the endless joking about the genitalia of these animals, which is parodied in the story of the child who, seeing a stallion with full erection, cries out, "What's that?" "It's nothing," the mother says evasively. The father beams. "She's spoiled," he says modestly. See the "flying fuck" under FLYING PHILADELPHIA FUCK.

RIM

To perform anal intercourse, also called a "rim job"; chronicled in *Naked Lunch:*

> "Darling, I want to rim you," she whispers.
> "No. Not now."
> "Please, I want to."
> "Well, all right. I'll go wash my ass."
> "No, I'll wash it."
> "Aw shucks, it ain't dirty."

(This seemingly impossible feat is accomplished with the aid of a dildo. The same fantasy appears in Gore Vidal's *Myra Breckenridge.)*

RIN-NO-TAM

A Japanese device for lonely and frustrated females, consisting of a small metal ball containing a minute amount of mercury. When set into the vagina, this ball will start moving about, due to the effect of body heat upon the mercury, and will continue rolling until the lady either collapses from the exhaustion of multiple orgasms or takes it out again This is a product of Akafune Drug Company, who have already brought joy to millions with such products as – well, to quote their current catalog:

> PLUSPIN CHOCLATE (MAKE HOT FOR WOMEN) . . .
> You shall, by using this medicine, drain the cup of pleasure to the dregs . . .

The Book of Forbidden Words

PLUSPIN (THE "HARD-ON" TABLETS) . . . Willi tills won derful drug, especially men over 40 years of age can obtain "Hard On" at any time as you want . . .

FINGER TICKLER. We have special shapes for one finger or fingers, and rub or tickle either clitoris or vagina. It shows the most pleasant effects. This can be used for keeping your prick erect for a long time, too.

GOLD MUSIC BALL . . . This is to be inserted in the female organ with your fingers. With every movement of it, an exciting sound will be heard to your excitement.

ROD

The penis; a simple euphemism quite old in England; in modern usage there might be a reference to *rod* meaning a GUN.

ROGER

To copulate with, as in "I'd like to roger her"; sometimes the penis itself, as in "I'd like to introduce her to Roger." It has been suggested that *roger her* means bull her, from the common use of Roger as a name for bulls.

It was once widely believed that women had an instinctive dislike for all forms of sex but conventional copulation. (In the Victorian Age, learned doctors claimed that the ladies disliked *that* too!) The opposite point of view is expressed in an anonymous folk poem:

> There once was a fellow named Fyfe
> Whose prudery ruined his life;
> He had an aversion

> To every perversion
> And only would roger his wife.
> At last the poor lady struck;
> She cursed and wept at her luck.
> "Where have you gotten us
> With all your monotonous
> Fuck after fuck after fuck?
> I once knew a lady named Lou
> (A saucy piece she was too!),
> After ten years of whoredom
> She died of sheer boredom
> When she married a jackass like you!"

And note the nice use of this name in the following limerick:

> There was an old maid from Cape Cod
> Who thought children were made by God,
> But it was not the Almighty
> Who lifted her nightie,
> It was Roger, the lodger, by God!

ROMAN CULTURE

Code in personal ads, signifying an interest in orgies, as in "Desires to communicate with young swingers devoted to Roman culture." Sexual intercourse with the woman on top is also called the Roman position. See ENGLISH CULTURE, FRENCH CULTURE, GREEK CULTURE, TURKISH CULTURE.

RUB

The technique of some frustrated males who relieve sexual tension by rubbing against female bodies in crowded places such as subways and buses. A "rub-off," on the other hand, is female MASTURBATION, perhaps by analogy with JACK OFF.

RUBBER

A CONDOM (male prophylactic).

RUG

The female pubic hair; but, also, in some circles, a man's WIG or toupee.

RUT

To copulate; from the rutting season (mating season) of animals, originally only of deer. The term is now used of human beings in a joking or insulting way: "Are you in rut again, you horny bastard?" Tennessee Williams used rut as a substitute for *fuck* to avoid censorship problems in *Cat on a Hot Tin Roof,* when Big Daddy, dying of cancer, is approached by a minister seeking contributions for new windows for his church: "Rut the Preacher! . . . Rut the cotton-pickin', chicken-eatin', memorial-stained-glass Preacher!"

SABER

The *penis.* See SWORD-SWALLOWER.

SANTA CLAUS

An old man keeping a young mistress; a SUGAR DADDY.

SAVING IT

Preserving one's virginity until marriage. See SIT ON IT.

SCARF

To FELLATE; not from the neck cloth, but from Old English *sceorfan,* to gnaw or bite, via the carpenter's "scarf" used in joining wood. Ed Sanders's short-lived newspaper, *The Dick,* startled New York's lower east side with its first issue's front-page headline: POET TED BERIGAN TEACHES PARROT TO SCARF COCK. Fortunately, Berigan was amused and did not sue for libel.

SCHMUCK

A Yiddish term that can mean either the penis or a foolish person; from German *schmuck,* a medal. It has been remarked that the English use of PRICK to mean a nasty or vicious person and the Yiddish use of *schmuck* to mean a simpleton indicate the differing phallic attitudes of the two cultures; a schmuck may get you in trouble through impetuosity or lack of foresight, but a prick deliberately sets out to SCREW you, FUCK you and SHAFT you. (New York lawyers' definition: a cosigner is a schmuck with a fountain pen.)

SCORE

To succeed in having coitus with a woman, as in "I scored with that chick twice"; from *running up a score,* keeping count of such conquests in competition with the known or imagined scores of other men. In the criminal professions, the "score" is the money taken (by force or fraud) from the victims, as in "The score in the bank heist was fifty Gs."

SCOTCH WARMING PAN

A woman, considered literally as an object, namely a bed-warmer.

SCRATCH

The vagina, as in "I'd like to get into her scratch"; also money, as in "Are you holding any scratch?" (But "Are you holding?" alone usually means "Do you have drugs in the house?") See ITCH, SPEND and SAVING IT.

SCREW

This word has a variety of meanings: as a noun, either sexual intercourse ("We had a good screw after dinner"), a prison guard or money; as a verb, to have sex with, to betray, injure, cheat or outwit, as in "I screwed him good on that deal."

The tool called a screw probably derives from Middle English *scrue* meaning to dig, since it "digs" into wood as one tightens it; but there might also be a link to *escroue,* Middle French for a female pig, since pigs dig into the earth with their snouts. (There is also an old superstition that boars have spiral-shaped penises.) *Screw* meaning intercourse, then, can come from the tool, or from the earlier *scrue* by the same process that made *plowing* a favorite sexual metaphor of poets. It's a mystery how *screw* (money) and *screw* (prison guard) evolved out of all this; psychoanalysis suggests obvious unconscious symbolism in the latter, involving homosexual sadism. *Screw* meaning to cheat derives from French *escroquer,* to swindle or cheat.

Screwy (insane) implies that sexual passion is a form of irrational compulsion; related terms are *screwed up,* meaning BALLED up or FUCKED up, and *screw off,* meaning get lost, disappear, go to hell, or FUCK OFF.

SCUM

The semen; from Middle English *scume,* the foam or cream on top of a liquid.

One would like to regard this as neutral and descriptive, but the truth is we have here some more Anglo-American sex hate. *Scum* was used by Marlowe in 1586 to mean worthless people, and the term *scum of the earth,* persons regarded as the lowest of the low, has been around almost as long. Hence, the scum on a liquid is now almost always considered something foul. The acronym SCUM (The Society for Cutting Up Men – an extremist women's lib group founded by Valerie Solanas, the lady who shot Andy Warhol) is linked with the idea that semen is revolting or offensive. This attitude is as widespread in the Christian world as the idea that the male ejaculate contains a magic Elixir of Life, a belief common in the pre-Christian world. Walter Winchell, a political sage of the 1940s, tried to popularize *scumunists* and *scummies* as nicknames for communists, and *scum bag,* lower-class slang for CONDOM, is used as a deadly insult by juveniles. (*You scum bag* will start a fight quicker than *you cocksucker.*) And finally: the homosexual-baiting joke about the QUEER who orders a second rice pudding in a restaurant. "Come again on the rice pudding," yells the waitress to the cook. "I knew it," the homo cries ecstatically, "I knew it, I knew it!"

SEAFOOD

Homosexual slang for sailors, as in "I think I'll go down to Sands Street and sample the sea food." The phrase *I like seafood* is a recognition signal used when one homosexual suspects another in a group of new acquaintances (when dining is being discussed, of course). If he is right, he gets a knowing stare in return; if he is wrong, the straights (heterosexuals) merely assume that the remark was meant in its literal sense. Curiously, this goes back to an earlier code, used during Prohibition, where *I want seafood* was a request for whiskey in a restaurant where government agents might be eavesdropping.

SEXPOT

An attractive female. This is a Hollywood ad-agency invention, based on *honeypot,* which means the vagina. See HONEY.

SHACK UP

To live together as man and wife without benefit of clergy. In Army slang, a "shack job" is the woman with whom one shacks up; both are from *shack,* cheap lodging.

SHAFT

The penis. When used as a verb, however, to "shaft" is to betray or injure a person, as in "He shafted all his partners and walked away with the profits." The movie, *Shaft,* depicted a tough black private eye named John Shaft who neatly embodied both meanings of this word. While in the service, John F. Kennedy became fond of the expression, *I've been shafted,* and his Boston accent made that sentence so unforgettable that he was nicknamed "Shafty" by the crew of his PT boat.

Shaft is also used to mean the clitoris in the book, *The Sensuous Man.* See VELVET BUZZ SAW.

SHAG

To copulate. This was popular in England from 1600 to 1900, and is now used in this country. H. L. Mencken notes that the contemporary English *shag,* a pipe tobacco, creates confusion in American visitors, especially those from the Midwest, when they see the London advertisement asking, "Are you looking for a good shag?"

SHAKE THE DEW OFF THE LILY

To urinate; used only of males, as in "There he was shaking the dew off his lily when his train came in." Variations are "He was watering the flowers," or "watering the old petunia."

SHEEP

Motorcyclists' slang for a young lady who willingly plays the starring role in a GANG BANG.

SHEIK

A Lothario, a seducer, a cocksman; either from *The Sheik,* a popular Valentino movie of the 1920s, or from *Sheiks,* a brand of CONDOMS.

SHIT

Excrement; from Old English *scoetan,* the source also of *shoot* and *scooter. Shit!* is a common expression of exasperation, similar to *hell!* or FUCK!

In American slang, when in trouble, you are "up shit creek" (sometimes "without a paddle"). If unpleasantly surprised, you might "shit green," blue, or even purple. A "shit-heel" and a "shit-head" are persons to be avoided, and one should never get on the authorities' "shit-list." On the other hand, to "shit in high cotton" is to obtain the ultimate in luxury, but this is an exception; more often one is "shit out of luck," or afflicted with the company of individuals who are "shit on wheels." If undecided or hesitant, you might be told to "shit or get off the pot." Most American of all, however, are the playful expressions *blivit* and *analocultectomy.* The former is defined as "ten pounds of shit in a five-pound bag," a perfect symbol of a restricted, uptight, constipated culture. The latter is highbrow humor and explained as "an operation on the back of the eye, in which the surgeon enters through the anus, to correct the shitty outlook on life that some people have."

The expression *when the shit hits the fan* (meaning when the trouble starts) merits a retelling of the old joke from which it derives. This yarn has it that a man in a saloon goes upstairs to the bathroom and finds it locked. In desperation, he looks around and sees a hole in the floor, where he quickly empties his bowels. Strolling back downstairs, he finds that the barroom, which had previously been crowded, is now empty except for the bartender, who is sweeping the floor. "Where did everybody go?" he asks. The bartender replies sourly, "Where were you when the shit hit the fan?"

Shit meaning narcotics, as in "What do you need that shit for?" has been around since the 1920s, but didn't achieve general public usage until it was used in Shirley Clarke's 1962 film, *The Connection,* which was banned in several states because the junkies in it, moaning that the pusher was late with the shit, were thought to be endangering public health and welfare by some form of verbal contagion. Curiously, this use of *shit* is selective; it means either addictive heroin or nonaddictive marijuana, but is hardly ever used for cocaine, amphetamines, barbiturates or LSD.

In the Fugs' album, *It Crawled Into My Hand, Honest,* is a song called "Wide Wide River." Ed Sanders, whose achievements are noted often in these pages, recites a "talking blues" about the gross dishonesty of recent Democratic and Republican presidents, while behind him the group sings mournfully:

> River of shit,
> River of shit,
> For twenty long years
> We've been swimming in it.

> Big brown river,
> River of shit . . .

And finally, a clever graffito often seen in public bathrooms:

> He who writes upon the walls
> Rolls his shit into little balls.
> He who reads these words of wit
> Eats those little balls of shit.

See CRAP.

SHIT-AND-PISS QUEEN

One who obtains sexual gratification from urine and feces, technically known as a coprophile. Some Paris whorehouses provide special rooms (in the cellar, for obvious and symbolic reasons) to gratify this fetish. People who are fond of the triple-barreled expletive *Shit, piss and corruption!* may be suspected of an unconscious drive in this direction, at least by psychoanalysts, but, more generously, we might guess that they are merely looking for an intensifier of the old-fashioned Victorian *Damn, blast and thunder!*

SHIT ON A SHINGLE

Army slang for chipped beef on toast; often abbreviated to S.O.S. and now common in civilian institutional slang, especially college cafeterias.

SHIT SHOOT

The anus; a deliberately offensive expression used to emphasize anger or contempt, as in "Get your mind out of the shit shoot and do something positive."

SHOOT

To have an orgasm; sometimes expanded to *shoot one's wad, shoot one's load, shoot one's* NUTS. As an exclamation, *shoot* is a seemingly meaningless oath, probably a last-minute substitute for *shit*.

SHOOT BLANKS

To copulate without orgasm or ejaculation; orgastic impotence as distinguished from erectile impotence. Also refers to male sterility.

SHORT ARM

The penis. A short-arm inspection is an examination for venereal disease in the Army. Compare with MIDDLE LEG.

SHORT HAIRS

The pubic hairs, as in "She has him by the short hairs" (he's trapped, he can't escape). More graphic alternatives are "She has him by the balls," or by "the short and curly."

SIFF

Syphilis, as used by Calder Willingham in *End us a Man:* "Why don't you tell us about the time you got siff from your nigger maid?" Also used in the world's most revolting limerick:

> There was a young lawyer of note
> Who thought he had siff of the throat,
> "But it wasn't a gal,"
> He confessed to a pal,
> "I got it by blowing a goat!"

SINK THE SOLDIER
To insert the penis.

SISTER BOY
A male homosexual, as in "Go away, sister boy." This is the origin of *sissie,* which in England has the same meaning but in America is used only by small boys and means a coward. See CAMP, which originally meant to flee from battle.

SIT ON IT
To preserve virginity; usually in the contemptuous question to a young woman, "Are you going to sit on it forever?"

SIT ON ONE'S FACE
To perform CUNNILINGUS on a woman is sometimes called letting her sit on your face. The following account from Hunter Thompson's *Hell's Angels* is interesting in this connection:

> A Hell's Angel who lived on Thirty-Seventh Street in Sacramento was continually being complained about for making suggestive comments to women who passed by his house . . ."Let's make it, baby" or "Hey, beautiful, come sit on Papa's face." A patrolman, checking on one of these complaints, first threatened the outlaw with jail and then asked him contemptuously if he couldn't find "something better to do." The Angel thought for a moment and then replied, "Not unless it was to be fucking a cop."

See *Diligence de Lyon* under RIDING SAINT GEORGE.

SIXTY-NINE

Mutual oragenitalism; a visual pun on the shape of the number 69. Some sexologists have suspected a similar reference in the origin of the astrological symbol of Cancer and the Chinese yinyang. Certainly, the act was held in great veneration by many of the ancients, and the Egyptians pictured the sky goddess, Nuit, her body covering the earth, engaged in perpetual sixty-nining with the sea god, Shu.

SKANKY

Black slang used for purposes of insult, it implies that the person so addressed is a PIMP, a WHORE, or in some way connected with the flesh industry; for example, "Shut your mouth, you no-account, skanky, low-life mammy-jammer."

SKIN FLICK

A pornographic movie.

SKIN FLUTE

The penis; also called the *silent flute* in 17th 18th Century slang. *Playing the skin flute* is old-fashioned homosexual slang for FELLATIO; it also means MASTURBATION in a schoolboy code on the Eastern seaboard.

SKINNY DIPPING

Swimming in the nude, also called swimming B.A. See IN THE ALTOGETHER and BIRTHDAY SUIT.

SKIRT

A woman, usually one who is young and attractive; 1920s slang, still occasionally heard.

SKY-CLAD

Naked, not clad at all; a term of unknown history used by surviving witch cults in England and America, who are "sky-clad" during their rites, as shown (quite accurately) in Roman Polanski's film, *Rosemary's Baby*, and also in his version of *Macbeth*. Compare ANGEL'S SUIT.

SLAUGHTERHOUSE

A whorehouse. Readers of Freud and De Sade might suspect that this term indicates unwholesome unconscious attitudes.

SLAVE

The masochistic partner in a sadomasochistic relationship.

SLEEP TOGETHER (or SLEEP WITH)

To copulate; an inept euphemism, as pointed out by numerous wits who have remarked that "Sleep together was the only thing we didn't do."

SLICE

An intrigue with a married woman, as in "Everybody in town has had a slice of her." Recorded nearly 200 years ago (by Grose); the origin is probably the old proverb that "a slice off a cut loaf is not missed." This may explain the odd imagery in *piece, piece of ass, piece of tail*.

SLIP IT TO HER

To engage in sexual intercourse, as in "Man, I'd like to slip it to that chick."

SLIT (or SLOT)

The vulva and vagina, by visual metaphor.

SLOPPY SECONDS

A man who HAS a woman immediately after she has had another man is said to get "sloppy seconds"; this occurs in brothels and in GANG BANGS. See also BUTTERED BUNS and WET DECKS.

SLUT

An insulting word for a woman, implying that she is immoral and revolting; from Middle English *slutte,* a WHORE, and older *sluched,* muddy or dirty. Similar expressions, implying both moral laxity and unattractiveness, are HEAVY CRUISER, HARD LEG, TANK and DOG.

S-M

Code in personal ads, meaning sadomasochism, as in the ad: "I want to observe wild S-M action. Write Box . . ." Popular confusion about this subject is immortalized in the two-liner:

> MASOCHIST: Beat me, whip me, humiliate me!
> SADIST: No, I won't.

Real-life sadists are not so subtle, however, and are glad to oblige.

SMACK

To kiss; from standard English *smack,* to purse the lips in pleasure (not to be confused with the other *smack,* meaning to hit).

Among heroin addicts, *smack* or, sometimes,

smeck, means heroin. This tends to substantiate the psychoanalytical theory that drug addiction is related to oral frustrations in infancy.

SMOKE

To FELLATE. In recent slang, a "smoke" was a black man, evidently from the alleged invisibility of Negroes in the dark, and is comparable to *spook,* another racist slur. A charming use of this occurs in the Broadway musical, *Hair,* where a protestor carries a sign proclaiming: SMOKEY THE NIGGER SAYS ONLY YOU CAN STOP GHETTO FIRES. *Holy smoke,* however, is neither a religious COCKSUCKER nor a pious Negro, but a variation of *Holy Ghost.* Oaths against this member of the trinity are rare because of the well-known passage in Matthew informing us that " . . . every kind of sin and blasphemy shall be forgiven to men; but the blasphemy against the Spirit will not be forgiven . . . either in this world or the world to come." A long heretical tradition, via the Gnostics, Alchemists and Rosicrucians, holds that the Holy Ghost is the semen, which makes the use of *smoke* for fellatio an especially interesting metaphor. Some cynics refer to the Trinity as "Pops, J.C. and Smokey."

SMOOCH

To NECK or PET; to engage in sexual foreplay; or sometimes merely to kiss. The origin is probably German *smauchen,* to smoke, with an implication of "getting steamed up."

SMUT

A term usually applied to pornographic material; deriving from the Middle English *smotten* and Middle German *smutzen,* meaning to stain or blacken. It is also related to *smudge,* and is a synonym for *soot.* Staining or soiling, of course, is the sin for which some unfortunate infants are punished during toilet training. Even though the word *smut* has very little to do with sex, censors and other critics consistently apply the term to sexual material they deem unacceptable. An example: A typical issue of *National Decency Reporter,* official organ of the Citizens for Decent Literature, had these headlines: "Smut Dealers Blamed in S.F. Tourist Slump"; "Smut is Harmful"; "Vatican Assails Smut."

L. L. White, in *The Next Development in Man,* points out that "civilized" (which means literally city-fied) disgust with sex may well be a result of the pre-plumbing period of city life, when sanitation and waste-disposal problems, combined with a lack of adequate washing facilities, were severe. With personal cleanliness in overcrowded conditions an impossibility, aversion to sex could result.

SNAFU

Army slang meaning Situation Normal: All Fucked Up. This was coined by some anonymous wit during the Second World War, and several related terms quickly came along in its wake, including *fubar* (*f*ucked *u*p *b*eyond *a*ll *r*ecognition); *tarfu* (*t*hings *a*re *r*eally *f*ucked *u*p); *cabfu* (*c*ombined *A*merican-*B*ritish *f*uck-*u*p); *commfu* (*c*omplete *u*tter *m*agnificent *m*ilitary *f*uck-*u*p), *janfu* (*j*oint *A*rmy-*N*avy *f*uck-*u*p); and *susfu* (*s*ituation *u*nchanged: *s*till *f*ucked *u*p). *Snafu* has proven the most durable of these expressions.

SNAKE

The penis. In some parts of the country one may also hear quasi-humorous variations, such as *snake venom* (semen), or *snake pit* (the vagina).

SNAPPER

A WHORE who is accomplished at performing the CLEOPATRA.

SNAPPING PUSSY

A talented vagina, capable of performing the CLEOPATRA (voluntary muscular contraction around the penis), as in "That gal has a real snapping pussy." An interesting variation of this occurs in *Blue Movie:*

> Angie's vage, "dry as a bone" though it may have been, had begun sweetening noticeably at the exact introduction of Boris' middle finger – which he then, for want of better, proceeded to agitate gently . . . and the girl, still gazing up at him with a nightmare grimace of hilarity, had responded by contracting her sphincter muscle with increasing speed and severity.
>
> "Say," said Boris, somewhat nonplussed by these unexpected developments on set, "that's uh, well, that's uh, some *control* you've got there."
>
> . . . she said, "You know what they call that back in Texas? . . . *Snapping-turtle* pussy."

See BITE.

SNATCH

The vagina. In 1969 a Women's Liberation demonstrator sported a placard stating, "No more bullshit up my snatch!"

SODOMY

The traditional name for male homosexuality, based on the Old Testament story of Sodom, which was destroyed because of the GAY ways of its men. (The word homosexual is recent, being first proposed in a medical journal of 1858.) In the statutes of some American states, however, sodomy is defined so as to include female homosexuality and, in fact, virtually any noncoital sex act, even those consentingly performed between a married couple. Worse yet, these laws are in many cases rather vaguely and evasively written due to the prudery of their authors, so that nobody is sure what is and is not sodomy in some states (one lawyer has sarcastically commented that any husband who kisses his wife below the neck might be in trouble). Some states, even more vaguely and hence more inclusively, prohibit "the crime against nature" without defining it. The antipollution people are going to take advantage of those laws some day.

The most famous use (or misuse) of the word *sodomist* in recent times inspired the Oscar Wilde-Marquis of Queensborough lawsuit. Queensborough, who wrote the rules that still govern boxing, was unpleasantly suspicious about the relationship between Wilde and his son, Lord Alfred Douglas, fearing that they loved each other not only dearly but somewhat QUEERLY. As an act of spite, he sent stinkweed, instead of the traditional flowers, to Wilde's club on the night of the opening of Wilde's play, *The Importance of Being Ernest.* The weeds bore a card saying, "To Mr. Oscar Wilde, posing as somdomist," which was seen by every member of the club. (The words *posing as* were inserted on advice of counsel, but the spelling "somdomist" was apparently Queensborough's own.) Wilde sued for libel and lost; the Crown then brought him to trial for sodomy on the basis of evidence produced in the first trial, but this led to a mistrial. Wilde was immediately rearrested and tried again; this time he was convicted, jailed, disgraced and ruined.

The most famous epic of sodomy in English is certainly the drama, *Sodom,* by "the E. of R." surreptitiously printed in London in 1684. The mysterious "E. of R." appears to be John Wilmott, the Earl of Rochester – the disguise was thin. Oddly, he frankly acknowledged authorship of various other bawdy works, but attempted to disown this one. The characters include such curiously named persons as Bolloxinion, King of Sodom; Cuntigratia, Queen; Swivia, Princess; Buggeranthos, General of the Army; Fuckadilla, Cunticula and Clitoris, Maids of Honor; Virtuoso, dildo maker to the royal family. The opening speech by Bolloxinion sets the tone of the whole play:

> . . . my nation shall be free,
> My pintle only shall my sceptre be,
> My laws shall act more pleasure than command
> And with my prick I'll govern all the land.
> To Buggeranthos let this charge be given
> And let them bugger all things under heaven.

The theme is not immediately pursued, and in the second scene we find Queen Cuntigratia planning an adultery with her maids of honor:

> *Officina*: Buggeranthos to a hair your cunt would rick.
> *Cuntigratia*: The general! Oh, I long to see his prick.
> They say he fucks all women to a trance.
> *Fuckadilla:* Madam, you'll say so when you

see his lance.
Cuntigratia: With open cunt then swift to him
I'll fly,
I'll hug and kiss, and bear up, till I die.

The rest of the play finally takes up the plot hinted at in the first scene, as the men all turn to homosexuality, and the women, in desperation, resort to various remedies, one seeking consolation with an elephant. King Bolloxinion, maddened with pride and lust, finally abandons mankind as he had previously abandoned womankind. He seeks higher things:

> *Bolloxinion:* I'll then invade and bugger all the Gods
> And drain the spring of their immortal code,
> Then make them rub their arses till they cry,
> "You've frigged us out of immortality!"

The biblical "fire and brimstone" follows quickly upon this blasphemy and all Sodom is destroyed.

SOUL KISS

An open-mouthed kiss; also called a "French kiss."

SPANISH FLY

Dust made by crushing the green blister beetle *(lyttu vesicatoria,* or *cantharides)*, alleged to be an aphrodisiac. Actually, in small doses, this merely irritates the urethral tract of the male and causes an erection that is painful rather than pleasant; in the female, it causes inflammation and burning sensations. In large doses, the result can be death. Other so-called aphrodisiacs have proven equally useless, except perhaps the famous "red powder" mentioned in Chinese erotic writings. According to Edwardes and Masters in *The Cradle of*

Erotica, this powder consists of cinnamon, mustard, pepper, ginger "and other irritating substances." Rubbed on the wet penis it reputedly causes a swelling of the vaginal walls, with corresponding intensification of mutual pleasure, creating an orgasm that is said to be so powerful that pain and pleasure are equally mingled. This would seem ideal for sadomasochist lovers. The Japanese call it *gokuraku-ojo,* "sweet death."

SPEND

To have an orgasm. This is virtually extinct today, but was standard usage for several centuries and still pops up occasionally. It mirrored the once widely believed theological-medical doctrine that each orgasm reduced one's vital energy and brought one closer to the grave. Moses Maimonides, for instance, wrote in the 11th Century that of 1000 premature deaths, only one was caused by other diseases and 999 by excessive sexual indulgence.

A similar attitude is reflected in the cynical jest that if a married couple place a bean in a jar each time they have intercourse during the first year of wedlock, and then take a bean out every time they copulate thereafter, the jar will never empty.

And there is the joke about the father who catches his son MASTURBATING and warns him that if he "wastes his seed" this way he will have none left when he marries and wants children. "Oh, that's no sweat," the boy says, "I've got ten Coke-bottlesful down in the cellar!"

In our own time, this economic approach to sex has been revived with a twist by Freudian revisionist Wilhelm Reich, who argued that orgasm is the "regulator" of the body's energy supply. According to Reich's "sex-economy" (the label is his own), the bioenergy needs to be discharged periodically in sexual climax, and, lacking this, the excess produces all the symptoms that are categorized as neurotic, psychotic or psychosomatic. One wit has suggested that the word *spendthrift* (a person who spends money lavishly) be applied to a woman who COMES several times during one erection – namely, a woman who makes thrifty use of the male's spend, while spending lavishly herself.

SPITTING CHICLETS

An insult implying that the person thus described is a cocksucker, as in "You been spitting chiclets again?" – a reference to the supposed resemblance between sperm and the white-coated chewing gum.

SPORTING HOUSE

A whorehouse. *Sporting woman* is old slang for a WHORE, but *sport,* in waitress's slang – "Got a sport out here" – means a customer rash enough to order corned-beef hash or similar ground-meat dishes.

SPREADING

Said of a woman, to signify that she has been having intercourse with more than one man: "She's been spreading for the whole town," or "She's been spreading, but only twice; once for the Army and once for the Navy."

SPREAD SHOT

A porno photograph in which the model's legs are spread to give the maximum visibility to her genitalia, sometimes aided by her hands pulling apart the outer lips; also called a split BEAVER shot. Ed Sanders's record, *Sanders Truckstop,* includes a tragic ballad about a man who is showing off his personal collection of spread shots to a friend in a bar when the friend's wife suddenly appears in one of them, with unhappy results all around.

STAND-UP JOB

A WHORE who provides a quick and inexpensive FUCK standing up in an alley or against a tree in a park; or the act itself. A "threepenny upright" is the recent English equivalent.

STARK NAKED

Totally nude; not from modern *stark,* unornamented, but from Middle English *start* or *stert,* a bird's tail. Stark naked, then, means tail-naked, or, as children say, "bare-ass naked."

STAVING CHAIN

The penis; from the logging industry in which the staving chain holds the logs being floated downriver This metaphor is memorably used in a 1920s blues song: "Pick it up and shake it/Life's sweet staving chain."

STEERER

A person who directs people to a brothel and receives a small commission; taxi drivers, bellhops and policemen sometimes supplement their incomes in this manner.

STERN JOB

Anal intercourse; adapted from BLOW JOB.

STICK

As a noun, the penis. Another *stick,* in England, is a stiff and stodgy person, related to a "wooden" performance in the theatre, a "stiff" grin, "unbending" authority. As a verb, one of its meanings is to FUCK, said by males, as in "I'd like to stick that chick."

Stick it up your ass is an insult and is often used in connection with an object of disdain, as in, "Why don't you take that shitty book and stick it up your ass?" This is sometimes followed by "Then you'll have it forever." Expurgated versions are: *stick it; take it and stick it; stick it in your ear; roll it into a cone-shape and stick it where it'll fit;* and *stick it where the moon doesn't shine.* Dick Cavett said the latter to Norman Mailer on his TV show, and Mailer replied by asking if Cavett had just invented the phrase or had been saving it for years, awaiting the proper occasion to use it. Cavett answered, "Is it possible, Norman, that you don't recognize a quote from Tolstoy?" (It is actually an old Russian idiom.)

STORM

An emotional cataclysm of one sort or another. To "work up a storm" is to quarrel; to "fuck up a storm" is to have very satisfactory coitus, and is comparable to Norman Mailer's "I slipped her a fuck the equivalent of a ten-round fight." Tempest Storm is a successful stripteaser who has been around since the 1940s. Gale Storm was an actress who had a brief career in the 1940s, only to disappear and then return on the Late Late Show and in a graffito saying, "Gale Storm lives."

STRAWBERRY SUCKLE

A technique of breast stimulation in which the man circles the lady's nipples with his tongue with increasingly rapid motions, alternating from breast to breast. First printed by the anonymous author of *The Sensuous Man.*

STRIKE OUT

To be unsuccessful at persuading a lady to enjoy your sexual ardors. Some women can make these rejections almost painless; others enjoy humiliating the man; but nobody quite equals the brutality of the heroine of William Bradford Huie's novel, *Mud on the Stars,* who gets rid of unwanted suitors by handing them five dollars and directing them to the town whorehouse.

STUD

A male who has demonstrated uncommon virility; a cocksman; from *stud horse,* a stallion kept to sire other horses; this is almost a redundancy, since the origin was Middle English *stede,* cognate with modern *steed.* Ghetto speech has an adverbial form, *studly,* as in "He's a studly old dude."

Studs came to mean steel nuts in a reverse process to the transfer of NUTS to mean testicles. James T. Farrell's hero, Studs Lonigan, earned that nickname by demonstrating his courage; "Iron Balls" is another title sometimes bestowed on the uncommonly brave.

SUCK

As a verb, to perform fellatio or cunnilingus. A "suck" (noun), or "suck-ass," is a flattering opportunist, even worse than an ass-kisser. This word, as a verb, became a political term in the 1960s and one reads graffiti stating that "Pentagon sucks, Johnson sucks, Amerika sucks," leading finally to such parodies as "Dracula sucks" and "Babies suck." The latest from Vietnam is "The Army is like a joint – the more you suck, the higher you get."

The "sucker" (victim) in a financial swindle is so named in reference to his infantile gullibility – he is like a babe at the breast (compare to *taking candy from a baby,* an easy theft). Professionals, incidentally, never use *sucker;* they refer to that party in the transaction as the "mark," the "savage," or, in an elegant mood, "Mr. Savage."

Whether or not Shakespeare was homosexual, he had an oral approach to sex, similar to that which we have found in GAY slang. When Ophelia speaks of "sucking the honey of his vows," she is using imagery that occurs again and again, not only in the plays but in the sonnets; Shakespeare always thinks of sex in terms of food ("If music be the *food* of love, play on" is the first line of *Twelfth Night,* for instance). His influence on popular speech through the touring Shakespeare companies of the last century probably has a great deal to do with the oral metaphors that appear in heterosexual lovemaking, such as *honey, sugar, cupcake, sweetie-pie. Go suck a lemon,* once a favorite exclamation of "polite" young ladies, got by only because, in this confectionary semantic environment, people could miss, or pretend to miss, its close brush with an explicit sexual reference. So, too, with the schoolgirl phrases *oh, fudge* and *oh, sugar.*

Behind the use of the word *suck* is the mood of oral sadism, the great unconscious theme in almost all horror films. The graffito saying "Dracula sucks" brought this forward humorously, and the Ernest Jones classic, *Nightmare, Witches and Devils,* had explored it psychodynamically long before. The wolfman is a similar oral nightmare, literally acting out the metaphor we all use when talking of "eating a pussy" or having a "box lunch at the Y" or speaking of the vulva as HAIR PIE or the FURBURGER. Jack the Ripper literally ate the genitalia of the women he killed, or at least claimed this in his famous letter to Scotland Yard. And, in moments of passion, almost everyone has said, "I could eat you all up."

SUGAR DADDY

An old man who keeps a mistress. It may sound cynical but this does not appear to come from *sugar,* meaning darling or lover, but from the underworld *sugar,* money.

SWEET ASS

Female passion, as in *She has the sweet ass for him.* Also a frequent substitute for *life,* in the expression *You bet your life,* as in "You bet your sweet ass, I will!"

SWINGERS

In personal ads, code for those who are exclusively interested in group sex or orgies. In standard speech, persons who are relatively free of the more idiotic taboos of the past.

Old English *swingan,* to beat with a whip, gave birth to *swing,* to move rhythmically; hence, swingers are people who regard life as a ball. The earliest use antedates "swing" music by 250 years; it appears in the Earl of Rochester's "Signor Dildo," 1678:

> The Countess of Falmouth of whom people tell
> Her footmen wore shirts of a guinea an ell
> Might save that expense if she did know
> How lusty a Swinger is Signor Dildo.

SWISH

A very effeminate male homosexual; from *swash,* as in *swashbuckler,* one who dresses in fine silks; the word is echoic of the sound such clothes make as the wearer moves.

SWITCH HITTER

A bisexual; from baseball where a "switch hitter" is a player who can bat left-handed or right-handed. A "switch club" is a heterosexual group in which males exchange wives for the evening, sometimes by throwing keys in a pile, each man taking the woman who owns the key he picked. Cynics suspect that the advertising slogan "*I'd rather fight than switch*" is a deliberate pun on one or both of these terms.

SWORD-SWALLOWER

A homosexual; by visual metaphor. See SABER.

TALLYWAGGER (or TALLYWHACKER)

The penis. The original is tallywagger, *tallywhacker* being a late corruption, perhaps influenced by WHACK OFF. This originated in the 17th Century, and the roots appear to be *tally,* a staff on which marks are made to measure time passed or money paid (from Middle English *tayl,* modern *tail*) plus *wag,* to wave or wobble. Thus, a tallywagger is a staff that waves or wobbles; as in the limerick:

> When a lovely young lady from Exeter
> Went abroad, all the men craned their necks at 'er.
> One, particularly brave,
> Had the courage to wave
> The visible sign of his sex at 'er.

TART

A prostitute. Originally, this was an endearment relating to *tart,* the pastry, and the general oral approach to sex suggested in *honey, sugar, cupcake* and similar terms of affection. As late as 1903, Farmer & Henley, in

Slang and its Analogues, defined *tart* as "a girl, chaste or not . . . a mistress." The connotation of whorishness came in around the First World War. An alternative etymology suggests a humorous and affectionate distortion of *sweetheart* to *sweet tart.*

TEAR OFF A PIECE

To have intercourse, as in "We were in the back seat tearing off a piece." The origin is suggested in PIECE OF ASS and SLICE, and the connotation is distinctly sadistic. William S. Burroughs, in his maniacally deadpan way, exposes the mood behind these phrases in a parable in *Naked Lunch,* in which a father takes his teen-age son to a whorehouse "to get his first piece of ass"; the boy quite literally slices a hunk off the prostitute's buttocks.

TEAROOM

Homosexual slang for the public lavatory. *Tearoom trade:* male prostitutes who hang around lavatories waiting for customers. A "tearoom queen" is a homosexual who CRUISES the public lavatories.

The identification of urine with tea goes back to the 18th Century when a chamber pot was called a "tea-voider," but an alternate etymology suggests that *tearoom* should actually be *T-room,* an abbreviation of *toilet room.* See also BOSTON TEA PARTY and WATER SPORTS.

TEASER (or TEASE)

A girl who promises much more than she delivers; this is a polite contraction of COCKTEASER. If such women are sadists, it must be admitted that many men are masochists, as illustrated by the popularity of the striptease. Then too, as Ring Lardner brilliantly observed, "Some like 'em cold."

Note the bitter masculine humor of the story about the fellow seen purchasing some odd items in a hardware store on his wedding morn: red paint, blue paint, a paintbrush and a hammer. A friend asks, "What are you planning to use that stuff for?" The answer: "She claims to be a virgin and has been holding out until we're married. I'm going to paint one ball red and the other blue and, tonight, if she blurts out, 'That's the oddest pair of balls I ever saw,' I'll hit her on the head with the hammer!"

TENT

Black and rural white slang for the bulge in a man's trousers caused by an erection, as in "You could tell she'd walked past – by the tents all the dudes on the street were sporting."

THREE-DOLLAR BILL

A homosexual; from the catchphrase *Queer as a three-dollar bill.* See QUEER.

THREE-WAY

Slang for a prolonged sex session involving vaginal, oral and anal copulation, as in "Me and that chick had a three-way that night." *Three-way broad* and *three-way frail* were 1930s expressions for lusty ladies inclined toward such sports. See NUMBERS GAME.

TIJUANA BIBLE

A book of pornographic photographs; from the fact that Tijuana is a city where such literature is readily available. "Hey, meestair, you wan' my mother? She cherry," is a frequently heard cry there. In one bar, the stripteasers walk from table top to table top being

CUNNILINGED by the audience, and CIRCUSES in which women perform with RANDY ponies are not unknown.

TIME

To "make time" with a woman is to successfully cajole her into a sexual affair. "Two-timing" is carrying on two affairs simultaneously, with neither party knowing about the other.

TIT FUCK

Insertion of the penis between a lady's breasts. Some women are quite skilled at pressing the breasts very tightly together to make this more enjoyable for the male, and the most enjoyable form of FELLATIO involves a simultaneous tit fuck and BLOW job.

TITS

The female breasts, as in "Dig the tits on that chick!" A "tit lottery," in journalists' slang, is a beauty contest. *(Tit for tat,* however, is a corruption of *tip for tap,* meaning blow for blow.)

The late Lenny Bruce once suggested that "Tits and Ass" would be the most accurate advertisement for most night-club acts, but this sane suggestion has not yet been adopted by the club owners. An earlier attempt at such honesty-in-advertising involved the eccentric millionaire Howard Hughes who in 1942 produced a film called *The Outlaw* chiefly notable for the frontal elevation of its leading lady, Jane Russell. This was advertised in Los Angeles by a skywriting airplane which formed the words *the outlaw* and then simply added two enormous circles with a dot in each. The film was banned from the American market for 12 years, although its chief offense was a special brassiere, allegedly designed by Hughes himself, which caused Miss Russell's breasts to bounce every time she moved.

T.L.
An ass-licker; from Yiddish *tuchus leker.*

TOMATO
A 1920s slang for an attractive young woman. When Ralph Ginzburg began publishing *Avant Garde* magazine, rival editor Paul Krassner asked sardonically, "How *avant garde* is a man who still calls women 'tomatoes.'?"

TOMCATTING
Seeking sexual adventure, as in "He's been out tomcatting every night this month." See CAT.

TONG
The penis; immortalized in the folk song, "Mr. Wong Has the Biggest Tong in Chinatown."

TOOL
The penis. *Tool check* is Army slang for a V.D. examination, or SHORT ARM inspection. A clever personal ad: "Gals: 34-year-old white carpenter with 10-inch working tool seeks generous women divorcees and cheaters who would like to do their own thing but never had the chance. Age no barrier. Satisfaction and discretion guaranteed. Generous women only."

TORCH JOB
An enema with Vicks Vaporub or Ben-Gay, one of the

odd pleasures for which masochists sometimes hire prostitutes. Recent underground ads indicate that there is now an "at-home-enema-on-call" service for enema freaks: "If giving or receiving enemas is your thing, there is now a very discreet enema service to cater to your desires at your residence or hotel. Serving male and female . . ."

There seems to be a rising interest in enemas as a sex kick, and the practice has already produced a criminal cleverly dubbed the "Enema Bandit" by newspapers. It seems that around a large midwestern university a man with a gun, a gym bag and a ski mask has been breaking into women's apartments, tying his victims with bedsheet strips and then proceeding to give them enemas. Police claimed at least 13 such enema rapes in one year.

TOUCH

Sexual intercourse; used by Joyce in *Ulysses:* "Give me a touch, Poldy. God, I'm dying for it." *Touchy* means nervous or irritable (see BLUE BALLS and GREEN SICKNESS); *Can I touch you?* or *Can I put the touch on you?* are requests to borrow money; and *touched in the head* means insane. The triple meaning here (sex-money-insanity) also appears in SCREW and its derivatives.

TOUGH SHIT

An ironic expression, sometimes sympathetic and sometimes hostile, used after somebody has recounted all the injustices of which he is the victim: "That's tough shit, fellow (or, sometimes, "tough titty"). In the Army, a complainer may be told to take his T.S. chit (tough-shit card) to the chaplain and have it punched. Similar, but more hostile, is the less vulgar "If you're looking for sympathy, try *S* in the dictionary."

TOWN BIKE

An insulting term for a woman, implying that she is a WHORE or COMMON carrier.

TRADE

Male prostitutes who service homosexuals for money while claiming to be straight (heterosexual) themselves; psychiatrists tend to doubt this claim. *Rough trade,* however, means virile-looking lower-class males (usually in construction, trucking or similar industries) to whom homosexuals are often attracted, as in the ad: "Masculine ex-sailor desires correspondence to masculine males such as construction workers, truck drivers, etc. . . . See SEAFOOD.

TRAMP

A WHORE; either from standard English *tramp,* a vagabond, or from *tramping,* walking, with a reference to the old euphemism *streetwalker.* For some reason the Hays Office, which enforced Roman Catholic censorship on American movies in the 1930s and 1940s, found this word less objectionable than other names for sporting women, and it pops up monotonously on the old Bette Davis, Ginger Rogers and Joan Crawford flicks on late-late TV. The invaluable Lenny Bruce offered the inevitable objection: "What do you mean, she's a tramp? She goes out in the woods and cooks mickies?" (Mickies: slang for potatoes.)

TRIANGLE

In ordinary speech, two people jealously in love with a third, or one person in love with another person who's in love with a third; also called the "eternal triangle" in the argot of commercial writers. In the GAY world, a triangle is an arrangement where a bisexual manages to keep two lovers of opposite sexes in one establishment without conflict, a feat attempted in the film, *Sunday, Bloody Sunday*. The French *ménage à trois* is an arrangement whereby a man lives with two women without their fighting (although the Chinese, more pessimistic than the Gauls, make their idiogram for *trouble* out of pictograms showing two women under one roof), and can also refer to a domestic situation in which two men share one woman.

TRIBADE

A female homosexual; from Greek *tribein,* to RUB. This word was once more common than LESBIAN, although it properly refers to only those lesbians who prefer to achieve orgasm through imitation heterosexual intercourse involving mutual clitoral stimulation.

TRICK

In WHORES' slang, either a customer or an act of copulation; to "turn a trick" is to service a client. Shakespeare cynically calls orgasm "the momentary trick" in *Measure for Measure.*

In the GAY world, "trick day" is the weekly, monthly or yearly occasion on which two partners give each other permission to go cruising for a one-night stand.

TRICK BABY

A child born to a prostitute, presumably fathered by one

of her customers or TRICKS. This is black slang and often used as an insult, in the manner of *son-of-a-bitch,* as in "Don't mess with me, you trick baby."

TURD

The singular of the collective noun SHIT; used by Chaucer circa 1300, "Your dratted rhyming is not worth a turd." In 1692, refusing to involve himself in the Titus Oates hysteria, King Charles II said, "The more you stir a turd, the more it stinks." The following limerick puns on the word:

> There was a young man named Clyde
> Who fell through an outhouse and died.
> Likewise his brother,
> He fell through another,
> And now they're interred side by side.

TURKISH CULTURE

Code in personal ads. "Interested in Turkish culture" means interested in anal intercourse. See ENGLISH CULTURE, GREEK CULTURE, ROMAN CULTURE, FRENCH CULTURE.

TV

Code for transvestites. One such person, advertising in a sex magazine, demonstrated a gourmet attitude: "Uninhibited bondage, loving 'French' TV loves to eat and drink all night long while firmly held between well-built white female's tasty smooth thighs, bald and bushy, 18-35, unattached and married, straight and lesbian . . ."

TWAT

The vulva. Of obscure origin, *twat* dates back to at least 1719 when it appeared in the ditty, "A Cellar at Sodom":

> In a cellar at Sodom, at the sign of the Twat,
> Two buxom young Harlots were drinking with Lot.

In a popular joke, the airline stewardess says, "Do you want some TWA coffee?" The male passenger answers, with a leer, "Just give me some TWA tea."

TWIDDLE-DIDDLES

The testicles; evidently suggested by both DIDDLE and TWAT, and perhaps also by the archaic *thingumbobs*.

TWIDGET

The vagina; immortalized in this limerick:

> There was a young coed named Bridget
> Whose clothes were too short for a midget.
> Every lad in the class
> Got a peek at her ass,
> And she'd wink at the prof with her twidget.

UPSIDE-DOWN KISS

CUNNILINGUS while the woman rests on her back with her buttocks and legs supported by a piece of furniture or the chest of the man. This term was first used by the anonymous author of *The Sensuous Man,* but the position is shown in ancient Greek and Roman frescoes.

VACUUM CLEANER

A WHORE who specializes in FRENCH JOBS; a COCKSUCKER. A BLOW job is sometimes called a Hoover, the brand name of a popular vacuum cleaner. The metaphor is too vivid to require comment.

VAULTING SCHOOL

A whorehouse. A variation on this became the title of a song banned from radio in the 1950s: "I'm The Greatest Broad-Jumper of Them All"

VEGETARIAN

A whore who refuses FRENCH JOBS.

VELVET BUZZ SAW

A technique of CUNNILINGUS described as follows in *The Sensuous Man:* "Stiffen your tongue, place it at the tip of her shaft, and move your head from left to right as though you are saying no – but do it rapidly so that your tongue is brushing her clitoris a dozen times a second."

VERSATILE

Code in personal ads, meaning that the advertiser is interested in all varieties of sex, however KINKY. Experience, however, has taught some of these folk to be more careful; thus, one frequently sees "Versatile – but NO discipline!"

VIXEN

A hot-blooded woman, with an implication that she is also probably fickle or treacherous. See FOX.

WALK-IN

A lady of easy virtue; from the use of signs saying walk in in many shop and restaurant windows.

WAND

The penis, a simple visual metaphor.

WANG (or WHANG)

The penis; from Old English *thwang* and modern English *thong,* with some influence perhaps from TONG and POONTANG.

WAP

To copulate; from Old English *wap,* to throw, an idea still current in rural American idiom – "I'd like to give her a throw." In Romani (gypsy language) a *wapping dell* is a prostitute.

WATER SPORTS

Code used in personal ads. "Interested in water sports" means that the advertiser wants somebody to urinate on him; for example in the ad, "Young male wishes introduction to Greek culture and/or water sports by experienced female. Prefer housewife, nurse . . ."

WEAPON

The penis; evidently directly from John Cleland's immortal *Fanny Hill:* "He produced a most formidable weapon." Shakespeare uses *pike,* a spear, similarly in *Henry IV,* Part Two: "He will spare neither man, woman nor child when his pike is up."

This term is one of a large family of "weapon" terms for the penis. See, for example, BAT, GUN, HOWITZER, PRICK, SABER. For sexual activity involving the penis, see BANG, BURY THE HATCHET, SHOOT, STICK, SWORD-SWALLOWER.

WEENY

The penis. Of obscure origin, this could be a put-down, from the childish distortion of wee, small, into *weeny*, or it could come from the GAY use of *weiner* to mean penis, by visual metaphor and by the same process which made such oral terms as LOLLIPOP, GROCERIES, SEAFOOD into homosexual slang for the penis (or for other males).

WET DECKS

A woman who has serviced several men in a row is said to have "wet decks." One of the only novelists to have recorded this term in literature is John O'Hara, in *A Rage to Live;* the husband refuses the advances of his unfaithful wife with the words, "I don't like wet decks." See BUTTERED BUNS and SLOPPY SECONDS.

WET DREAM

An orgasm experienced during sleep; a nocturnal emission.

WHACK OFF

To MASTURBATE; a variation on JACK OFF, intended to show greater vigor and more passion.

WHALESHIT

A metaphor for the absolute bottom, as in "He's lower than whaleshit and that's at the bottom of the ocean." See BULLSHIT, CHICKENSHIT, OWLSHIT.

WHISTLING

Performing FELLATIO. *Whistling in the dark* (which Red Skelton used as the title of a movie), means performing CUNNILINGUS, as well as having the more innocent and better-known meanings of "barking up the wrong tree" or pretending bravery.

WHITE SLAVE

An archaic term for a prostitute, still used occasionally by tabloid writers. The implication behind the term goes back to a time when it was very widely believed that many women of the profession had been drugged, kidnapped and forced into a brothel by professional "white slavers."

WHORE

A prostitute. *Whoremonger* has two meanings, depending on how the speaker interprets the *monger,* some, reasoning by analogy with *ironmonger,* use it to mean a PIMP, a dealer in whores; others, thinking of *warmonger,* employ it to signify a patron or devotee of whores, a steady customer, also called a "whore-hopper."

WIFE-SWAPPING

Group sex, as practiced by suburban SWINGERS. With the rise of Women's Lib, this term is beginning to change into the less sexist *mate-swapping.*

WIG

The female pubic hair. Another *wig,* a verb meaning to go mad or throw a temper tantrum, is a contraction of the 1930s *blow your wig.* Lately, somebody suspected of having gone mad may be called a "wig," as in Terry Southern's story, "The Blood of a Wig," concerning a novel twist of vampirism in which jaded drug-trippers find a new high by injecting themselves with blood from a schizophrenic patient.

WOLF

A Don Juan or cocksman; from the carnivorous animal. The Romans called whorehouses *lupercales*, wolf-houses (compare to the modern cat-house).

WRITE OUT A CHECK

To go to the lavatory. "Pardon me while I write out a check" is considered an elegant euphemism, on a par with "Pardon me while I see a man about a dog" or "Pardon me while I water the daisies," which have the same meaning in certain segments of the population.

YODELING IN THE GULLY

A three-person daisy chain with two females and one male; the man performs CUNNILINGUS on one woman while himself being fellated by the second female. This is not a recent term at all; it is used in a 1932 porno comic showing Skeezix performing in this fashion with two of his female schoolmates (who, after he is worn out, are shown in the next panel sixty-nining each other, as Skeezix bemusedly watches, saying, "Golly, I sure started something").

ZOOPHILIA EROTICA

Bestiality; being sexually aroused by animals. There are a surprising number of books dealing with this perversion; more often than not, they depict women, rather than men, copulating with dogs. This practice is recorded in more limericks than any other perversion. Among the most memorable are:

> There once was a hermit named Hollis
> Who took crocodiles for his solace.
> The results had scales
> And long, furry tails
> And voted for Governor Wallace.

There was a young lady named Thalia,
With men she was always a failure,
But what she could do
With a male kangaroo
Quite astonished the folk in Australia.

Said a merry old judge named Magoo,
"Perversions? Yes, I've tried a few,
But the best that I've balled
Were Lee Harvey Oswald,
The Singing Nun and a pink cockatoo!"

There was a young man named McGill
Who made his neighbors exceedingly ill
When they learned of his habits
Involving white rabbits
And a bird with a flexible bill.

%!@$

%!@$
SELECTED BIBLIOGRAPHY

Chase, Stuart and Marian. *Power of Words.* New York: Harcourt, Hi ace, 1954.

Chase, Stuart. *The Tyranny of Words.* New York: Harcourt, Brace, 1938.

Crist, Clifford. *Playboy's Book of Limericks.* Chicago: Playboy Press, 1972.

Edwardes, Allen. *The Jewel in the Lotus.* New York: Julian Press, 1964.

Fraxi, Pisanus. *Encyclopedia of Erotic Literature.* New York: Documentary Books, 1962.

Frazer, Sir James. *The Golden Bough: A Study in Magic in Religion.* New York: St. Martin's Press, 1955 (3rd rev. ed.).

Freud, Sigmund. *Three Essays on the Theory of Sexuality.* London: The Hogarth Press, Ltd., 1905.

Garrison, Webb B. *Why You Say It.* New York: Abdingdon Press, 1955.

Gillette, Dr. Paul J. *Complete Sex Dictionary.* New York: Award Books, 1969.

Gilmore, Donald. *Sex in Comics.* San Diego; Greenleaf, 1971.

Goldberg, B.Z. *The Sacred Fire: The Story of Sex in Religion.* New York: University Books, 1958.

Grose, Francis. *Dictionary of the Vulgar Tongue.* Northfield, Illinois: Digest Books, 1971.

Hayawkawa, S.I. *Language in Action.* New York: Harcourt, Brace and World, 1940.

Kinsey, Alfred, et. al. *Sexual Behavior in the Human Female.* Philadelphia: W.B. Saunders Co., 1953.

------ *Sexual Behavior in the Human Male.* Philadelphia: W. B. Saunders Co., 1953.

Lawrence, D.H. *Sex, Literature and Censorship.* New York: Viking, 1959.

Legman, Gershon. *The Anatomy of the Dirty Joke.* New York: Grove Press, 1968.

------ *The Limerick: 1700 Examples.* New York: Brandywine Press, 1970.

------ Oragenitalism: An Encyclopedia of Techniques. *New York:* Julian Press, 1969.

Masters, R.E.L. and Edwardes, Allen. *The Cradle of Erotica.* New York: Julian Press, 1964.

Masters, R.E.L., *Sex-Driven People.* Los Angeles: Shelbourne Press, Inc., 1966.

Masters, William, and Johnson, Virginia. *Human Sexual Inadequacy.* Boston: Little Brown, 1970.

------ *Human Sexual Response.* Boston: Little Brown, 1966.

Mencken, H.L. *The American Language.* New York: Alfred A. Knopf, 1936.

------ *The American Language Supplement One.* New York: Alfred A. Knopf, 1945.

Partridge, Eric. *Dictionary of Slang and Unconventional English.* New York: Macmillan, 1970.

------ *Dictionary of the Underworld.* New York:

Macmillan, 1961.

------ *Origins.* New York: Macmillan, 1962.

Reisner, Robert. *Graffiti: 2000 Years of Wall Writing.* New York: Cowles Book Co., 1971.

Smith, Homer. *Man and His Gods.* Boston: Little Brown, 1952.

Taylor, Rattray. *Sex in History.* New York: Vanguard, 1954.

Wentworth, H., and Flexner, S.B. *Dictionary of American Slang.* New York: Crowell, 1971.

HILARITAS PRESS

Publishing the Books of Robert Anton Wilson
and Other Adventurous Thinkers

www.hilaritaspress.com

www.ingramcontent.com/pod-product-compliance
Lightning Source LLC
Chambersburg PA
CBHW070049080526
44586CB00013B/979